Data Dynamics

Aligning Teacher Team, School, & District Efforts

Edie L. Holcomb

Solution Tree | Press

a division of

Solution Tree

555 North Morton Street
Bloomington, IN 47404
800.733.6786 (toll free) / 812.336.7700
FAX: 812.336.7790

email: info@solution-tree.com
solution-tree.com

Visit **go.solution-tree.com/schoolimprovement** to download the reproducible in this book.

Printed in the United States of America

15 14 13 12 11   1 2 3 4 5

Library of Congress Cataloging-in-Publication Data

Holcomb, Edie L.
  Data dynamics : aligning teacher team, school, and district efforts / Edie L. Holcomb.
    p. cm.
  Includes bibliographical references and index.
  ISBN 978-1-935542-23-0 (perfect bound) -- ISBN 978-1-935542-24-7 (library edition)
  1. Educational evaluation--United States--Data processing. 2. School improvement programs--United States--Data processing. I. Title.
  LB2822.75.H585 2012
  379.1'580973--dc23
                     2011037523

Solution Tree
Jeffrey C. Jones, CEO & President

Solution Tree Press
President: Douglas M. Rife
Publisher: Robert D. Clouse
Vice President of Production: Gretchen Knapp
Managing Production Editor: Caroline Wise
Senior Production Editor: Lesley Bolton
Proofreader: Elisabeth Abrams
Text Designer: Amy Shock
Cover Designer: Jenn Taylor

Acknowledgments

I would be ignoring what I stress to others about "family first" if I did not begin by expressing my heartfelt gratitude for the faithful, patient support of my husband, Lee Olsen, in this and all my endeavors.

Turning from the personal to the professional, I must thank Gracia Alkema, first president of Corwin Press, for initially pushing me to become an author—and then for connecting me with Robb Clouse, who has stayed with me as my editor through every one of my books as he acquired loftier titles and moved on to Solution Tree. Thank you, Robb, for your skill, loyalty, and friendship.

My friend Jane Goetz Chadsey has shared ideas and insights over many years. She and her husband, Terry, of the Center for Courage and Renewal, always challenge my thinking and sometimes soften my rhetoric.

Hardworking educators across this great continent inspire me with their questions, their successes, and their endeavors. I owe gratitude, credit, and admiration to:

Steve Clarke, Principal, Bellingham High in Washington state, for your inspiring examples of student focus and staff support.

Amelia Mills, a Pennsylvania friend, for your assessment expertise and ideas.

Dr. Roberta Selleck, Superintendent, Adams County School District 50, Westminster, Colorado, for your leadership of the most courageous and comprehensive implementation of standards-based practices I've seen. Cooperation and assistance came from many, including Steve Saunders, Director of Communication; Dr. Oliver Grenham, Executive Director of Learning Services; Jeni Gotto, Director of Assessment and Instructional Technology; Dr. Copper Stoll, Director of Secondary Schools; James Duffy, Executive Director of Student Services; Sarah Gould, Principal, Josephine Hodgkins Elementary School; James Stewart, Principal, Hidden Lake High School; and teacher Craig Sherman of Hidden Lake High School, who created student benchmark and evidence charts for the staff and students in his district.

Susan Baston, Principal, McClure Elementary School, Tulsa, Oklahoma, for sharing the Benchmark Tracker and your reflections about teacher preparation.

Dr. Vickie Brown Gurley, Assistant Superintendent of Teaching and Learning, Kenosha Unified School District, Wisconsin, and the staff of the Department of Teaching and Learning, for Success Steps.

Donna Cloud, Principal, Highland Park Elementary School, Mid-Del Public Schools, Oklahoma City, for sharing the Data Chat Log and letting me spend extra time exploring your Data Room.

Kim Fischer, Principal, and the staff of Bullen Middle School in Kenosha, Wisconsin, for being a source of inspiration and a reality check as I charted the course of Mode Middle School.

Robert Fisher, Principal, Coatesville Area High School (Pennsylvania), and Assistant Principal Michele Snyder, for great examples of data to document implementation and results.

Dr. Angela Houston and Dr. Rochelle Converse, principals of Eisenhower Elementary and Stonegate Elementary in Oklahoma City, for your 2010–11 Academic Profile template.

Susan Howe, Instructional Support Teacher, Media Elementary in Pennsylvania, and team members Sandy Gruber, Rebecca Harrison, Brittani Lutterman, Carol Mitchell, Patrick Murphy, and Christine Seeley, for sharing authentic meeting notes.

Robb MacGregor, Assistant Superintendent, Renton, Washington, for many years of friendship and collegial work on school improvement.

Rita Martin, Principal, McAuliffe Elementary School, Broken Arrow (Tulsa), Oklahoma, for sharing your Collaboration and Feedback Form.

Gordon Oliver, Principal, Rockwood Elementary in Oklahoma City, and Ginger Bunnell, Principal, Byrd Middle School in Tulsa, for ideas about data walls.

Michele Rennie, Celeste Blay, and Katelyn Hubert, for your excellent example of teacher team leadership.

Naomi Samuels, Fifth Grade Team Leader, Highland Elementary School, Montgomery County, Maryland, and your team members Scott R. Steffan, Principal; Michelle Piket, Assistant Principal; Melissa Wilkins, Staff Development Teacher; Meghane Vaughn, Reading Specialist; Adrienne Gadoci, Fifth Grade Teacher; Erin Radzinschi, Fifth Grade Teacher; and Sonya Vasilios, ESOL Teacher, for letting me listen in on your team meeting.

Hundreds of unnamed educators whose interactions unknowingly influence my thinking and direction—I am humbled by your trust and awed by your passion. Thank you.

Solution Tree Press would like to thank the following reviewers:

Alfredo G. Barrantes Santamaria
Assistant Director, Student Achievement and Program Evaluation
Cartwright School District #83
Phoenix, Arizona

Erika Bolig
Director of Assessment and Data Analysis
West Ottawa Public Schools
Holland, Michigan

Gladys I. Cruz
Assistant Superintendent for School Improvement
Questar III BOCES
Albany, New York

Bridget Hermann
Principal
Ladue Horton Watkins High School
St. Louis, Missouri

Visit **go.solution-tree.com/schoolimprovement** to download the reproducible in this book.

Table of Contents

List of Figures and Tables

About the Author

Edie L. Holcomb, PhD, is highly regarded for her ability to link research and practice on issues related to school leadership, improvement, and reform, having been a principal, district administrator, and university professor. Holcomb's classroom experience includes teaching heterogeneous classes at all grade levels, the inclusion of students with multiple disabilities, and the coordination of services for gifted and talented students. Her building-level administrative experience is in settings ranging from affluent suburban to schoolwide Title I with racial/ethnic diversity and English learners.

At the university level, Holcomb served as associate director of the National Center for Effective Schools, developing School-Based Instructional Leadership, a training program for site-based teams. As an associate professor of educational administration at Wichita State University in Kansas, she coordinated the principalship course and internships and taught applied inquiry in the field-based doctoral program.

Holcomb is familiar with the challenges of districts with enrollments of 3,000 to 45,000, having served as director of standards and assessment and later as supervisor of twenty-one schools in the Seattle School District in Washington. She was also executive director of curriculum and instructional services in Kenosha, Wisconsin.

Holcomb has provided technical assistance for the implementation of school improvement efforts throughout the United States and in Canada, Guam, St. Lucia, Hong Kong, and the Philippines. She helped develop Washington State's *School System Improvement Resource Guide* and worked with the Ohio Department of Education on its plans for technical assistance and support for districts and schools identified for improvement under No Child Left Behind. She has also worked with statewide models in Kentucky and Pennsylvania.

She holds a BS in elementary education, an MS in gifted education, and an EdS in educational administration. She received a PhD in educational administration from the University of Minnesota.

To book Edie L. Holcomb for professional development, contact pd@solution-tree.com.

Introduction

Data Dynamics is a book about the deliberate and continuous tasks of accessing and using information in the context of district and school improvement processes and teachers' instructional planning. It includes advice on group dynamics through teaming structures and activities to engage the hearts and minds of educators. It will help you empower the data dynamos within your sphere of influence and increase your ability to make sound decisions and implement change.

While working as an external partner with schools and districts across the United States and Canada, I've met more and more educators who describe themselves as "discouraged" and "overwhelmed." They hear the accusations that they are failing and read admonitions like "work smarter, not harder." They are hurt by the implications that they are too dumb to know what to do or too lazy and uncaring to do it. These educators don't appear to me to be getting up in the morning pondering whether to leave Jose or Denisha behind today. On the contrary, I observe that:

- Educators want to be good at their jobs.

- Educators believe they *are* doing a good job.

- When new research comes along and is introduced at a theory and awareness level, educators think they *are* applying it in practice.

- Sometimes when educators explain what they would *need* to be able to apply the new research in practice, they are labeled as resisters.

- Only after doing everything that they know to try and discovering it isn't working fast enough—*only* when faced with what seem to be outrageously impossible expectations—do these educators sometimes resort to less-noble reactions like blaming their students and parents, protesting the tests, adhering without question to daily pacing guides regardless of student needs, and, in some drastic situations, even enabling dishonest testing practices.

The purpose of this book is to help hardworking educators like you further advance the progress that has been made, correct misuses and replace unintended negative consequences, and more skillfully employ the range of data that can help you be more effective in your work with students. For some of you, the description of basic steps will help you begin to deal with data or expand the number of people involved in the data discussions. For others of you, the examples and critical questions will redirect or renew your efforts. For many of you, these descriptions will affirm and applaud your work and challenge you to expand into new sources and uses. For all of you, this book will help you grow from being data rich and information poor, past being data-driven, to being data-guided. Almost anything we decide and do, we can do better with skillful use of appropriate data.

A meaningful context for the use of data to improve student achievement is provided as readers are introduced to Mode Middle School. Mode Middle School is not a single case-study site. True to its statistical namesake (*mode* meaning "most frequent response"), it is a composite of real examples played out in a typical middle school setting. A middle school was chosen because examples from elementary schools are already prevalent. High schools, on the other hand, are so unique as to be less easily generalized, and fewer examples of high school data use are available. Each chapter includes sections called "Elementary Exceptions" and "High School Highlights," which identify variations of the events and concepts of the chapter pertinent to those grade levels. The main focus of the book is the schoolwide data team, which utilizes data for overall school improvement and supports the data work of grade/course teacher teams within the school.

In response to practitioners' requests for steps, approaches, and processes, each chapter includes protocols that may be followed for staff engagement, generally based on critical questions for data discussions. Examples of data are linked to the kinds of decisions and actions they should inform.

Data Dynamics begins with a review of how the focus has shifted from voluntary data use to federal mandates, and outlines current needs and trends that should drive immediate shifts in purpose and action. Chapter 2 describes conditions that enhance the use of data, including structures and processes that engage staff and tap the leadership of data dynamos.

Chapter 3 focuses on the examination of data about student learning. The data presented are not from a specific state test or single school site. Instead, they are created from a variety of real examples for three reasons: (1) no specific school is identifiable, (2) the examples are more transferable, and (3) they help tell a story of school change. In chapter 4, the examination of nonacademic student data shapes an understanding of the skills, background knowledge, dispositions, and perceptions of the students. Chapter 5 illustrates the importance of considering staff qualifications and perceptions, while chapter 6 highlights information that is needed about parent and community stakeholders.

Chapter 7 turns the attention to data use within school improvement planning and implementation. The use of data by teacher teams to plan instruction and monitor and motivate student success is highlighted in chapter 8. Chapter 9 describes ways in which instructional and school improvement depend upon appropriate leadership and support from the district. Chapter 10 provides tools to diagnose use of data in your setting and identify next steps to make your data work technically correct and powerful.

Using the tools and structures in this book, your data work can move from mundane and dreaded to motivated and dynamic!

Shifting the Dynamics of Data Use

Data. A four-letter word that seems to evoke negative reactions of fear, anger, and suspicion. But call it *facts*, *figures*, or *information*, and it becomes clear that it's a valuable resource. Who would venture to make a major decision—financial, personal, or educational—in the absence of facts and information?

The key to greater comfort and confidence is in the *dynamics* surrounding the data. Merriam-Webster Online (2011) provides helpful definitions. As a noun, *dynamic* is defined as "an underlying cause of change or growth." As an adjective, descriptions of *dynamic* include "marked by usually continuous and productive activity or change" and "energetic, forceful." *Dynamics* represent "a pattern of change, growth, or activity."

Data dynamics, then, are the use of information in a continuous way as the energy and force to stimulate and guide change. This is our work in schools on behalf of the current and future success of students—our moral purpose. It requires teamwork at the district, school, and teacher levels, which involves the complications of group dynamics, "the interacting forces within a small human group" (Merriam-Webster Online, 2011). The skill and commitment of key leaders at every level of the educational system are critical. A *dynamo* is "a forceful, energetic individual" (Merriam-Webster Online, 2011), and every district and school must find, nurture, and support its own data dynamos who have a balance of technical expertise and student-centered passion.

Voluntary Data Use

My personal interest and investment in the use of data go back to when I was a rookie principal. In those days, my mentor referred to me as a "data nut," which is probably the source of my emphasis on a new term, *data dynamo*. At that time, use of data was advocated but was still voluntary and apparently the exception more than the rule. Researchers including Wilbur Brookover and colleagues (Brookover et al., 1978; Brookover, Beady, Flood, Schweitzer, & Wisenbaker, 1979) and Ron Edmonds (1979, 1981, 1982) had identified schools in which children were more successful than their counterparts in schools with similar demographics of race and poverty. Examination of those schools had revealed a set of characteristics that became popularly known as the correlates (Lezotte & Jacoby, 1990) of effective schools: safe and orderly environment, a climate of high expectations for success, instructional leadership, clear and focused mission, opportunity to learn and student time on task, frequent monitoring of student progress, and home/school relations. Even then, there was controversy around parent involvement, with Edmonds (as cited in Lezotte & Jacoby, 1990) stating:

> It is certainly desirable to have the most exalted level of parent participation you can get, and we never design school improvement programs that don't include parent participation, but you are never to depend on it. One of the great implications of this work is that programs of school intervention must fix their attention exclusively on those characteristics over which the school has control. (p. 153)

I wanted my school to be effective, and these characteristics were the variables to study. Surveys were administered and yielded data to indicate which correlates were perceived as strong and which were deemed to need attention in order to improve the school as an organization and the student success within it. The characteristics (correlates) themselves became the goals or targets to achieve. School improvement guides were created, and successful case studies were documented (Lezotte & Bancroft, 1985; Lezotte & Jacoby, 1990; Taylor, 1990). We worked to increase the evidence of the presence of the correlates, presuming that improved student learning would follow.

In my school, it did. The scores of Title I students improved so much from fall testing to spring testing that the inspectors from the state department of education became suspicious and came to check our records and testing practices. When they found nothing amiss, an article in the state's Title I newsletter (1985–86) described my school as "the best-kept secret in the state." From that experience, I learned the value and power of data to create positive visibility and to obtain resources.

As I later moved into a leadership role with the National Center for Effective Schools, researchers and school leaders realized that if being effective meant impacting student learning, we needed to reemphasize evaluation based on actual evidence of improved student learning, not just enhancing the empowering characteristics (correlates). So the crusade for increased use of student learning data began. Disaggregating data by student subgroups was a new approach, purely voluntary, used mostly in large urban districts and not at all common in suburban and rural districts.

On a hot day in August, I visited one such suburban district. Because this district had no racial diversity, the new data we explored consisted of student performance data disaggregated by socioeconomic status. By reputation, this was a top-notch district, and the numbers representing achievement of "all" students were impressive. But when they isolated the scores and grades of students whose families qualified for free or reduced-price lunch benefits, they saw a very different picture.

First, they were surprised that there were enough students in this category to constitute a statistically significant subgroup. Then they were startled to see the degree of difference in test scores and grades attributed to students in this group. One high school teacher voiced his reaction with a fist to the forehead: "I'm really shocked! We've been focused on the high averages of all and not even realizing that there's a whole set of kids we're neglecting. We just didn't see it." I concluded my summary of the day with the declaration, "Disaggregating data is such a powerful tool, there should be a law that every school has to do it!"

Federal Data Mandates

We know all too well that a law *was* passed, based on the belief that all children can learn. It included a requirement to check data and determine which students really *are* learning. But it happened further back than most current practitioners realize.

The origin of federal education law was a realization that resources must be sufficient and equitable to carry out the mission. As part of Lyndon Johnson's Great Society movement, the Elementary and Secondary Education Act (ESEA) provided federal funds to help districts educate students who became their responsibility due to federal impact, such as proximity to a military base. In fact, at one time, the funds were referred to as "federal impact funds." By design, expenditures under ESEA had to be reauthorized every six years. So every senator who served at least one term had a crack at it. And every president who served during the right term or got reelected to a second term got to knot the strings attached to federal aid to education. Thus, new versions of ESEA appeared around 1971–72, 1977–78, 1983–84, 1989–90, 1995–96, and 2001–02, though they sometimes fell behind schedule. Nixon tried to undo the whole thing in 1973. Reagan overhauled it through budget reductions in 1981. The report *A Nation at Risk* stirred things up for the 1984 version. For his iteration, Clinton gathered governors and businesspeople to create national goals for education. The goals were very idealistic, but punishments for failure were not meted out.

Then came the George W. Bush version in 2001–02, known as No Child Left Behind (NCLB). Not only did it raise the bar, it added threatening acronyms and punishments. Getting over the bar meant every child in the school (100 percent of the students, including those in most special needs categories) had to reach "proficient" on state assessments of both reading and math by 2013–14. Lines were drawn from a school's current status to 100 percent to create the trajectory for how much progress would be necessary (adequate) each year in order to reach that goal. If a school failed to make AYP (adequate yearly progress), it might be called a SINI (school in need of improvement) and the state might send out a SIF (school improvement facilitator). If multiple schools in a district failed to make progress, the district might be called a DINI (district in need of improvement) and the state might send a DIF (district improvement facilitator). After two years of failure, parents would be offered the choice to move their students to a different school. At three years of failure, funds could be redeployed to help parents access supplemental services to support their children's learning. After another year of not keeping up, corrective action would kick in—meaning somebody would get kicked out, usually the principal. If failure continued, the prospect of being shut down or taken over by some other governance entity was real.

School and district administrators have worked hard to build acceptance and skill for use of data to improve schools and increase instructional effectiveness. They have redeployed resources as long as they could and then cut to the bone, while holding the high-road ideal as the climb got steeper and steeper. State departments of education have created school improvement systems and developed cadres of technical assistance providers to help districts find solutions that match their challenges and barriers. Their sincere efforts should be applauded, while we also disseminate and address their concerns, so they can and will maintain their efforts and their commitment to all students.

The underlying ideal of NCLB was and is inarguable. We *shouldn't* neglect or overlook any child. We *should* prepare every child for a productive future. We should *not* make prejudgments about who would and wouldn't be capable of learning in our classrooms. We *shouldn't* rest or rust on our laurels if many or most are successful and some aren't. More learning for every student was the ideal we sought even before NCLB. So I continued to look for ways to help schools and districts use data to address new challenges.

School Data Uses

The need to use quality data in worthwhile ways has been advocated and guided by many who are referenced throughout this book, including Victoria Bernhardt (2004), Deborah Wahlstrom (1999), and Nancy Love, Katherine Stiles, Susan Mundry, and Kathryn DiRanna (2008). School improvement experts from Larry Lezotte (Lezotte & Snyder, 2011) to Mike Schmoker (2001) have stressed the need for data-based or data-driven decision making. Assessment gurus from Rick Stiggins (2007) to Robert Marzano (2010b) to Douglas Reeves (2007) have pushed for more frequent assessments to generate data for formative uses to guide instruction.

In the early 2000s, I studied reports about high-performing schools and districts, variously defined as those that were remaining consistently high in student achievement, maintaining exemplary performance through changes in their student populations, or making significant improvement in previously low performance. Common themes in those reports are outlined in figure 1.1. They are numbered only for ease of reference and are not in either priority order or sequential order. All need to be present, and the starting point may be different in each setting.

In addition to my ongoing study of the uses of data, I have shared responsibility for student learning in two large urban districts and have worked as an external partner with schools and districts across the United States. I have observed progress with many of these aspects of data use. I have also seen misuse of data and unintended negative consequences emerge. The following sections provide a status report on current data use in schools. Numbers in the section headings correspond to the eighteen uses of data summarized in figure 1.1.

Creating Collective Responsibility (#1)

The good news is: educators don't argue anymore about whether they should use data. The bad news is: schools are using some of the wrong data, in some of the wrong ways, while leaving behind more critical and useful information. The danger is a tendency to work on increasing data for the sake of more data, without creating the context that determines what data become useful information.

1. Create a culture of collective responsibility for all students.
2. Understand that assessment is an integral part of the instructional process.
3. Test results against the espoused mission.
4. Make clear distinctions between inputs (by adults) and outcomes (for students).
5. Use both objective and subjective (perceptual) data appropriately.
6. Focus on the most critical priorities to conserve time, energy, and money.
7. Drill down for student- and skill-specific data in priority areas.
8. Plan forward as students rise—to respond to individual skill gaps.
9. Plan backward to fill gaps in the instructional program.
10. Look around at research, best practices, and exemplary schools.
11. Look within to analyze curriculum and instructional strategies.
12. Select proven strategies for implementation.
13. Identify and plan for student populations with specific needs.
14. Identify formative assessments to balance large-scale, high-stakes tests.
15. Monitor rates of progress over time—student and cohort.
16. Gather evidence of both implementation and impact of improvement strategies.
17. Consolidate multiple plans.
18. Take the initiative to tell the rest of the story.

Figure 1.1: How high-performing schools and districts use data.

Source: Holcomb, 2004.

The goal of NCLB was and is correct and critical. Its public focus on equity has provided a forum and visibility for advocacy groups, including the National Association for the Advancement of Colored People, the National Council of La Raza, the Citizens' Commission on Civil Rights, and the National Center for Learning Disabilities (Shirley, 2009). In many schools and districts, the use of disaggregated data on state assessments has raised awareness of achievement gaps that were previously hidden or ignored. Though much remains to close those gaps (Barr & Parrett, 2007), the reality is now abundantly clear.

The public visibility of state assessment systems and results has begun to build a sense of collective responsibility in another way. When we first began to have tests in reading and math, and at only one grade in each level (elementary, middle, high), those test results were often studied only by teachers of that grade level or subject. With the entire school now judged "adequate" or not and with data provided for more students, more staff members are included in the data discussions. Even at the high school level, non-state-tested disciplines are being asked to contribute to schoolwide efforts on behalf of student learning.

However, too many conversations still focus on finding excuses and blaming the victim. Edmonds' advice to focus on characteristics over which the school has control has not been universally applied, by any means. And in our hyper-focus on reading and math, we've failed to engage many teachers of other content areas. We've left them to shrug their shoulders in relief and wash their hands of responsibility because the burden of accountability doesn't apply to them. Or we've left them to sigh in disappointment and wring their hands in despair that their treasured field is not valued because it's not considered important enough to be assessed.

Another disturbing pattern is the focus on "bubble kids," those almost-but-not-quite-yet-proficient students most likely to make it over the cut score with the amount of extra help that's available. Comments about targeting resources toward "the kids who will help our scores the most" are incongruent with responsibility for all students. I recently had a conversation with a teacher in an alternative high school. She had been searching for her old desk from last year, trying to scavenge it from the boneyard of desks discarded by the "regular" high school teachers, who were all getting new furniture. When I asked why that purchase didn't extend to all high school teachers, she reported—and seemed to accept—the rationale that "not many of our kids reach proficiency, so they don't bring in funding, so we don't get any new things." In the process of trying to accomplish what's considered "adequate," we've left behind proficient kids and highly creative kids and complex kids and the most school-dependent kids. How dare we define the worth of a student in terms of how close he or she is to a state cut score?

Testing Results Against Mission (#3)

The use of data in comparison to a stated mission is closely related to the development of the school culture. Although some consider it passé, I still advocate for active dialogue among professionals about the moral purpose at the heart of our endeavors. Authentic involvement in articulating our shared beliefs is less than half of the picture. Identifying and analyzing data aligned with each lofty phrase fill in the view of whether an organization actually walks the talk. The pressures of NCLB and its implication that the sole mission of a school is to ensure reading and math proficiency have overshadowed attention to more general discussions of beliefs and values. Many educators have essentially said that "since NCLB, we don't have to bother with a mission statement anymore. We just have to meet AYP."

Focusing on Priorities (#6)

In much the same way, assessment and accountability reports have focused the attention of the school on the fundamental skill areas of reading and math. There is no argument that these are crucial building blocks for present and future learning. But they have led to school improvement plans that target only reading and math—and that ignore what's been learned about all the other factors that make a school a better, more effective learning organization.

Consolidating Multiple Plans (#17)

In this area, there has been considerable change that may not actually represent progress. Previous discussions highlighted the need for coherence of school efforts, which were often fragmented into school improvement plans, technology plans, professional development plans, curriculum adoption cycles, and so on. Now the situation is nearly reversed. With high-stakes tests and targets, and scarce resources, it appears that everything is being directed toward basic reading and math, and important factors that attract and motivate teachers and students are being deferred. Less attention and action are focused on the climate for learning, students' social and emotional needs, teacher leadership, and embedded professional development.

Studying Research, Best Practices, and Exemplary Schools (#10) to Select Proven Strategies (#12)

Not long ago, it was difficult to access research and identify best practices. Readers were cautioned to look for data documenting that practices advocated in journal articles had actually produced results. Now the pendulum has swung almost too far in the opposite direction. Clearinghouses of "what works" and state school improvement training and templates have provided lists of programs that are research-based, or evidence-based. This certainly improves access and simplifies confusion about the quality of research designs. Unfortunately, it has created a tendency to choose a program from the pull-down menu and has become a way to shortcut the critical logic flow of analyzing current practice, examining root-cause factors, and matching solutions to a more detailed understanding of needs. We've begun to focus on adopting new stuff from lists of approved programs and neglected the rigorous reflection and diligent diagnosis of the programs and practices already in place and paid for that might yield results if implemented with fidelity.

Drilling Down for Student- and Skill-Specific Data (#7)

One of the barriers to data use listed in the first edition of *Getting Excited About Data* (Holcomb, 1999) was the "feast or famine" nature of data availability. Some schools had very little data to examine, while others were overwhelmed with tables and charts. No one seems to be suffering now from too little data. In fact, another pendulum swing has occurred in this aspect of data use. After studying 180 schools in forty-three districts in nine states, Karen Seashore Louis, Kenneth Leithwood, Kyla Wahlstrom, and Stephen Anderson (2010) report that "most principals have and use considerable amounts of evidence about the status of individual students and their student populations," but "very few principals have systematically-collected evidence about the school and classroom conditions that would need to change for achievement to improve" (p. 179).

Analyzing Curriculum and Instructional Strategies (#11) and Filling Program Gaps (#9)

These two uses of data are closely related, as both refer to curriculum and instructional programs. As noted earlier, progress has included greater access to validated programs, and evidence-based strategies appear more often in school improvement plans. Districts have actively pursued alignment with state standards and assessments. Many have continued their work to include the creation of pacing guides to prioritize time on heavily tested skills and ensure that instruction moves along through grade level and course expectations.

These are appropriate responses and recommended actions, but they also raise concern about unintended implications. First is the dilemma that arises when formative uses of data clearly reveal that students have not achieved a benchmark but the pacing guide requires moving on. Second is the persisting reality that the taught curriculum may not be as written, and the new program may not be in use as researched. The prevailing assumption, often wrong, is that because a program was selected and teachers received initial training at the start of the year, it is in place. The result of such an assumption can then be a knee-jerk decision that the program didn't work and needs to be replaced.

Planning Responses to Individual Skill Gaps (#8)

When state assessment results reach school districts, most take the following steps. First, principals and teachers ascertain whether the school reached the mandated levels of performance overall and for each subgroup. Then they look for more specific areas of deficiency within the tested area(s) or group(s) of concern.

In fewer cases, individual student results are analyzed in terms of the specific needs of each student, and that information is moved *forward* and used to help the student fill in gaps while also experiencing the grade-level curriculum. This is of particular concern in states with spring testing and for transition grade levels such as fifth and eighth grades. In such cases, students have literally moved on to different schools when the results come in. This management of data needs further refinement, and the district must play a supporting role in expediting such coordination and communication.

Planning for Student Subgroups With Specific Needs (#13)

The retrospective earlier in this chapter reviewed the roots of data disaggregation as a check for equity of access and achievement, especially related to race and poverty. The federal mandates of NCLB stimulated progress in this aspect of data use. NCLB directly reports results and requires improvement plans aimed at subgroups of the student population who do not reach AYP.

The Individuals with Disabilities Education Improvement Act (IDEIA) of 2004 increased requirements for general education to support struggling learners in multiple ways *before even considering* whether they might be classified as having "special needs." Response to intervention (RTI) was created as "an organizational framework for *instructional and curricular decisions and practices based upon students' responses* . . . to integrate assessment and intervention within a multilevel *prevention* system to maximize student achievement and reduce behavior problems" (DuFour, DuFour, Eaker, & Karhanek, 2010, p. 19, italics mine). The levels in this system have been described as tiers, with the first tier (universal) including modifications teachers make in the general education classroom as they observe students, assist them, and differentiate instruction. A second tier includes additional time and support, such as small-group tutoring, for students who have not responded to classroom instruction by achieving proficiency. The third tier is reserved for those students who still do not respond and need more intensive intervention. This may include formal evaluation to determine whether there is evidence to identify a learning disability or other condition. In such a case, the next step would be preparation of an individualized education plan (IEP) for related services that some models would consider as a fourth tier.

The point of emphasis is that RTI is not focused on identification for special education. It is a systematic approach to differentiating instruction and providing extra help based on evidence of student progress toward learning goals. Students with disabilities are not the intended beneficiaries of RTI—all students are.

Few would quarrel with a sequence of support for struggling students, but in too many places, errors are occurring in uses of data for RTI. RTI has been perceived in some places as a "more cumbersome way" to get students into special ed. That is not the intent, and if it is the focus of implementation, unintended negative consequences will accrue. For example, I have seen students being labeled as "Tier 2 kids." The use of tiers or levels terminology refers to the type of help the student should be given on a specific skill, not an appellation generalized to the student as a whole person. Conversations such as the following occur far too often:

"We have a great intervention plan in place for Raquelle. She'll go to class for the first twenty minutes and then to the math intervention group for thirty minutes. She'll be back in time for the whole-group reading, but then when they split up for groups, she can head to the computer lab for the online math program. During lunch, she can do her basic facts packet while the volunteer's watching the library, and in the afternoon, she'll have the regular math period with her class."

"Is she on grade level in reading?"

"Well, no, but we made AYP in reading, and we really have to get to AYP in math this year."

"What is Raquelle's favorite subject?"

"Hmm . . . she loves PE. But there are just some sacrifices she'll have to make so she can get proficient in math."

"How does Raquelle learn best?"

"I'd say she's a pretty social kid. Before school starts in the morning, she usually has a little group around her, and she's always getting them organized for this, that, or the other."

What a great plan for Raquelle. She gets to miss her favorite subject, work on the computer and with a learning packet by herself when she's a social kid, have the whole-group instruction but not the small-group help in reading, and devote two and a half hours of her school day to mathematics. Her teachers want to do right by her. Their grant doesn't provide a late bus, so her options are limited to the school day. But what will happen to the sparkle in Raquelle's brown eyes?

Data meant to be used to plan interventions in response to specific student needs can easily be misused. An error of commission is to characterize all members of a special population as the same, such as assuming that because AYP was not reached for African American students, a program should be designed specifically for black males, and all black males are then regarded as poor readers. An error of omission is to disregard the full range of school activities that keep students engaged and motivated for the long haul, focusing only on the short-term need to increase test scores.

Distinguishing Inputs From Outcomes (#4) and Gathering Evidence of Implementation (#16)

Inputs by adults include factors like the instructional programs and strategies discussed previously. Outcomes are the actual results, hopefully increased, that occur in student learning related to those actions. The visibility of reports from high-stakes tests has made it very clear that a school or district can no longer describe itself only in terms of teacher qualifications, professional development opportunities provided, and new initiatives promised. The question of whether those actions made a difference for students must be answered. But before the impact on students can be documented, there must be assurance that implementation is occurring consistently across the school. (That is why statement #16, "Gather evidence of both implementation and impact of improvement strategies," is separated in this discussion.)

Progress has been made in the form of classroom walkthroughs specifically customized to focus on evidence of the new practices agreed upon for schoolwide action. Further action is needed to engage teachers in collaborative discussions of their successes and challenges and what support they need to continue to improve. Other sources of data about implementation include self- and peer-reviews of video segments and student input on classroom activities.

Understanding (#2) and Balancing Assessments (#14) for Evidence of Impact on Student Learning (#16)

The measure of teacher and school success with new practices will be seen in new state data about student learning, but a whole year is a long time to wait and does not provide immediate validation. The anxiety of waiting for state results and the questions about whether they are fair, reasonable, valid, reliable, and so forth have created fertile ground for changing assessment practices and beliefs. Educators want to be able to predict how their students will do and be clearer about who needs help. The work of Marzano (2010b), Stiggins (2007; Stiggins, Arter, Chappuis, & Chappuis, 2004), Reeves (2006, 2007), Thomas Guskey (2007), and others has encouraged the use of classroom data in real time to guide instructional planning.

Whether and how data on student learning become linked to teacher performance are being studied by researchers, explored in some state accountability models as "growth" or "value-added" data, and, in some places, are contested in the context of collective bargaining. Doing this right will require precision and patience. Michael Fullan (2005) describes three "big requirements for the data-driven society: drive out fear; set up a system of transparent data-gathering coupled with mechanisms for acting on the data; and make sure all levels of the system are expected to learn from their experiences" (p. 202). Driving out fear refers to one of W. Edwards Deming's (1986) prescriptions in the days of total quality management. Leaders in the use of data for teacher rating and ranking must pay careful heed to the fear factor and its effect on morale and recruitment as they move forward. This book will focus on the last two of these three big requirements: mechanisms for data work and engaging all levels of the system.

Monitoring Student Progress (#15) and Telling Your Success Story (#18)

Monitoring the rates of progress for individual students and cohorts of students is essential for quality decision making and provides information to help the community understand the real accomplishments of its schools. Elementary schools often receive entering kindergarteners who have not been exposed to print-rich environments, have heard and used a very narrow range of vocabulary, and have missed the socializing and academic readiness-building advantages of early childhood education. Secondary schools receive students who have limited English proficiency and/or a jumbled academic history due to high mobility. These gaps may not be closed in the short term of *one* academic year but can be narrowed significantly *each* year.

Figure 1.2 shows the story told by an elementary school, tracking a cohort of kindergarten students as the number of original members of the kindergarten class grew smaller due to mobility and the percentage of that cohort meeting proficiency standards increased year by year. Few, if any, state assessment systems report results for cohorts of students, so this task must be supported by individual districts. It does make a difference to know that hard work implementing powerful practices is worth the long haul.

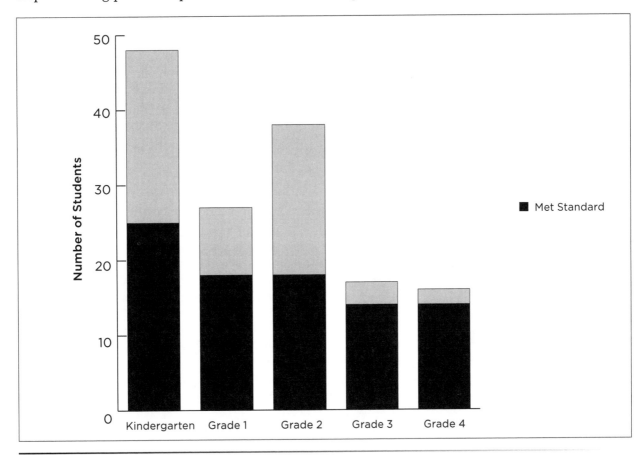

Figure 1.2: Tracking a kindergarten cohort.

Source: Adapted from Holcomb, 2004.

Using Both Objective and Subjective Data (#5)

The terms *hard data* and *soft data* are sometimes used to refer to data from objective measures, such as standardized assessments, and data based on human perceptions of their experiences with the school or district, respectively. Prior to the demands of NCLB, school accreditation and school improvement models included a cycle of gathering input from stakeholders, typically through surveys.

When asked about stakeholder input, the answer too frequently now is, "Well, yes, we used to give a survey to community, staff, and students so we could get their opinions and compare their perceptions, but we haven't done that in quite a while. We've had to really focus on just getting our state scores up." Both parents and nonparents have perceptions, concerns (accurate or not), and visions for their schools that may be broader and loftier than making AYP. In order to communicate with and engage a community, it's critical to hear from them and to use the perceptual data as clues to find points of leverage that will move the school forward.

Current Needs and Trends for Data Use

The preceding section reviewed eighteen previously cited uses of data and described both progress and problems that have emerged with shifts in data dynamics. This section reinforces those observations and highlights next steps from the perspective of practitioners and new research on use of data.

During recent data workshops, participants have been engaged in activities to review the eighteen ways that high-performing schools and districts use data, diagnose their present practices, and generate questions and topics that will be the priorities of the day's activities. Their responses have fallen into three categories that reflect the current needs of principals and teachers:

1. **Gathering other types of data**. Principals and teachers want to know how to gather information other than the state test results that already come to them. They specifically mention formative assessments, classroom practices (walkthroughs), and how to keep track of individual student progress toward proficiency.

2. **Organizing the data work**. Principals, teachers, and central office administrators ask for an approach that includes easy, practical steps for their schools and for K–12 and districtwide coordination and coherence.

3. **Using data with staff**. Principals and central office administrators want to make it easier to engage teachers in data discussions. They raise questions about how to communicate the data, how to develop the school culture around assessment and accountability, and how to achieve staff buy-in.

These ongoing challenges are reflected in the findings of the six-year *Learning From Leadership* study funded by the Wallace Foundation. Louis et al. (2010) examined test data, conducted classroom observations, and gathered perceptual data from a wide range of respondents in 180 elementary, middle, and high schools in forty-three school districts in nine states. A seventeen-page section of the report focuses specifically on "Data Use in Districts and Schools," providing observations and recommendations about types of data and how schools organize and use the data with staff.

Types of Data Used by Principals and Teachers

All but one principal in the *Learning From Leadership* study (Louis et al., 2010) referred to state-mandated assessment results when identifying the types of data used in their schools. Sixteen of twenty-seven also referred to district-mandated measures of student achievement. Only a few of the respondents talked about the development of diagnostic and formative assessments used by teachers to track student performance and provide targeted interventions. In schools that were rated as high data-use schools, there was particular emphasis on the development and systematic use of diagnostic and formative assessments of student learning.

Principals also referred to evidence about their students as a group, including mobility rates, attendance rates, graduation rates, eligibility for free or reduced-price lunch, and various disabilities. At a minimum, they used these data to comply with policy requirements for reporting student test results and allocating student and district resources. Less frequently, school and district personnel used background information for help in interpreting student and school performance data. This more complex use of data was more likely to occur in high data-use schools.

Organizing and Using Data With Staff

One central finding of the *Learning From Leadership* study was that "high and low data-use schools differed little in respect to the data available to them. Differences were more evident in the *uses* schools made of the available data" (Louis et al., 2010, p. 191, italics mine). Activities more typical of high data-use schools included:

- Actively using data to monitor the outcomes of school improvement plans
- Using formative assessments of student progress at regular intervals throughout the year
- Using data in making decisions about professional development plans
- Using data in conversations with parents about student performance and programming
- Using data to move beyond problem identification to problem solving—gathering additional data to better understand the causes or factors related to the problem in question

Differences in Data Use by Level of School

Differences in uses of data between elementary and secondary schools were even more marked and paralleled the differences between high and low data use. When all schools were considered together,

> the typical approaches to data use by districts and principals had no measurable influence on student learning . . . In elementary schools, however,

> data use may account for a significant proportion of the variation in student achievement, over and above the effects of student diversity, poverty and school size. (Louis et al., 2010, p. 196)

Throughout the report, districts are advised to focus intensive support toward their secondary schools. As stated in the concluding section, districts should

> provide assistance for teachers and school level leaders in accessing, interpreting, and making use of evidence for their decisions about teaching and learning . . . Increased support will be especially important for secondary schools, where state testing data is typically more limited, and data must be examined at the department, as well as the school and grade levels. (p. 216)

In order to provide a coherent story of data use and school improvement, the case of Mode Middle School is used as the principal framework for the application of data work in chapters 2–8. Each chapter also contains sections called "Elementary Exceptions" and "High School Highlights" to help district and school leaders recognize and respond to the unique challenges and needs of the various levels of school/grade configuration.

Conclusion

The dynamics of data use have shifted from voluntary use in a limited number of settings to legislated use in the United States and nearly universal use in developed countries around the world. Comparisons are made between countries, between states, between districts, and between schools within districts. Unfortunately, the cost of this progress can be measured in shifts away from use of a full range of types of data and decreased consideration of organizational and social factors that impact learning. As the bumper sticker states, "Shift happens."

It is now time to intentionally focus on deliberate shifts in what data are used, why, how, and with whom. Visit Mode Middle School, and discover how Mr. Good works with staff to shape the culture and implement new structures and processes. Think about your school or schools, compare the challenges, and identify your data dynamos. Whatever your official title, you are a leader when you raise questions and share ideas from your professional reading and reflection. Help your colleagues shift from doing the data work as compliance with an external mandate to fulfilling the commitment of a dynamic internal drive. Make your data dynamics a force that will energize teaching and learning for students and staff together.

Creating the Culture and Structures for Data Use

Mode Middle School is a typical (modal) school serving 744 students in grades 6–8 in a city that once prospered with industry and now suffers from unemployment and declining property values. As staff discover that school performance has also declined, defenses are going up.

Mr. Good comes to Mode Middle School as principal and recognizes conditions that concern him. But he waits a year to incorporate any changes so he can learn more about the school's history, staff, and students. As part of his entry plan, he created a set of questions that he uses as a protocol for many interactions during the year, especially in get-acquainted conversations:

- What's going well here that should be continued?

    - How can I learn about that?

    - What can I do to support it?

- What do you think needs to be improved or changed?

    - How can I help or contribute to your goals? (Holcomb, 2009, p. 184)

Some staff members and stakeholders initiate conversations with him right away in the fall. At midyear, he reviews his log and begins to intentionally seek out those who have not yet engaged in dialogue.

As the school year winds down, Mr. Good reviews his notes from various conversations to look for common themes, and he begins to organize and look more closely at the various reports that have landed on his desk over the course of the year. It is a jarring juxtaposition of input. People have told him about wonderful things that his evidence indicates just aren't quite so. And they never mentioned some problems that seem to leap out at him from the pages of some of the reports. He pauses to scratch his head and mutter, "Haven't these people even seen these data? How am I going to get them to face reality? I can't just shove this in their faces. I'm going to have to appeal to some more intrinsic drive to get them to pay attention."

Mr. Good has made several valuable discoveries. By seeking out the perspectives of many people, he has learned what they want to continue and what they feel should be changed—and he has recognized the need to create a culture of reflection and responsibility. As he wonders how to move his school from good to great, he realizes that his own actions will be key, and he wants to grow from being good to great as an instructional leader.

Reporting on the *Learning From Leadership* study, Louis et al. (2010) emphasized:

> Leadership is second only to classroom instruction as an influence on student learning. After six additional years of research, we are even more confident about this claim. To date we have not found a single case of a school improving its student achievement record in the absence of talented leadership. (p. 9)

The authors also reported:

> Where principals do not make data use a priority—where they do not mobilize expertise to support data use and create working conditions to facilitate data use in instructional decision making—teachers are not likely to do it on their own. (p. 179)

As the principal ponders the challenge of creating motivation for data use, words like *vision*, *mission*, and *passion* come to mind. He will begin to tap his background knowledge about shaping the culture of a school.

Tapping the Passion

Underlying every major endeavor is a theory of action, which Fullan (2009) describes as "a way of understanding the world that identifies insights and ideas for effectively improving it" (p. 275). For a theory of action to be powerful, he states, it must have the possibility of addressing the whole system, must be able to demonstrate potential for positive movement, and "must demonstrably *tap into and stimulate people's motivation*" (p. 275, italics mine).

Such a theory of action helps school leaders respond to the perennial change question "Why?" Though plagued by the semantics of whether to call the product a vision or mission or belief statement or core value, the process of engaging in deep discussion about purpose is critical. That is why, despite the pendulum swings that make it fashionable or less so, I have steadfastly included this step as part of school improvement work. Developing a mission statement may indeed be a diversion of time and energy if it is simply written and filed, just printed across the bottom of the next order of letterhead paper, or only added to the electronic template and website. But if used as a continual frame of reference (Holcomb, 2004, 2009), it provides an organizational conscience that slows the drift away from the central purpose and sparks commitment when energies flag. This ability to stay grounded and to persevere is part of what Fullan (2005) refers to as *sustainability*: "the capacity of a system to engage in the complexities of continuous improvement consistent with the values of human purpose" (p. ix).

Mr. Good thinks about ways to surface the soul-searching questions of: Who are we? What do we believe? Who do we serve? What is our unique purpose? What criteria will show us that we have achieved our ultimate success? He has heard people talk about going through an affinity process to create a mission statement (Holcomb, 2007). Apparently, they each used sticky notes to generate meaningful words and phrases, then compiled them in small groups and added headings for common groupings, and eventually synthesized the beliefs and values that had the strongest affinity for the most people. Now he realizes that he hasn't really followed up on that in any meaningful way over the past year. As he thinks about creating greater data use and a sense of urgency, he plans to resurrect the mission statement and ask people to think about how they would know if they were really accomplishing it. He also realizes that it's not just a technical matter of getting people to understand the data. There needs to be a change of culture so people will value the evidence and be willing to act on it.

Cultivating the Culture

According to Fullan (2005), "cultures consist of the shared values and beliefs in the organization" (p. 57). If those beliefs are not spelled out in some fashion and used to ennoble efforts and create a striving for higher purpose, they remain at a level of nonchalant routine and slide away from true commitment during times of stress. School leaders must devote attention to cultivating the culture of the school while it swirls around them.

The end goal is to create a culture with the three commitments described by DuFour and colleagues (2010):

1. A commitment to high levels of learning for all students. The fundamental purpose of our school is to ensure all students learn at high levels, and the future success of students depends on how effective we are in achieving that fundamental purpose. There must be no ambiguity or hedging regarding our commitment to learning, and we align all practices, procedures, and policies in light of that fundamental purpose. We recognize that a commitment to the learning of each student means we must work together to clarify exactly what each student must learn, monitor each student's learning on a timely basis, provide systematic interventions that ensure a student receives additional time and support for learning when he or she struggles, and extend and enrich learning when a student has already mastered the intended outcomes. We also recognize that if all students are to learn at high levels, we must also be continually learning. Therefore, we must create structures to ensure all staff members engage in job-embedded learning as part of our routine work practices.

2. A commitment to a collaborative culture. We cannot achieve our fundamental purpose of learning for all if we work in isolation. Therefore, we must build a collaborative culture in which we work together interdependently and assume collective responsibility for the learning of all students.

3. A commitment to using results to foster continuous improvement. We will not know whether or not all students are learning unless we are hungry for evidence that students are acquiring the knowledge, skills, and dispositions most essential to their success. We must systematically monitor each student's learning on an ongoing basis and use evidence of that learning to respond immediately to students who experience difficulty, to inform our individual and collective professional practice, and to fuel continuous improvement. (p. 21)

This end goal is clear, but how does a principal accomplish it? In the meta-analysis of principal leadership practices associated with student achievement conducted by Marzano, Timothy Waters, and Brian McNulty (as cited in Reeves, 2007), only three of twenty-one behaviors were associated with both first- and second-order change. In other words, the three behaviors stimulated the quick and easy reforms as well as those that produce lasting systemic improvements. The three were (1) belief systems about the efficacy of leaders and teachers, (2) research-based practices, and (3) monitoring and evaluation. Of those three, reforms of the recent past have focused attention on the last two and ignored or even undermined the first.

As they move to create a sense of urgency and accountability, leaders must pay conscious attention to the morale of the troops. Conveying confidence in the ability and willingness of the staff, believing in them, and building their capacity are as critical as focusing their attention on the needs revealed in the data.

Leaders who are working to strengthen cultures would do well to consider taking some of these steps:

- Periodically assess the culture in a formal way through a climate survey or externally facilitated focus groups.

- Constantly assess the culture through informal chats with both certified and support staff.

- Identify opinion leaders in various parts of the building, and connect with them regularly to get a glimpse into what is current in people's hearts and minds.

- Use the formal and informal assessment information to identify positive and negative factors and trends.

- Accentuate the positive, and take steps to mitigate the negative.

- Create space for people to vent their frustrations through brief, planned icebreakers and openers, but keep them short. (One principal commented, "It's OK to vent your feelings. It's not OK to wallow around in them.")

- Support the positive, and work with the willing. Don't alienate the slow to believe, but don't obsess over them either.

- Set new norms through group discussions (Holcomb, 2009), and then articulate and model them consistently.

- When norms are violated, follow up individually, gently at first, but don't hesitate to defend and reinforce collaboratively developed norms.

- Be open and public about a new skill you are learning on the job, and reveal some of your own challenges.

- Develop new stories of success, renewal, and accomplishment from within the staff.

- Bring in new voices, and provide them with an audience.

- Identify teacher leaders as spokespersons for the initiatives that are under way.

- Provide praise and recognition, not because people are doing what *you* want, but because they are supporting the collective effort identified in *their* school improvement plan and individual goals.

Mr. Good reflects on what he has learned about shaping school culture and is pleased to realize that he has done some of the right things already: assessing the culture through his informal conversations and using those notes to clarify his perceptions. He also brainstorms some activities he could include in various sessions at the start of the school year. Before jumping right into challenging the mission statement with data, he thinks it might lighten things up to start with a quick-write and ask staff to express themselves using the sentence stem:

When I think about data and graphs, I feel like a/an _____ because _____.

That will give them the chance to be honest. Sharing their statements in table groups will be a good icebreaker. If each table shares one with the whole group, there will certainly be some humor as well.

Mr. Good knows that he has staff who don't hesitate to voice their strong opinions, so he thinks about engaging them in a "vote with your feet" activity. He will post signs spread out on the wall like a living Likert scale: strongly agree, agree, disagree, strongly disagree. Then he'll make some mildly controversial statements and let them walk to their positions. He might try:

- All kids can learn . . . based on their ability.

- All kids can learn . . . if they take advantage of the opportunity.

- All kids can learn . . . if their families are involved and actively support them.

- All kids can learn . . . and we will establish high standards of learning that we expect all students to achieve.

- All kids can learn . . . and we will accept responsibility for their growth.

Sampling a few voices from each opinion group will stimulate thinking that Mr. Good can build on as he describes his concerns and goals for their work in the coming year. It may even help him identify the believers who could be nurtured into leadership roles.

But Mr. Good is no fool. He knows where some of his staff will stand if they are honest. Some will disagree with statements they should agree with and just the opposite. But he's confident that there will be others who will raise their voices with countervailing thoughts. Over time, though, Mr. Good wants to shape the beliefs in the culture. So he wonders how to deal with the resisters and get buy-in from staff for using data and accepting responsibility for student learning. Two ideas come to his mind: work with the willing and build commitment through engagement.

Reflecting on Resistance

As noted in chapter 1, needs expressed by practitioners include using data with staff, developing the school culture around assessment and accountability, and achieving staff buy-in. The term *buy-in* implies that there's a manufactured product and that the customer must be convinced or coerced into paying for it, generating mental images of the stereotypical used car salesman pulling out all the stops to unload a lemon on some unsuspecting victim. If a mission statement or school improvement plan or district initiative has indeed been manufactured elsewhere—and that does happen sometimes—then *buy-in* might be an appropriate term. In my experience, investing energy at the *end* to create buy-in is not a good use of resources. A better term than *buy-in* would be *build-up*. Engaging people *throughout* a process is a much better way to gain their commitment than expecting them to accept and support a done deal after it's been created by someone else.

Even with ample opportunities for all stakeholders to hear and be heard, a certain amount of conflict is unavoidable in organizations. In fact, Bob Garmston (2006) considers conflict to be among five principles of successful meetings. He stresses the need to "respect cognitive conflict by eliciting disagreements and respecting other viewpoints" (p. 1). He also affirms that "groups that discuss substantive differences of opinion produce better decisions, increased commitment, cohesiveness, and follow-through" (p. 6).

Fullan (1997) also points out that "learning organizations will legitimize dissent" and that "the value of resisters has been missed. Trying to manipulate the change process to eliminate resistance is futile. A more successful process is listening to those who are resisting and seeking to understand what lies behind their resistance" (p. 223).

The chicken-and-egg dilemma—which comes first, changed beliefs or changed behaviors?—enters into discussions about commitment to use data and to accept responsibility for the results. Sometimes beliefs do not change until the professional behavior and actions of others actually change the *data* and prove what students can accomplish. While challenging beliefs, the leader must be willing to focus on behavior. Staff members may not initially share a universal high regard and enthusiasm for working with data, but they must not be allowed to sabotage the effort with such actions as skipping meetings where data will be involved, undermining colleagues' efforts, and criticizing leaders' efforts in classrooms with students. Anthony Bryk and Barbara Schneider (2002) write about trust in schools and point out that unwillingness to confront inappropriate behavior sends the message to everyone in the organization that the behavior is acceptable and actually reduces the levels of trust teachers express in their principals.

At some point in time, leaders must be ready to hold crucial conversations with individuals whose behavior is limiting the effectiveness of others. These are private conversations in which the leader states his or her concerns very directly with specific examples and identifies steps that each party must take to remedy the situation. The leader also asks how he or she can help and support the other person as they move forward (Patterson, Grenny, McMillan, & Switzler, 2002).

The reality is that 100 percent buy-in is rarely, if ever, attainable. When DuFour et al. (2010) describe how the specific change process of implementing professional learning communities played out in several schools and districts, they note:

> In almost every instance, not everyone was convinced of the need for change, and a very few chose to leave to seek out more comfortable environments where they would not be expected to embrace the premise that they had a responsibility to help all students learn, collaborate, or provide evidence of student learning. (p. 205)

Mr. Good is on the right track. Initially he plans to focus on working with the willing and engaging all staff in nonthreatening ways. But for some, any change is a threat, and he will need to be ready for resistance, willing to hold crucial conversations when necessary, and able to deal with resignations or transfer requests if they arise.

Creating Team Structures and Processes

On a hot August day in the Napa Valley, District Superintendent John Sugiyama gathered his administrative team to review the district's priorities for the coming year and plan opening-day activities for staff. His charge was to shift attention from adult issues to outcomes accomplished for students. He realized that this would require a transformation of the culture of his schools and stated that "the key to changing a culture is to create structures, processes, and activities that cause people to think about different things in different ways with different people than they ordinarily would." The "different things" are data. The "different ways" are planned, structured, facilitated, collaborative conversations that require careful preparation and skilled leadership. The "different people" are colleagues who may have interacted informally but have not yet become part of purposeful, ongoing collaboration.

Mr. Good has identified some initial activities that will engage his staff and begin to build commitment. Now he needs to create structures and processes that will embed use of data into the ongoing sequence of events at Mode Middle School. One new structure will be the formation of a schoolwide data team. New processes will include communication links and feedback loops, data gathering and previewing, and collective data analysis, decision making, and progress monitoring.

As Linda Lambert (2003) points out:

> the benefits of participation—improved relationships, altered assumptions and beliefs, shared goals and purposes, increased maturity and cognitive complexity—emerge in a spiraling way: the greater the participation, the greater the development; the greater the development, the higher the quality of participation. (p. 12)

Mr. Good is initially looking at staff participation through the lens of working with the adults in the school: shaping the culture and building commitment to new practices of using data and new beliefs about responsibility for student learning. He would be thrilled to know that collective leadership also pays off in terms of student achievement.

In separate sections on "shared leadership" and "collective leadership," Louis et al. (2010) reported effects on teachers and students. *Shared leadership* was used to "denote teachers' influence over, and their participation in, school-wide decisions with principals" (p. 41). *Collective leadership* referred to the broader participation of "organizational members and stakeholders" (p. 19).

Key findings included:

- Almost all people associated with high-performing schools have greater influence on school decisions than people in low-performing schools.

- Higher-performing schools award greater influence to teacher teams, parents, and students, in particular.

- School leaders have an impact on student achievement primarily through their influence on teachers' motivation and working conditions; their influence on teachers' knowledge and skills produces less impact.

- When principals and teachers share leadership, teachers' working relationships are stronger and student achievement is higher.

- Leadership effects on student achievement occur largely because effective leadership strengthens professional community—a special environment within which teachers work together to improve their practice and improve student learning. Professional community, in turn, is a strong predictor of instructional practices that are strongly associated with student achievement.

Figure 2.1 illustrates the dynamics among various combinations of individuals who use data within a school and district. Mr. Good's role is represented by the "P." He is a pivotal connection between his administrative team, the school improvement/leadership team, and the schoolwide data team. Every teacher team feels his influence and the support of the schoolwide team structures on their own uses of data. As noted previously, that influence from the principal is associated with higher student learning.

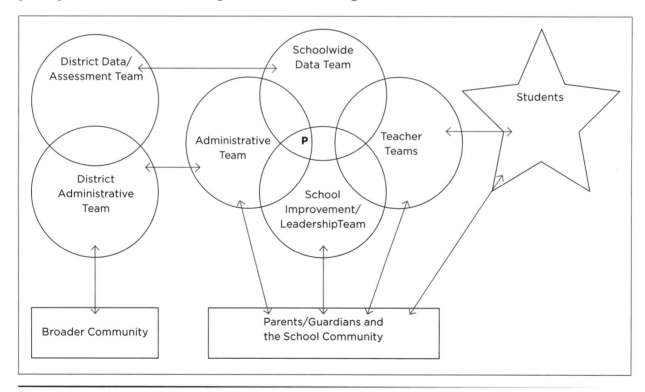

Figure 2.1: Data team structures.

The Administrative Team

In large elementary schools and in middle and high schools, the administrative team is composed of the principal, assistant principals, and sometimes other administrators or quasi-administrators such as an activities director or dean of students who supervises counselors. As the overlapping circles in figure 2.1 indicate, some members of the administrative team participate on the schoolwide data team, and some participate on the school improvement or school leadership team. Based on all the findings quoted thus far, the head principal should play an active role with both of these groups and not delegate this leadership role to an assistant.

The School Improvement/Leadership Team

The school improvement process should be open and participatory, involving teachers, administrators, support staff, students, parents, community representatives, and business partners in a variety of ways. Students belong in a category by themselves. They are the most intimately involved with and aware of the school's needs and successes; at the same time, they are the least integrated into analysis, decision making, and planning processes.

Composition and Characteristics

The school improvement/leadership team should include representation from every segment of the school, such as grade levels and/or content departments, special education, general education, support staff, and so on. In addition to representing an identified constituency, members of the school improvement/leadership team should be teacher leaders who are respected by their colleagues. They may have firm individual philosophies but must be motivated by a sense of "the good of the whole."

Roles and Responsibilities

This team does not *make* the decisions about how to improve the school. The team decides how and when to engage peers, students, and constituents in the decision-making processes and facilitates those activities. School improvement/leadership team members prepare, plan, coordinate, orchestrate, and follow up on data activities that involve the entire staff. Full engagement of all staff will be crucial at the following decision points:

- Developing and affirming the school's mission
- Identifying significant, meaningful data to be compiled for the school portfolio
- Interpreting the data, requesting more data, and identifying areas of concern
- Focusing areas of concern to a few priorities and developing goals
- Participating in study groups to further analyze data in priority areas and recommend validated strategies
- Affirming the completed achievement plan
- Participating in staff development to learn the use of new strategies and assessments

- Discussing evidence of progress with implementation and impact on student achievement (Holcomb, 2004, pp. 46–47)

The Schoolwide Data Team

Lambert (2003) emphasizes the importance of teachers as the heart of the "high leadership capacity school" (p. 32). She eloquently states:

> Teachers who exhibit vitality are energized by their own curiosities, their colleagues, and their students; they find joy and stimulation in the daily dilemmas of teaching and are intrigued by the challenge of improving adult learning communities. Teachers become fully alive when their schools and districts provide them with opportunities for skillful participation, inquiry, dialogue, and reflection . . . Because teachers represent the largest and most constant group of professionals in schools and districts, their full participation in the work of leadership is necessary for high leadership capacity. (p. 32)

Although the entire school improvement process should be participatory and decision making should be shared, teachers must be given special status in the actual gathering and analysis of data. All constituents have a right of access to data. But teachers should have the first chance to explore, analyze, and prepare to discuss the data with others. In some cases, this is new, unfamiliar, uncomfortable work. Leaders should be sensitive to these feelings and provide shelter for teachers—not to shield them from the data, but to provide a safe environment for their explorations.

Composition

The schoolwide data team should be an expanded subset of the school improvement/leadership team. The data team is a smaller group and may not include a member from every grade or department. There may, in fact, be additional members of this data team who are *not* members of the overall school improvement team but who possess the skills and interests needed. For example, some schools have found that retired teachers are willing to volunteer time to help in this endeavor.

Although constituents do not have a major hands-on role with the data work and development of the school improvement plan, they do need to be regularly informed and have an opportunity for input and reaction to the decisions made at each critical step. Representation of parents and community is more typical on the school improvement/leadership team than the data team, due to the time and type of work and the privacy issues around student information. However, broad involvement of stakeholders at key decision points is possible and valuable through the use of ad hoc groups to accomplish specific tasks. Unlike standing committees, which have a limited number of seats available and require a long-range commitment, a series of ad hoc groups, each with a specific task and defined time frame, can provide more opportunities and connections.

Characteristics

Members of the schoolwide data team should be individuals who get excited about and are comfortable working with data. They may not have the time to devote to or interest in the full set of responsibilities of the school improvement/leadership team but can help identify, prepare, and interpret data in preparation for consideration by the school improvement/ leadership team or for sharing with the whole staff. They should, of course, be assessment literate. Fullan (2003a) describes assessment literacy as:

- Ability to gather dependable student data
- Capacity to examine student data and make sense of it
- Ability to make changes in teaching and schools derived from those data
- Commitment to communicate effectively and engage in external assessment discussions

These skills will enable data team members to determine whether the data are dependable and help others make sense of them. A key skill in helping translate data is the ability to convert columns and rows of numbers into line and bar graphs, stacked bar graphs, Pareto charts, and pie charts.

In addition to having these technical skills, the members of the data team should also be individuals who have established strong relationships of trust with other staff members. If the school is on data overload, this team will help sort out the most significant data elements for first review, which gives them the power to portray a picture that highlights their personal interests and issues. They must have the respect of staff and the reputation for being totally objective.

Roles and Responsibilities

The school improvement/leadership team and data team work in tandem with each other and the administrative team to support schoolwide decision making. The school improvement/leadership team identifies information that is needed for school decision making, and the data team determines whether it already exists and/or how to collect and compile it. The data team also supports teacher teams in the use of data for the decisions they make about their classes and individual students. Specific tasks of the data team include:

- **Gathering existing data**. After years of standards and accountability, most schools have access to more data than they realize or may routinely use. In fact, a new challenge is sorting out which data are most informative for the issue(s) being considered. (The next section of this chapter describes categories of data that should be utilized.)

- **Identifying the critical questions of importance for discussion and decision making**. What do the teams really need and want to know?

- **Previewing data for relevance and usefulness**. With so much data now collected, time is too scarce to expect everyone to know everything there is to know about their school. A valuable role of the data team is to preview the existing available data in terms of its relevance to questions arising and decisions pending in the school. A courageous school improvement/leadership team will also notice patterns and trends that *should* be rising to the awareness of the school and will bring them to the fore.

- **Creating user-friendly data displays**. When it comes to working with data, the saying "a picture is worth a thousand words" could be paraphrased as "a graphic is worth a thousand cells of numbers." When the data team has identified facts or findings that are important for staff use, their role is to display it in graphs or charts that Schmoker (2010) describes as "simple data that even a child could construe" (p. 51). The purpose is to create and ensure an objective, commonly held reality that either confirms or confronts the stories that have shaped school actions in the past. Readers of *USA Today* will recognize good examples of graphics that include the fundamentals of good graphs and tell a story at a glance.

- **Planning and facilitating data events and conversations**. Traditions and rituals surround certain times of the year in schools, and the annual release of state assessment data has become a significant event. It is certainly a time for all staff to be updated on the results. There are also times in the cycle of school planning that create opportunities for the school improvement/leadership team and the data team to engage all staff in review of schoolwide data. However, the true goal of the schoolwide data team is to create and support an environment in which use of data is an assumed aspect of ongoing conversations and collaboration. In this role, the data team helps teacher teams tease out the data related to their own students and practices. When teacher teams identify new questions and challenges, the data team (or team member) advises them on available data that may be helpful.

- **Summarizing significant trends and findings for dissemination and future reference**. This task is related to the use of data to "tell the rest of the story" (see chapter 1). Rather than try to challenge or explain or defend data that are reported in the media, a better expenditure of energy is to be proactive and create short, effective descriptions of results achieved by the school. Even factoids of interesting information (for example, did you know that nineteen different languages are spoken by our students?) generate a better understanding of the school's challenges and accomplishments.

- **Leading the search for better data and data management**. As teacher teams become more data-oriented, they will identify needs for better assessments, will look for better ways to keep records of student progress, and may engage in action research that entails data to make comparisons before and after or between groups and classrooms. The schoolwide data team should lead, guide, and support these efforts.

- **Interfacing with the district data team**. As schoolwide data teams support their administrators, the school improvement/leadership team, and teacher teams, needs and ideas will arise that go beyond the scope of the individual school. In figure 2.1 (page 24), a two-way arrow illustrates interaction between each school's data team and the individuals/groups responsible for overall district data management. In a large district, this would be the Assessment and Evaluation Department or Office of Accountability. The schoolwide data team would bring forward assessment issues, policy issues (such as grading), and data warehousing issues. For example, as teachers experiment with ways to monitor student proficiency on critical benchmarks and manage interventions, they may develop simple spreadsheets that work well for their purposes, perhaps even better than canned commercial software. Learning of their usefulness, the schoolwide data team helps to refine them so they can be aggregated to the school level. These homegrown tools then provide models for selecting or creating district systems.

Data for Initial Use

As noted earlier, the first task of an emerging data team is gathering existing data. The data should be gathered into an organized, accessible collection—electronic and/or hard copy.

Data can be divided into four categories. The first category represents the first and ultimate goal—student learning. State assessments are a part of this category and may be the only or most readily available data. Other sources and ways of using data on student learning will evolve over time. Clues to unlock student learning challenges are often found in the information gathered as nonacademic student data, the second category. The third category represents data that are available related to staff qualifications and perceptions. This information will also provide insights for planning and professional development. The fourth category contains data related to parents and the community of the school. For example, it can be useful to know how the demographics of the student population resemble the neighborhoods served by the school.

Teacher Teams

Although the responsibilities of the school improvement/leadership team and schoolwide data team include interaction with the district level, their two priorities are focused on schoolwide issues related to learning and the learning environment, and support of teachers working directly with students. Teams of teachers who share responsibility for student learning in a particular grade or course content area must also be data users. These teacher teams are similar to Reeves' version of data teams or the DuFours' Professional Learning Communities at Work™ structure. They have the most direct connection to students.

Composition and Characteristics

The underlying criterion for "team-ness" is that these are professionals and paraprofessionals who share students and are responsible for similar curricular expectations. The teams are commonly divided by grade levels at the elementary level, houses in middle schools, and departments at high schools.

Roles and Responsibilities

Teacher teams share responsibility for students achieving proficiency on essential learning targets. Their tasks include planning instruction, checking for student understanding, adjusting instruction and providing additional help, assessing student progress, and keeping track of student progress.

Teacher teams use data that are created by the schoolwide data team. They also make requests to and through the schoolwide data team for access to or development of other kinds of data they need. For example, teacher teams may discover that assessments currently in use do not provide them with data they need to keep track of each student's progress on the specific concepts and skills for which they are accountable. Frequent two-way communication and teamwork between teacher teams and the schoolwide data team are important. Some of these interactions will result in needs and concerns moving forward through the schoolwide data team to the district data/assessment team for attention.

Teacher teams also interact with the school improvement/leadership team. They inform and affirm the choice of new practices for schoolwide implementation. They provide input about support that is needed and progress being made on those new practices and programs. And they provide the ongoing information about student learning that lets the school improvement/leadership team know whether and how changes are actually benefiting students.

Team Tools

All teams, by whatever name and composition, need some basic tools in order to function effectively. These include shared norms, communication and feedback processes, and templates for agendas and summaries of meetings.

Shared Norms

In Fullan's (2003b) discussions of moral purpose, he uses the phrase "treating people with demanding respect." We take these words at face value, often without exploring the specific ways individuals may interpret them. Some readers will hear the "demanding" resonate loudly, while others focus on the softer "respect" and have an entirely different impression. Assumptions about "what we mean by . . ." can be disastrous later on, so it's important for any group that will work together regularly over a period of time to articulate specific norms for its interaction. All members of the group, but only members of the group, should establish the norms by which they will conduct themselves. A facilitator may be helpful but must maintain a neutral role.

In most settings, norms can easily be identified from the knowledge and understandings of the group. If the group is large, it can be divided into smaller groups and a think-pair-share format can enable them to reflect on their previous experiences in groups and generate characteristics of successful teams that they would emulate. If the group has fewer than ten members, this can be done as a whole group. All of the contributions from individuals or subgroups are considered, and a small number (approximately six to eight) are selected. If the initial list of suggestions is lengthy, similar items could be clustered as in an affinity process, and then common wording could be selected. Norms such as "be respectful to each other" may need more specific wording to make the expectation clearer. "No interrupting" is a specific, concrete example of respect.

Norm-setting discussions should generate a list of items written on chart paper. These meeting notes may be saved electronically, but posting the original charts at each meeting until they become tattered and torn provides valuable evidence of these commitments and increases continuity and consistency.

An alternative to starting with people's own experiences is to create a shared knowledge base by introducing content of norms and examples for discussion. I recommend and use the norms of an adaptive school from Bob Garmston's work (Garmston & Wellman, 1999). The seven norms are:

1. Pausing
2. Paraphrasing
3. Probing for specificity
4. Putting ideas on the table
5. Paying attention to self and others
6. Presuming positive intentions
7. Pursuing a balance between advocacy and inquiry (p. 37)

In some cases, discussing someone else's set of norms is safer for individuals than volunteering their own desires. The discussion may even provide an opportunity to surface and heal pain from previous interactions. With some wordsmithing to increase ownership, Garmston's norms can be accepted by all members of the group. However, the concepts behind the simple words are complex, and skillful use takes practice. Training or reading of Garmston's material will be helpful to ensure that these norms are really understood by all and that skill in their use will continue to develop.

Once norms are accepted, the group must also deal with the issue of what they will do when one of the norms is violated. In a healthy environment, the answer is usually, "We'll just say the number of the norm on the chart, and people will get the point." Sometimes a good-natured penalty may be assigned. For example, the United Way drive in one school district benefited from a $5 fine per cell phone ring heard in administrative meetings. Sometimes an uneasy group will ask the facilitator to "remind us when we're not sticking to it." Eventually, they become comfortable enough to pick up that role on their own.

Communication and Feedback Processes

After the school improvement/leadership team or data team meets, information must be shared with all other staff members in each member's representation group (department or grade). Input should also be gathered for future discussions on ongoing issues still being considered. This sharing "out" of updates and gathering "in" of ideas create feedback loops that need deliberate attention.

Templates for Agendas and Summaries of Meetings

Time for teamwork is one of the scarcest resources in the educational setting—and that leads to the need for assurance that the time is spent well and achieves results that benefit staff and students. As Lambert (2003) points out, "Discussion during unskilled collaborative time tends to focus on two main topics: individual problem students and instructional materials and activities" (p. 21). She goes on to describe an elementary school where teachers take turns leading teams and all-staff professional development sessions in discussions of teaching practices and student work. Every time the teams meet, they complete a communiqué that informs the school of their activities, needs and accomplishments. Teachers learn to facilitate different teams and capture the key ideas of each session for the school community. (p. 21)

Figure 2.2 provides a template for similar communication of results from the group and of information to the entire school. A school in western Washington used five clipboards hung on nails in the teachers' lounge to provide transparency to the ongoing work of teams in the school. After each meeting, the team put their quickly summarized note on the clipboard, and any staff member or visitor could readily observe the topics and progress of the teamwork that was occurring.

Team Time

A common pattern in the past has been monthly meetings of the school improvement/ leadership team, with meetings of the schoolwide data team interspersed to prepare data for use in schoolwide settings such as faculty meetings and designated professional development times. This is now a minimal commitment. Teacher teams need to get together even more frequently. Three trends have increased the need for time for data work:

1. Expanded emphasis on use of data for both schoolwide and instructional planning

2. Greater numbers of data reports to be utilized

3. Emergence of data use in teacher collaboration, such as professional learning communities and grade-level or content-area teacher teams

Ideally, teacher teams meet every week, which can lead to increased requests for participation and support from the data team, which will then need to meet more frequently as well.

The first step in finding time is to maximize all existing opportunities by handling announcements and housekeeping items through electronic communication and consecrating gatherings on shared work to improve teacher practices and student learning. A frequent practice has been to provide substitute teachers so this team can meet during school hours. In some cases, the scarcity of substitute teachers—or the awareness that student learning is negatively impacted when the "real teacher" is away—has led to a different format: school improvement/leadership teams and data teams meet for two to three hours outside the school day and are compensated accordingly.

Some member(s) of the data team may need additional time for hands-on tasks such as preparing data displays. In some schools, this key individual is provided additional time by having one fewer teaching preparation period (secondary) or being relieved of supervisory duties (elementary lunchroom, recess, and such).

The collective bargaining agreement in some districts provides for a stated number of hours for individually directed professional development. Data work and support of colleagues definitely qualify as professional learning, and this makes it possible for team members to "pay themselves" by counting their hours toward that contract provision.

Team Meeting Date:	Your Representative:

Members Present:			

Goals for This Meeting:	Data to Be Used:

I. Issues Discussed (for each issue, use bullets for main points and asterisk the input you provided from your grade/department)

II. Decisions Made (list each decision, who will be affected, and when it will take effect)

III. Tasks Accomplished (list project, process, or product completed and how it will be distributed and used)

IV. Next Steps and Meeting Date

V. Input/Data Needed (for each topic, include method for gathering data/input and deadline)

Figure 2.2: School improvement/leadership and schoolwide data team agenda and report form.

Source: Adapted from Holcomb, 2004.

The Adams County School District 50 in Westminster, Colorado, has made major moves toward standards-based education and supported the continued development of data systems for teacher use. As part of their systemic reform effort, the collective bargaining agreement was renegotiated so that forty-five minutes before or after school every day are available for meetings of school improvement teams, data teams, teacher teams by grade/content, and "verticulation" teams up and down the grade levels. The time was made possible by eliminating positions through attrition and consolidation, thus providing funds for raising teacher pay to compensate for an eight-hour teacher workday.

The school calendar in Coatesville Area School District in Coatesville, Pennsylvania, dedicates four professional days as PLC-data days. They are scheduled in September, October, February, and May to match times in the year when testing has been done, so that teachers review student performance on recent districtwide benchmark assessments and plan instructional strategies to address the precise needs of their students. Schools are encouraged to schedule additional time for teacher meetings such as grade-level, team, and department meetings.

Connecting to Other Levels

Observers of school reform have frequently noted the discrepancies between pace and degree of change in elementary schools and pace and degree of change in secondary schools. These levels of schooling are distinct in many ways, most noticeably in terms of size of enrollment, type of teacher preparation, and physical setting. These differences must be acknowledged and variations made, as will be noted in these sections of every chapter.

Elementary Exceptions

Elementary schools are typically smaller than secondary schools, which means there is a smaller number of people to share the same critical tasks. In addition, elementary teachers "do everything." The norm is still the self-contained classroom, with perhaps some specialization at upper grades if students rotate so one teacher handles the hands-on science activities, for example.

The school improvement/leadership team and data team may be smaller, and there may be more overlap of representatives serving on both. Because elementary teachers are responsible for student learning in all subjects, they have more data to examine and monitor. These realties increase the need for time for data work without taking away from student contact.

High School Highlights

At the secondary level, the administrative team may include assistant principals, dean(s) of students or counselors, and perhaps the activities/athletic director. Because the ultimate accountability for the school rests with the administrative team, the school improvement process and development of the achievement plan must be a primary focus of all the administrators. The head principal must play an active role with both of these processes and not delegate this leadership responsibility to an assistant. Where there are multiple administrators, decisions about delegating responsibility must be carefully weighed in terms of the unspoken messages they convey. An assistant principal may lead the data team as a component of the work, but the head principal must be closely involved with the overall analysis and plan development. Assignment of the school improvement plan to an administrative intern weakens the impact on the culture.

Because of the content-area focus of most secondary teachers, typical structures for staff representation on the school improvement/leadership team and the schoolwide data team have naturally tended to rely on department heads. Findings from the Louis et al. (2010) research call this into question: "Indeed, one major finding is that department heads provide little to no instructional leadership. They appear to be particularly well-situated to offer leadership to their colleagues, but that potential for leadership appears nonetheless to be a squandered resource" (p. 91). The researchers synthesized implications for district policy and practice, and among these is a recommendation that "the role of department head in secondary schools should be radically redefined" (p. 93). When creating new structures and processes, it is important to resist the natural tendency to assume that people in old positions are necessarily the best to lead change.

While elementary teachers are generalists and monitor student data for a smaller set of students in all content areas, secondary teachers work with more students but within one content area or even a single course. As part of teacher teams, they may focus solely on the standards and benchmarks aligned with their teaching assignments. However, the unique challenge of the school improvement/leadership team at the secondary level is to ensure interdisciplinary conversations across content. For example, reading expository text and technical writing are skills that transcend content areas, and students' prior knowledge, current status, and improvement in those skills should be part of all conversations.

Secondary teachers should also be engaged in whole-school data conversations about the nonacademic characteristics of students. All teachers have assumptions about why students don't reach proficiency, which students don't or won't, and which need to be challenged in mixed groups. Such assumptions need to be intentionally pursued with data to confirm or, in most cases, contradict their accuracy. Use of a cause-and-effect diagram can lead to decisions that better match root causes.

Because secondary teachers see more individual students in a given day or year than elementary teachers do, another unique role of the secondary schoolwide data team is helping to ensure that all pertinent information from multiple teachers is coordinated on an individual student basis. In *Raising the Bar and Closing the Gap: Whatever It Takes*, DuFour et al. (2010) describe how three-week progress reports were generated and used at Adlai Stevenson High School. The teacher(s) would meet with the student, suggest strategies for improvement, and offer a pass from study hall to the tutoring center. An adviser would receive a copy of the progress report and meet with the student to review the concerns. The counselor would get a copy of the progress report and stop in during advisory period to meet with the student, express concern, and ask the student what he or she was going to do to improve. The parents would also get a copy of the student progress report, with a request to discuss it at home. As a result, "students begin to get the impression that they are being quadruple-teamed from people harassing them about their unacceptable academic performance" (DuFour et al., 2010, p. 54). Creating the processes by which student performance information is gathered and disseminated in a coordinated fashion is one of the ways that a schoolwide data team can support staff, students, and parents.

The District Data Team

The primary internal role of the district data team is to respond to schoolwide and teacher team needs. An external role of the district is to connect with the broader community (greater than one school's boundaries) of taxpayers and voters. The *Learning From Leadership* study (Louis et al., 2010) reported the extent of influence exercised by most stakeholders in and around schools on decisions in the school and found "considerable variation across schools in the nature and extent of stakeholders' influence" and suggested that "student achievement benefits from relatively greater influence by all stakeholders in school decisions" (p. 16).

Conclusion

Skillful, collaborative use of meaningful data is one of the keys to making good decisions that benefit staff and students: "Increasing teachers' involvement in the difficult task of making good decisions and introducing improved practices must be at the heart of school leadership. There is no simple short-cut" (Louis et al., 2010, p. 53).

Mr. Good has taken on the leadership tasks that are at the heart of serving the students in his school. He has analyzed the anecdotal entry data that he gathered on the culture of Mode Middle School and identified its need to confront realities. He has begun to design some new activities for the critical first days of the school year, so that new traditions and rituals can be invented and embedded. He has also decided that he needs to expand the existing school improvement/leadership team and create a schoolwide data team. He wants to start the schoolwide data team with a teacher in the math department and needs to get her lined up before she leaves for the summer. Then they can brainstorm together about other possible members. The team will begin to gather existing data about student learning, student characteristics and perceptions, staff qualifications and concerns, and community perceptions of the school. The time frame will be tight for gathering this initial data, because they will want to be ready for an all-staff data review early in the school year as they kick off the new work of developing their school improvement plan and enhancing professional practice through professional learning.

Using Student Achievement Data

Prepping for his second year at Mode, Mr. Good expands his school leadership team to be sure every grade, content area, and staff category is represented. To keep the group to a manageable size, he makes some combinations. All secretaries, aides, and lunchroom workers are one constituency with one representative, as are the electives teachers who cross over grade levels. He holds small-group meetings to be sure that all staff members know who the representatives are and how agendas and notes will be handled so they are kept informed and can provide input.

He also forms Mode Middle School's first schoolwide data team. A few members of the original leadership team agree to double up and be the links between the two groups; several others express interest in staying with just the leadership team. They begin to talk about what "the data part" of the work will entail.

All summer, Mr. Good has been counting on one of the math teachers to become Mode's data dynamo. They have exchanged several emails about how to begin. But she's already having second thoughts. He's very worried because of what he overheard her say to a friend . . .

"Oh, my goodness. I *knew* I should have hit the parking lot right after the kids cleared out instead of staying to clean my room and file my math materials a little better before summer school. Instead, there I was, still hanging around, and wouldn't you know Mr. Good finds me and hits me with another one of his great ideas: 'You're always asking how we're doing as a school and whether we're making a difference for kids, and you've got excellent math and communication skills, so I think it would be a real benefit for us if you'd take on a special role as leader of our data team next year.' Yeah, right. Be leader of a team that doesn't even exist yet. What kind of an honor is that? I ask questions because I really care, and it turns into another no-good-deed-goes-unpunished type of thing. So why in the world did I hear yes coming out of my mouth? Guess I was just too tired at the end of the year to have any energy to resist. So . . . I'm going to forget about it for a bit . . . maybe he will, too. It does seem kind of interesting, though. Wouldn't it be great if everybody in the school was paying attention to the same things and everybody got on board to do what would really help kids?"

This developing data dynamo has noticed that the people on the new schoolwide data team seem to use data terminology as though they each have their own definitions. And she is worried that the whole effort will get bogged down because there is so much data in so many different forms. Most of all, she doesn't want the rest of the teachers looking suspiciously at the data team as though they have some hidden agenda.

Mr. Good reassures her that he'll work with the team initially to review some fundamental concepts about data use. Then they'll organize the data that's readily available and coordinate an activity so all staff can review and discuss it. That will give everyone a big-picture view of the school from many perspectives and a chance to express their viewpoints. In this way, they'll begin building both the knowledge base of the team and the comprehensive school portfolio that will include four types of data: (1) student achievement data, (2) nonacademic student data, (3) staff data, and (4) parent/community data. Student achievement data will come first, of course; it's both the top priority and the bottom line. But Mr. Good knows that improving as a whole school will necessitate looking at some of the other information for clues about causes and solutions.

Fundamental Concepts for Use of Assessment Data

The first category of data in the school portfolio is student achievement data. A positive development of the recent past is that more of these data are now available, and state education agencies are working to provide them in more timely and user-friendly ways. An unintended negative consequence is that, due to shortages of time and pressures from politicians, attention has become focused almost solely on an annual review of the results from the most recent state assessment. Of course, such an annual review should take place. But it must be placed within the context of other important data, and care must be taken not to violate some fundamental concepts about large-scale assessment data.

High-Stakes Decisions Should Not Be Based on One Measure or One Year

This principle was articulated clearly in Public Law 94-142, the "original special ed law" formally known as the Individuals with Disabilities Education Act (IDEA). It stressed that a child could not be placed in special education based on only one test. The special provisions of IEPs are a great benefit to many children—but we need to be fully aware that when we create the plan, we also create a label of disability attached to that child.

It is illegal and unethical to make a high-stakes decision about a single individual based on one criterion, yet we have begun to routinely make high-stakes decisions about whole schools full of children based on just such limited information: "We didn't make AYP in math this year; ergo, we should change math programs, and/or put kids into tracks [by other euphemistic names, of course], and/or send them to math interventions during other subjects."

All Tests Have Errors, and Some Data Are Already Old

One of the realities about standardized assessments is a statistic called the *standard error of measurement*. In nontechnical terms, this means that if a single student took the same test repeatedly (with no new learning taking place between tests and no memory of the questions), he or she would not get the exact same score every time. The amount of variation in the scores is referred to as the standard error of measurement. (These calculations are typically described in the technical notes provided with score reports.) For example, a student might receive a score of 100 on a test, but after applying the standard error of measurement, the student's *true* score would fall between 94 and 106. If it also happened that the cut score for proficient was 102, this variation would have a significant impact. This is why, in a statistical sense, all test scores are not exactly true, so no single score should have the degree of impact on a student that is occurring with some state tests.

State assessments have improved in some ways over time, and considerable effort has been exerted to speed up the scoring process. Even so, schools in states with fall testing windows often receive results in April, and schools in states that test in the spring may not receive final results until August or September. In both cases, the scores are months old by the time school leaders study them. When spring results come in August, they don't reflect "summer losses" due to lack of learning opportunities in the lives of many students. When fall results come in the spring, they don't reflect "winter gains" as the result of ongoing teaching and learning. So in a time-sensitive environment, state assessment scores are almost always obsolete. Recommendations for an ongoing flow of current information from real-time assessments are simply logical, compared to the illogical practice of making decisions based on inaccurate, obsolete data.

The Quality of Data Matters in Decision Making

The standard error of measurement and the time lag between administering assessments and receiving results are two factors related specifically to large-scale assessments and the annual state tests required by NCLB. In a more general sense, the cliché of garbage-in/garbage-out applies to data use in schools. If the data are flawed, the accuracy of decisions reached from them may be compromised to such an extent that scarce resources of time, energy, and money are misspent.

Although this chapter and the next three suggest a range of data sources, not all will be available. Of those available, not all will be useful for a variety of reasons. Considerations in judging the value and quality of data include:

- **Alignment**. Student learning data that are not aligned to specific concepts and skills from the standards-based curriculum may be too generic to identify where new practices or programs are needed. This is not to say that the data should be discarded or ignored, but users must realize that the data will not, by themselves, lead to good decisions about the specific changes that need to be made. For example, percentile scores and normal curve equivalents from norm-referenced tests may be statistically valid and reliable, but they are not particularly useful for the evaluation of school programs and practices.

   There is also an alignment issue in the case of perceptual data gathered through surveys and focus groups. In this case, the alignment must be between the questions asked and the issues for which information is needed. There must be a direct relationship between survey items and the local need to know. Packaged surveys may need to be revised for specificity (and often reduced in length) in order to provide good data. More items do not necessarily yield better information, and participants may not complete a lengthy instrument.

- **Validity**. This term is related to alignment in the sense that it is a measure of whether the items in a test really assess the skill or concept that they claim to assess. Professionally developed assessment instruments have generally been field-tested, and calculations of validity are provided. Locally developed student assessments are, by nature, less sophisticated in this regard, so rigorous discussions of "what are we really seeing here?" become essential in the development of common assessments to provide student feedback and guide instruction.

- **Reliability**. The term *reliability* refers to whether the assessment will generate similar results when given multiple times. A measure of reliability is generally included with commercial assessment packages. Local assessments may not be as reliable, but because they are more specific and frequent, they can provide dependable information for decision making.

- **Sample size**. Sample size is acknowledged as important even in the context of NCLB, as states determine the number of students in a subgroup (most often between twenty-five and fifty) that would constitute an appropriate focus for identification and accountability. Sample size is also important when considering a recommended program or practice. The advocates may have achieved outstanding results—but only in one grade in one school in one year. Sample size is also very important when deciding on the use of perceptual data. If less than 10 percent of potential respondents provide input, confidence in acting on that input is greatly reduced. The higher the response rate, the more likely it is to represent the overall perceptions of constituents.

- **Representation of subgroups**. In the case of perceptual data, the overall response rate must also be evaluated from the perspective of subgroups within the pool. For example, a school with a diverse population may code responses by address or ask respondents to indicate their racial category in order to ensure that the responses do not overly represent perceptions of some at the expense of others.

- **Understandability**. The value of subjective data from surveys and focus groups is also subject to a review of the terminology and grammar used in the items and questions. An instrument of this nature should be reviewed *before* use to make sure that items are succinct and clear. When analyzing the data, items that seem to yield surprising or confusing results should be reviewed with the question in mind: "What might the respondents have thought this meant?"

Use of Data Should Match the Purpose and Design of the Instrument

An additional consideration when evaluating the usefulness of data for decision making is the original purpose and design of the data source.

The mandate for each state to buy or build a state assessment system was aimed at judging schools, not diagnosing individual student needs. Although many states have developed, revised, and refined their assessments by articulating grade-level expectations and aligning test items, these assessments are still primarily a measure of the school's performance. But the designation of failure is also felt by communities and students.

When school leaders (principals *and* the school improvement/leadership teams) examine the details of the state assessment reports, it *is* appropriate to do an item analysis to judge the curriculum, program models, and instructional priorities. Yes, drill down into the data to see where *multiple* students in *multiple* years consistently struggle. Then examine current practice within the school to see how, how often, how much, with what, and when those skills are included in classroom reality.

By contrast, it is *not* appropriate to do an item analysis of an individual student's right and wrong answers on a large-scale standardized test several months old and use it solely to label the student and choose a tier of remediations for him or her. Such an item analysis must be considered only a hypothesis to be confirmed or contradicted by more recent information from more real-time assessments.

A disturbingly frequent pattern I have observed illustrates this point. An area of math assessment that is usually lower than other areas is the standard related to probability and statistics. Conversations with teachers often reveal that they are not confident with this part of the mathematics curriculum and either do not "get around to covering it" or know how to properly assess it. In this situation, more interventions for the students or a new math program is not the answer. Appropriate curriculum guidelines, careful matching of teacher qualifications to teaching assignments, and differentiated professional development to build specific teacher confidence and competence are the interventions most needed. A score of pull-out programs will not address the underlying omissions from classroom instruction.

As Stephen Chappuis, Jan Chappuis, and Stiggins (2009) point out, assessment-literate teams would not use a state test score to determine reading group placement. Nor would they use SAT scores to determine instructional approaches, rely on performance assessments to check factual knowledge, or use multiple-choice items to assess a procedural skill that must be observed.

Subgroups of Students Are Not Always Homogeneous

Our sense of social justice demands that we disaggregate data to test our actuality against our espoused commitment to equity. This is essential. But good information can be used in wrong ways. When needs are attributed to all members of a group, the solutions may not be the right fit for some and may actually contribute to lowered expectations. For example, some advocates recommend specific programs aimed at certain subgroups, such as African American males. A school with a population that includes black males may assume that they need such a program, when in fact, the data do not indicate that is the greatest need or gap in student achievement. If such a gap *is* clear in the student performance data, the discussion of what to plan for black males (or any other subgroup) must include these follow-up questions:

- Is *every* black male failing?
- Of those failing, do they all have the *same* strengths and challenges?

If the answer to either question is no, planning must proceed very carefully to avoid over-generalizing and perpetuating the very patterns and perceptions we are trying to overcome. Generic approaches, such as identifying more appealing reading materials, are helpful but are not sufficient in the absence of explicit instruction customized to match specifically needed skills. Two critical caveats are: (1) don't make assumptions about groups just because they are present in the school—check the data, and (2) don't assume that one program will match the specific needs of every member of a subgroup—check the individual student data.

Trend Data Trump Snapshot Data

As mentioned previously, high-stakes decisions should not be made on the basis of one year and one instrument. Programmatic decisions are high-stakes in that they absorb huge quantities of teacher energy to retool and make changes, and affect entire student populations. Decisions about how students will be labeled and placed are high-stakes for individual students, because they affect self-perception, motivation, and future opportunities. Given the serious nature of high-stakes decisions about schools and students, such decisions should never be made on the basis of a single data point. Current-year data should be presented as an *additional* data point on a trend graph that shows at least two previous years of results. Trends and patterns are more accurate and fair than a single year's score on a single measure.

The concept of statistical significance must be applied to the highs and lows of the trend line. Statistical significance is the probability that the results did not occur by pure chance (Bernhardt, 2004). A designation of "$p<0.05$" means there is less than 5 percent probability the results occurred by chance and, therefore, a 95 percent probability that changes are significant and related to the actions that were taken. Some test companies and state departments provide trend data as part of their score reports and include the degree of significance for variations. In many cases, it's the role of the district data team or assessment department to make this calculation.

One superintendent of a large city district learned this the hard way. The district made a 2 percent gain in test scores, and he was elated. His assessment staff reminded him about the standard error of measurement and statistical significance and suggested cautious optimism in his public pronouncements of the breakthrough. He proceeded nonetheless to call a press conference and grandly trumpet the proof of his leadership and initiatives. One year later, he was trying to explain why a gain of 2 percent was significant but a drop of 1.5 percent was nothing to be concerned about due to expected variability in standardized testing.

Conclusions Must Be Verified Through Triangulation

Historically, triangulation was used by the ancient mariners to calculate their position using two stars, and mountaineers determined locations using two geographical features (White, 2007). Now the same concept operates global positioning systems. The underlying principle of triangulation is that it takes at least two other data points to establish your true position. Bernhardt (2004) uses the term *triangulation* "for combining three or more student achievement measures to get a more complete picture of student achievement" (p. 297). Anne Davies (2007) describes triangulated data as being "collected from multiple sources and in multiple forms and collected over time" (p. 35).

The application of triangulation to use of data may be simply translated as: "Make sure you have three indicators that all point in the same direction." When school leaders make decisions about the status and needs of their schools, they must check state assessment results against at least two other indicators, which may be previous years of state assessments, more recent district assessments, and/or teacher observations.

Cohort Data Are Needed to Monitor Progress of the Same Group of Students

The use of trend data is recommended as a way to look at assessment results over time. However, even such an effort to take the long view has a flaw. The reality of trend data is that each year, the tested population is a *different* group of students. Cohort data represent the performance of the *same* group of students over time and can illustrate the results of teacher effort. Cohort data measure the gap-closing effectiveness of a school or district by observing whether students are getting closer to proficiency levels as they move through the system and experience the instruction and interventions provided for them. A critical question to ask is this: are more and more of our students reaching proficiency as they have more time in our instructional approach?

Of course, these data also have a flaw. It is impossible to keep the cohort pure. Some students will leave, making the size of the cohort smaller, and the accuracy of the data will be compromised if data from newer students are added.

By this time, it's apparent that there are no flawless data—which simply reinforces the importance of looking carefully at a variety of data sources and analyzing them through the lens of multiple questions. The following section reviews the definitions and purposes of four types of assessment that yield student achievement data. A balanced assessment system will provide the best collection of information to guide schoolwide action and instructional planning.

Assessment Definitions

Because the schoolwide data team will lead discussions of data with all members of staff, their assessment literacy is essential. One of their roles will be to clarify definitions of assessment so that everyone is not only speaking the same language, but understanding what they are talking about and what it implies for their instructional practice. Four terms of assessment in common usage are *diagnostic*, *benchmark*, *summative*, and *formative*.

Diagnostic Assessment

In the medical context, diagnostic tests attempt to determine what's wrong so a course of treatment can be prescribed. In the school setting, diagnostic tests provide detailed information about a specific skill or set of skills so that the course of instruction can be determined. *Diagnostic assessment* may occur formally with sophisticated instruments if a student is still struggling after instruction has been adjusted at the classroom level and additional support, such as extra tutoring, has not accelerated his or her learning. Diagnostic assessment may occur in less formal ways, such as kindergarten screening or pretesting at the start of a course or unit. The more that an assessment provides detailed information about the specific strengths and needs of a certain student, the more likely it can be considered diagnostic.

Benchmark Assessment

The term *benchmark assessment* has emerged in the standards-based environment to refer to periodic (or interim) checking of whether students are progressing at an appropriate rate to demonstrate needed proficiency on large-scale state assessments. These tests are constructed around the benchmarks, or grade/course expectations, measured on the state test, and the intent is to be able to predict how students will do on those high-stakes assessments. They are typically given three to four times over the course of a school year. An end-of-quarter exam in a high school course may or may not be a benchmark assessment, depending on the degree to which it is linked to specific concepts and skills that are described in the standards-based curriculum and measured on a large-scale assessment.

Summative Assessment

The large-scale, high-stakes state test is a primary example of a *summative assessment*. It occurs at a single point in time and measures a large body of knowledge that students are expected to have acquired. No change in status can be demonstrated until a year later, when a different set of concepts and skills will be measured. The twin aspects of "comes at the end" and "can't be changed" are the hallmarks of a summative assessment. When those criteria are applied, even a ten-point Friday quiz can be considered a summative assessment if it represents the end of instruction on the measured skills and if nothing can or will be done to improve the outcome.

Susan Brookhart (2004) makes the distinction between summative and formative assessments clear: "Formative assessment means information gathered and reported for use in the *development* of knowledge and skills, and summative assessment means information gathered and reported for use in judging the *outcome* of that development" (p. 45, italics mine).

Formatively Used Assessment

For the category commonly called "formative assessment," I have substituted the term *formatively used assessment* to express the idea that no measure of student learning is formative solely by virtue of its construction or the frequency of use. A quiz, grade, project, or product cannot be automatically described as formative. Just because an assessment is shorter, focused on just one or two skills, or given more frequently (every two to three weeks), that does not mean it is formative. An assessment is just a source of data; what is *done* with that data determines whether it is formatively used or not. The intended purposes of short, frequent, formatively used assessments aligned with specific standards (or benchmarks, grade-level expectations, or learning targets) are:

- To help teachers understand how students are *form*ing skills and their understanding of concepts

- To be used by teachers to in*form* instructional planning

- To be used by teachers to *form* flexible groups for reteaching, clarification, and additional practice (as well as enrichment and extension)
- To in*form* students about what they do well and what they need to do to improve, so they will *form* goals and have a chance to re*form* their status

W. James Popham (2011) recently raised the importance of using a hyphen to change terminology from *formative assessment* to *the formative-assessment process*. He referenced the "four decades' worth of empirical evidence attesting to the instructional dividends" of using assessment in formative ways and emphasized that "when this process is well implemented in the classroom, it can essentially double the speed of student learning" (p. 2).

In a classic study, Paul Black and Dylan Wiliam (1998) examined more than 250 studies on formative assessment and concluded that the body of research

> shows conclusively that formative assessment does improve learning. The gains in achievement appear to be quite considerable . . . and among the largest ever reported for educational interventions. As an illustration of just how big these gains are, an effect size of 0.7, if it could be achieved on a nationwide scale, would be equivalent to raising the mathematics attainment scores of an "average" country like England, New Zealand, or the United States into the "top five" after the Pacific rim countries of Singapore, Korea, Japan, and Hong Kong. (p. 61)

A process with such powerful potential must be included and used appropriately in every school and classroom.

Assessment methods that yield themselves to formative *use* include quizzes, oral questioning, teacher observations of students at work, student-created concept maps, and learning logs (McTighe & O'Connor, 2005). Student response cards, displays of work on whiteboards, and exit tickets to gather student perceptions of their learning during class are also valuable—depending on what the teacher does with them.

Two aspects of formatively used assessment are hotly debated, and scholars differ on the answers:

1. Are grades (usually meaning letter grades) formative or summative?
2. Should performance on formative assessments count toward a student's grade?

With regard to whether letter grades are formative or summative, my position is that it depends. A letter grade that has been calculated at the end of a term or course and posted to an electronic data system is irrevocable and permanent and unquestionably summative. A letter grade that is placed on an assignment and has been derived from a standards-based rubric or learning scale with specific descriptors of levels of proficiency and is not the last and only opportunity for the student to demonstrate his learning may indeed be used formatively.

As to whether results of formative assessments (referring to a series of student attempts) should count toward a summative grade, my position has been that letter grades convey very little accurate and meaningful information to parents or students but may be a necessary reality based on community pressure and perceived college entrance demands. Teachers should keep track of student progress on the specific skills and concepts for which they are accountable and make conversions to mandated letter grades at the last possible point in time.

Mode Middle School's Initial Data

Mr. Good and the Mode Middle School data team are ready to begin their data work. As the team gathers in Mr. Good's office, they see notebooks and file folders of test reports piled on the table and shelves where Mr. Good has put them as he tried to organize his office—and his thoughts—over the past year. He knows that state test scores are not the only valuable and needed information, but they are there, and sense needs to be made of them. So that's the place to start.

Gathering the Data

Most schools have large-scale assessment data and use them in some way each year when they are received. Beyond that, there is a wide range of available data and processes for using them. There are at least two ways of dealing with the question of what other data to gather and analyze.

One approach is to take inventory of all the types of student learning data that are available somewhere in the school or district and try to compile them all in one place, electronically or as documents. Figure 3.1 lists some of the student learning data sources that may be available. It could be used as a shopping list or set of treasure-hunt clues to find additional student achievement information. When a schoolwide data team goes shopping to gather all the available data, they must be selective in terms of the quality of the data they will use. The team should identify the questions about student learning that they are pursuing and evaluate how well each source of data may answer their query.

- State assessment data—multiple years
- Summaries of collaborative analyses of student work samples
- National norm-referenced tests—such as Iowa Tests of Basic Skills, California Achievement Test
- Criterion-referenced (standards-based) tests—such as state, local, National Assessment of Student Progress
- Local unit tests
- Ratings from team projects and exhibitions
- Curriculum-based classroom assessments
- Districtwide benchmark assessments
- Common formative assessments
- College entrance tests—such as SAT, ACT
- Beginning and end-of-year tests
- Midterm, semester, and course exams
- Grades and grade point averages
- Performance checklists

Figure 3.1: Sources of student achievement data.

A second approach to gathering data from multiple measures is to become familiar with the formal and informal assessment system as it exists in the school and district. Figure 3.2 illustrates a pattern of assessments that is recommended to balance large-scale, district, and classroom methods and create an ongoing flow of information about student learning. In this illustration, the state test "floats" in midair for two reasons. It acknowledges the reality that different states do their state testing at different times of the year and that sometimes the state assessment is disconnected or poorly aligned with other forms of assessment.

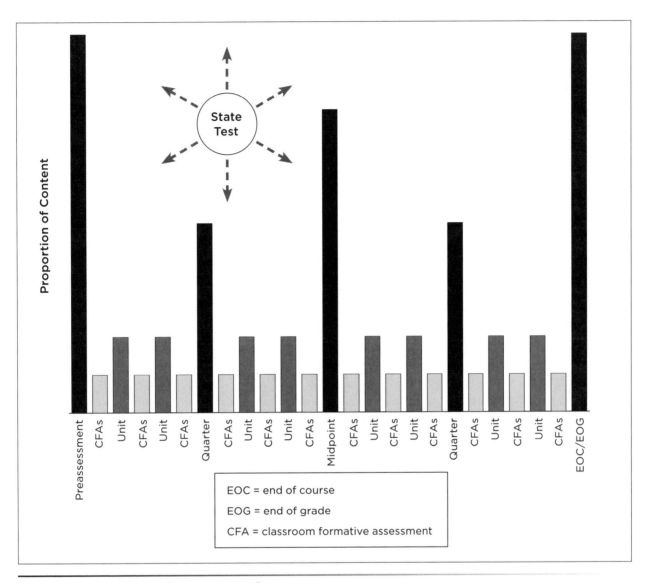

Figure 3.2: Pattern of assessments.

Source: Adapted from Holcomb, 2009.

The time period spans a school year, culminating in an end-of-course (EOC) or end-of-grade (EOG) test. The first bar on the left represents the testing that is often done at the start of the school year for diagnostic and placement purposes. The height of the bars represents the amount of content assessed, with a major assessment at midpoint of the year or course and quarterly assessments further breaking up the content. The quarterly assessments may also be referred to as benchmark or interim assessments, if they

> fall between formative and summative assessments in both timing and purpose . . . [are] administered on a regular preplanned schedule, evaluate student progress on the content standards that students must master to be on track to reach end-of-year learning goals . . . [but] take place in time for teachers to adjust instruction to address any identified gaps in student mastery. (Huebner, 2009, p. 85)

In large districts, the end-of-year and quarterly assessments are sometimes purchased. Often, they are developed by teacher teams from across the district to provide curriculum consistency. Interspersed are unit tests, which may be included in curricular packages, and classroom formative assessments (CFAs). These CFAs may be common assessments given by all teachers of the same course/grade and include informal indicators of student learning like exit tickets that individual teachers use in a formative way to adjust instruction. Working from this pattern of assessments will do more than identify data that may be available for collection and organization. It will also begin conversations about frequency and appropriate types of assessment to inform instruction and collaboration.

Displaying the Data

Mode Middle School's data team is starting with the information most readily available—three different sets of annual state assessment results. They want to capture as much information as possible in one place, so they design a set of stacked bar graphs for each grade level that shows proficiency levels for subgroups for the past three years.

Figure 3.3 shows the reading results for eighth graders. In actual use, color coding would indicate the proportion of each group who attained advanced, proficient, basic, and emerging status. The hope is that blue (advanced) and green (proficient) portions of the bars are largest and become bigger each year. Achievement gaps are easily spotted when some bars have considerably more yellow (basic) and red (emerging) than other vertical bars.

The stacked bar graphs answer a lot of questions about the pattern of proficiency for different groups of students, but Mode's schoolwide data team wants to know what happens to students as they move through three years in the school. They hope they can see that a set of students leaves their school with greater numbers attaining proficient and advanced levels than when they entered. Although figure 3.4 (page 50) is not provided in the state test reports, they tap the three years of information and create it for themselves.

Recognizing the vital importance and transferability of reading skills, the schoolwide data team wants more specific information than proficiency in overall reading. They want to look at the major strands for which results are reported. They display them as a profile with all three grades, as shown in figure 3.5 (page 50).

As they work together, the schoolwide data team is gaining familiarity with the data, setting priorities for data that will inform their questions, and creating displays that capture information in ways that will expedite data discussions among the whole staff. They know that everyone needs a common understanding of the challenges and are looking ahead to engage their colleagues in the type of rich discussions they are having. They also know that some teachers are not "numbers people" and will need to feel a more intrinsic tug at the heartstrings to really connect with the urgency of student learning needs. For this purpose, they decide to create a bulletin board in the private teachers' work area that will add the personal touch of names to match the numbers. The "data wall" will be ready when teachers start the school year. Figure 3.6 (page 51) represents their commitment to show every student's status in reading and challenge every staff member to help move performance upward, literally one student at a time. Each sticky note contains a student's name (Juan Doe in fig. 3.6) and his or her reading score (462) compared to the required score (400).

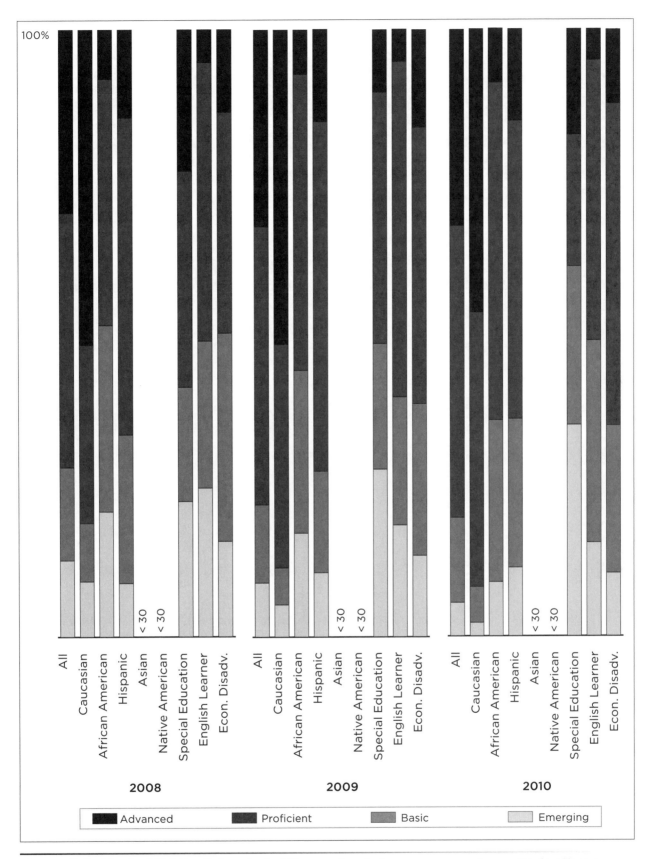

Figure 3.3: Mode Middle School eighth-grade state assessment results for three different classes.

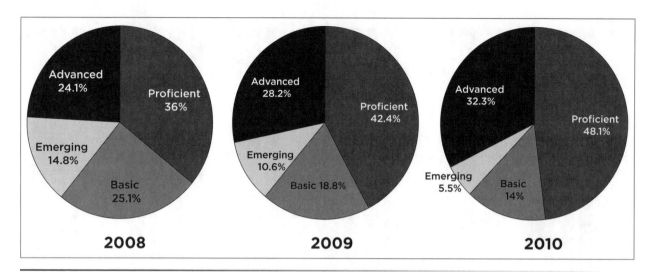

Figure 3.4: Mode Middle School reading, eighth-grade cohort, all three years.

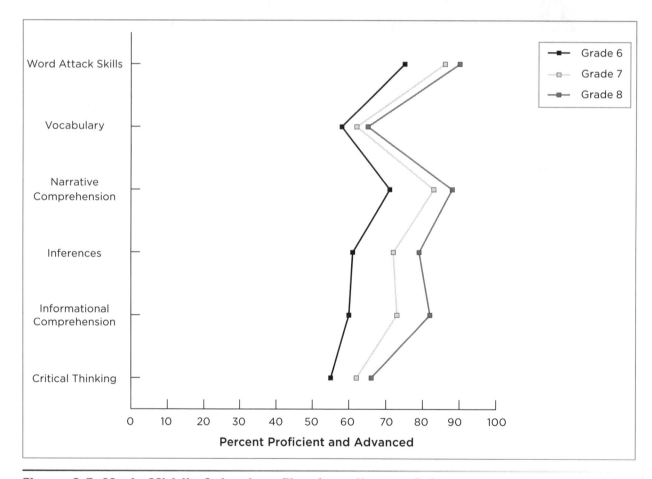

Figure 3.5: Mode Middle School profile of reading proficiency.

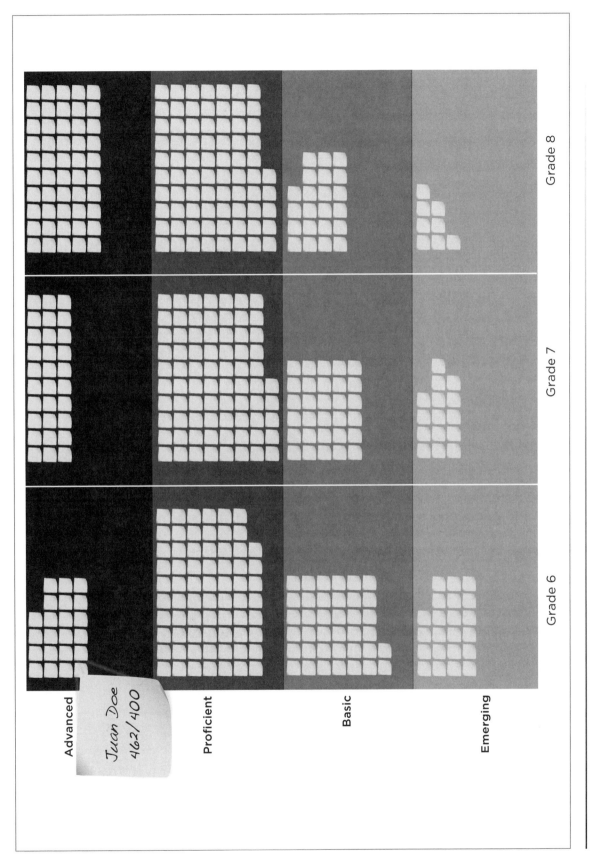

Figure 3.6: Mode Middle School's data wall, reading.

Source: Adapted from Byrd Middle School, Tulsa, Oklahoma.

Discussing the Data

As the schoolwide data team assembles and organizes data, their initial discussions are somewhat random and exploratory. They find that valuable in their small group but realize they will need a more focused approach when they share the experience with all staff. The set of questions that they develop as a protocol for discussing student learning data includes:

- In which strands (for example, benchmarks, skills) are our students making the most progress? Some progress?

- In which strands do many students have ongoing challenges?

- Do all student groups show evidence of the progress we're making? If not, what are the differences?

- Do all student groups experience the same challenges? If not, describe the differences.

The schoolwide data team wants to make sure that some of the questions will yield good news of progress to celebrate so the focus is not totally on the concerns that are identified. They also want the entire faculty to see specific strand data like the breakdown of reading proficiency in figure 3.5 (page 50), so they will realize that there are foundational skills (for example, knowledge of academic vocabulary, comprehension of informational text, and expository writing) that are essential parts of teaching and learning in every content area. As they work, they begin a summary of what they discover, shown in table 3.1.

Mode Middle School's data team will also study the data for sixth and seventh grades, similar to figures 3.3 and 3.4 (pages 49–50), and discuss data from math and other tested areas displayed like figures 3.5 and 3.6 (pages 50–51). Their summary shown in table 3.1 will expand as they make note of these celebrations and concerns. They will emphasize skills that affect content areas that are not state-assessed—for example, constructed response items. The social studies teacher on the team knows that department discussions have focused a lot on poor written work, and these concerns provide insights about student learning that impact test scores in other disciplines. Other team members realize that the electives teachers want to help the overall school effort but don't want to weaken their own curricular areas. They include these comments in their summary so they will remember to follow up in future discussions.

Although they are excited about what they see, they resist the temptation to publish their findings. They want to help their colleagues form and confirm common observations. And they definitely want to avoid being perceived as a group that studies data in secret and sits in judgment. They will remember the *d* words: Don't *declare* the data. *Display* the data to help others *discover*.

Deciding on Action

Although the only justification for time spent studying data is to translate that data into action, a big challenge for a schoolwide data team is to *not* rush toward decisions on the actions that should be taken. Team members will have lots of ideas already in mind about what should be done, but they must hold those lightly until more momentum is built around the data and more people identify the same patterns of need. The actions that the schoolwide data team plans are the ways to present the data and engage the staff in processes that will lead to action in the context of school improvement and instructional planning. First, they will help the whole school look at schoolwide patterns and needs that cannot be resolved at the classroom or department level. Then they will provide guidance for teacher teams to go more in-depth, such as conducting item analyses and using more real-time assessment information. With the support of the schoolwide data team and the insights and input gathered from staff, the school improvement/leadership team will coordinate the selection of schoolwide actions, and teacher teams will identify classroom-based action.

Table 3.1: Summary of Mode Middle School's Student Achievement Data

Content Area	Celebrations	Concerns
Reading	✚ Over 80% of students are proficient. ✚ Each grade level is showing gains. ✚ All cohorts increase percent proficient as they move through grades (for example, 60.1% to 80.4%). ✚ Strategies to support African American, Hispanic, and economically disadvantaged students are paying off. ✚ Gains occurred in all strands of reading assessment.	− Gaps still remain. − The largest gap is special education, followed by EL. − Proficiency with informational text is lower than with narrative. − In general, reading proficiency is lowest for all grade levels in vocabulary and in critical thinking related to informational text.
Math	✚ Each grade level is showing gains.	− Only 67% overall meet proficiency. − Proficiency is the lowest in the algebraic sense strand.
Writing (no separate state test)		− Constructed responses are lower than multiple-choice items in all tested areas.
Science (state test only used in one grade)		− Constructed responses are lower than multiple-choice items.
Social studies (no state test)		− Teachers observe that reports submitted by students are loosely connected links of quotes from the Internet. − There is a lack of critical thinking and organization.
Electives (no state test)		− Teachers are concerned about how to assist with academics and still honor their own curriculum.

Future Student Achievement Data Needs

As Mode Middle School's data team assembles graphs from existing state assessment data, they struggle to keep from leaping to conclusions about schoolwide actions until others are also engaged in the discussion. At the same time, they also realize that the data most available to them (state tests) will not inform them as accurately as other types of data that provide more specific and timely feedback. Their "parking lot" of ideas to explore further begins to resemble a list of future data needs, including comments like:

- We need real-time assessments in smaller chunks so we can see how kids are doing.

- We need to give the same assessments, or we can't have collaborative teacher discussions about how our students did.

- We need some common agreements about the most essential skills to teach and assess, or we won't know what to include in the assessments.

- We need a way to keep track of different things—not just points earned, but skills reaching proficiency—for each student.

- Besides developing other sources of data in our own school, we need to get data from the elementary schools about our incoming sixth graders. Then we might not have to spend so much time at the start of the year giving placement tests and so on.

As Mode Middle School continues its data work, ideas for school improvement work and instructional planning will continue to emerge. After they've looked at nonacademic student data, staff data, and parent/community data, they will be ready to identify school and classroom strategies to support their students.

Elementary Exceptions

One of the unique challenges at the elementary level is the lack of schoolwide assessment data from grades K–2. This is not to say that even more students should participate in high-stakes, large-scale tests. It *is* to say that schools and districts need to determine how they will diagnose needs and monitor progress in these critical early years. Many struggling schools that received Reading First funding used Dynamic Indicators of Basic Early Literacy Skills (DIBELS) tests to meet grant requirements but often abandoned the assessment when the funding expired. Even when the tests were given, there was wide variation in how thoroughly they were used to plan instruction.

The nature of the skills and the developmental stages of young children suggest that performance assessment, observation, and anecdotal evidence are appropriate and necessary. But those same factors can contribute to lack of consistency as individual teachers make idiosyncratic decisions about how to determine proficiency. Teachers must use common criteria, and the district must help shape and ensure that there is appropriate assessment of foundational skills in the primary grades and that data are purposefully collected and aggregated to begin the flow of information about student progress through the elementary years.

The plan for primary data was evident at Rockwood Elementary in Oklahoma City. Even though it was only the third week of school, two bulletin boards were prepared to serve as their data walls. One had been divided into sections with headings for each of the upcoming assessments: Comprehensive Benchmark 1 (district assessment), Quarter Benchmark 1 (district), Quarter Benchmark 2 (district), 5th Grade Writing (state), and so on. Green, yellow, and red rows across the bulletin board were ready for data to be posted to note student levels of proficiency. The other wall was labeled "DIBELS Data Wall," and each section was identified with a teacher's name and contained a strip of green, yellow, and red paper. The first DIBELS testing had occurred, and students had decorated stick figures to represent themselves and placed their stick figures on the green, yellow, or red strip to indicate their level. No names were publicly displayed. Only the student would recognize how he or she had decorated the stick figure and would be proud and rewarded to move the paper doll to a higher level on the next assessment.

Another way of involving students is through the use of a private learning journal or data folder. This can include charts such as the examples in chapter 8, as well as student notes about what they learned each day. Students can also use a variety of codes and icons to reflect on their progress. Stars, question marks, happy and sad faces might represent success, confusion, or needs for help.

High School Highlights

Just as the early or entry years represent a data challenge for elementary schools, the exit years represent a challenge for high schools. With mission statements that often promise things like "success in school and the workplace," high schools need data on their graduates. For example, the state department of education in Colorado gathers information from postsecondary institutions about the percentage of students who need to take remedial courses or do not complete each year of their chosen community or state college program. These data are then aggregated back to the high schools to provide them with insights on how their students fare in those settings.

High schools also face data challenges due to their structure by academic disciplines and the requirement for just one grade level to be tested in the state accountability system. First, these realities must be addressed by engaging staff of all disciplines in identifying student skills that are required for success in their content areas, whether tested by the state or not. Examples of such generalizable skills are academic vocabulary, comprehension of informational text, and expository/technical writing. Second, assessment practices of all teachers who deliver the same courses must be shared and become more common in order to provide data on student success in content areas and grade levels that do not participate in large-scale assessments.

Conclusion

The top priority and bottom line of our work in schools is to ensure that students learn to high levels and are prepared with the skills they need for future success. Understanding the appropriate use of assessment data is essential for members of the schoolwide data team, and part of their role is to nurture the assessment literacy of all staff. This chapter has provided examples of data displays that convey important insights about student learning and outlined critical questions for discussion of the student achievement data. The need for a broader range of information about student progress is clear and will be explored in later chapters. Meanwhile, the search for other kinds of data about the students at Mode Middle School is under way.

Using Nonacademic Student Data

Mode Middle School's data team is building its school portfolio. They have assembled and decided how to display three years of state test data as a starting point. In the process, they have had several aha moments, realizing the limitations of the large-scale data, and identified future steps to provide up-close, real-time data to inform instruction and increase learning. They will capture those insights for future discussion with all staff because they know that implementing better assessment practices schoolwide is a change that should be included as a strategy for school improvement.

Now they are immersed in gathering the data that are most readily available to supplement the large-scale assessment data that have been the main focus for the last few years. Even though they have tried to stay focused on what is in the data, they have found it humanly impossible not to veer off course into the "why" territory of assumptions about causes or the "what if" of prematurely brainstorming the actions that should be taken. The upside of their mental wanderings is that they have begun to wonder what *else* they need to know in order to make sure their theories are well founded and their intuitive solutions will match the reality of the situation.

Fundamental Concepts for Use of Nonacademic Student Data

The title of this chapter includes the term *nonacademic*. Some authors use the term *noncognitive* to describe data, such as attendance, that are not a direct indicator of student learning. I prefer the term *nonacademic* because I believe there *are* cognitive and metacognitive aspects to student thinking and decision making about issues such as attending school and how to behave there. This second category of data about students focuses on the enabling or empowering characteristics that support learning. The study of factors such as demographics, attendance, discipline, and engagement in school activities yields clues to find leverage for improving student learning. It also challenges assumptions that are made intuitively, and sometimes unconsciously, about students and their learning. For example, the Mode Middle School data team will be happy to celebrate the discovery that one of its assumptions about attendance patterns is not really true.

One aspect of data use in high-performing schools and districts, as outlined in chapter 1, is using both objective and subjective (perceptual) data appropriately. Figure 4.1 lists both objective and subjective sources of nonacademic student data. This combination of data types is critical in regard to students, as well as staff and parent/community members. It is commonly accepted that behavior data are relevant because bad behavior interferes with the learning of the misbehaver and the entire class. It is well understood that students won't learn the intended curriculum if they are not present for the instruction.

Student demographics	**Attendance**
• Gender	• Overall
• Racial/ethnic groups	• By identifiable subgroups
• Home language	• Chronic absenteeism
• Socioeconomic status	
• Mobility	**Disciplinary referrals and actions**
	• Overall numbers of referrals and actions
Graduation/dropout rates	• Number of referrals and actions by subgroup
• Overall and by subgroup	• Proportion of referrals to actions
Status of graduates	• Ratio of referrals to actions by subgroup
• 2 years after graduation	
• 5 years after graduation	**Participation data**
	• Co/extracurricular activities
Homework completion rates	• Community service
	• Overall and by subgroup
Observation logs	
• Staff	**Journal entries, anecdotes**
• Students	• Staff
	• Students
Checklists, rating scales	
	Career/interest inventories
Student survey data	
	Student focus group data

Figure 4.1: Sources of nonacademic student data.

It is *not* so common for school staff to accept the idea that students know what good instruction is and what they need in order to learn successfully. Principals and teachers diligently analyze their test data to identify student needs, but few schools tap into a more direct source of essential data—the students. Based on over forty years in and around classrooms as a teacher, principal, central office administrator, associate professor, author, and consultant, I am convinced that students as young as fifth grade (and even younger) are very articulate, responsive, and accurate when they are asked what they need in order to learn. We need to listen to them for their sake and ours. For our own benefit, we need to hear their insights. A decade into his or her career, a teacher may have had ten repetitions of a similar experience in the same surroundings. A decade into his or her schooling, and a student has had many different experiences in different classrooms and schools. Isn't it fair to say that students may have valuable—at least interesting—comments about what they have observed and experienced? We need to listen to the voices of students for the insights they can give us.

We also need to listen to students for their own sake. They need to feel that they are a part of what goes on around them. They need to see themselves as having an opportunity for advocacy. They need to feel that they are active participants in their schools, not passive recipients of an education designed far away from where they sit until they reach the age to formally exercise their right to be elsewhere.

Objective Nonacademic Student Data

The Mode Middle School data team is weighing the importance of various kinds of nonacademic student data and reviewing what they have readily available for immediate use. They are starting to realize how much better schoolwide decision making could be with more supporting information, but for now, they are limited to student demographics, attendance, and behavior. The power of that data will depend on the questions they ask as they plan how to display and discuss it with staff.

Gathering Objective Nonacademic Data

Objective (purely quantitative) data sources include various breakdowns of demographics, attendance, disciplinary referrals, participation, homework completion, and graduation rates and success.

Demographics

Teachers sometimes live outside the community and may represent different races and levels of education and income than the students they serve. As a result, it is easy to overlook changes happening in the neighborhoods where students live. A government survey reported in *USA Today* noted that "the kindergarten class of 2010–11 is less white, less black, more Asian and much more Hispanic than in 2000" (El Nasser & Overberg, 2010). Based on the study of 4 million children, the writers concluded that about 25 percent of five-year-olds are Hispanic, up from 19 percent in 2000 and outnumbering African American students almost two to one. Awareness of such changes is critical for schools to prepare for the human dynamics of interaction and the language development challenges that may be part of such a shift.

Attendance

The topic of attendance is easily oversimplified, as pointed out in a sequence of observations made by Hedy Chang (2010):

- "One in 10 kindergarten and 1st grade students misses at least a month of school every year."
- "Chronically absent kindergartners demonstrated lower academic performance than their peers once they got to 1st grade. For many low-income children, the poor performance persisted through 5th grade."

- "A long-term study in Baltimore showed that many chronically absent 6th graders later dropped out of high school."

- "In Chicago, poor attendance in 9th grade was a better predictor of dropping out than 8th grade test scores."

- "An elementary school of 400 students can have 95 percent of its students showing up every day and yet still have 60 children missing 18 days—or 10 percent of the school year."

The last of those findings should alert every school to dig deeper than the overall percentage of students present and test the reality of how good attendance really is and whether they are correct in the predictions and assumptions they make about who is and is not taking advantage of the opportunity to learn.

Participation

Although the term *participation* in some contexts refers to whether the student took the state assessment, it is used here to describe actual participation in the community of the school. Students behave and learn better when they feel connected to the school and are actively engaged. Information about student participation in extracurricular activities can provide insights about whether all students participate in some club or sport and whether there are patterns of academic performance or race in certain endeavors. Although it would be idyllic if students all came to school purely for the joy of learning, the truth is that students need to feel they belong in a more personal sense to something that is going on around them. Another measure of the culture of a school is the extent of student participation in school decision making, community service, and service learning. Any school proclaiming a mission like "to create caring, contributing citizens" should be looking for evidence that the characteristics of such a patriot are emerging in the developmental years.

As Kathleen Cushman (2006) reminds us:

> Clubs and activities—especially those that do not involve competition—can foster a tone of inclusion that often comes as a relief to students. Tracy [a student] related that one club is "a small place where kids feel equal to each other, where people know your name, where no one is advanced or not advanced." (p. 36)

Displaying Objective Nonacademic Data

The Mode Middle School data team has chosen a set of pie graphs to illustrate their discoveries about the changing proportions of race in their student population (see fig. 4.2).

As they work, they note that the proportion of Caucasian students has remained relatively stable, and as a result, staff have assumed that the population is not changing. As the pie graphs clearly illustrate, the racial background of the minority population is shifting with decreases in the population of African American students and increases in the Hispanic population. When the whole school observes this trend, it will prompt many questions about issues like service for English learners and communication with families.

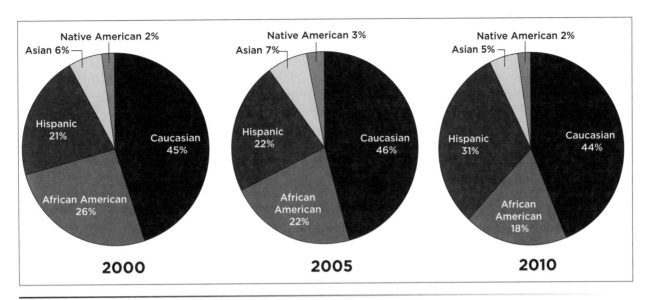

Figure 4.2: Mode Middle School enrollment demographics.

The staff at Mode Middle School have been rather complacent about attendance because their overall percentage of attendance is quite respectable. To learn more, the schoolwide data team chooses to break down attendance by subgroup for each month of the school year (see fig. 4.3).

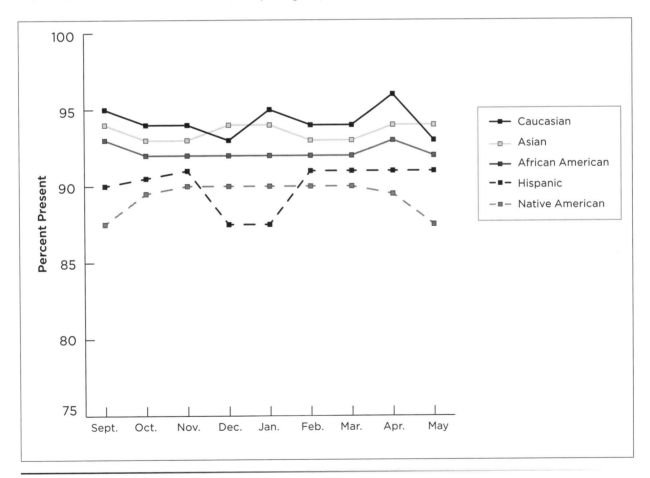

Figure 4.3: Mode Middle School attendance.

The pattern of attendance that emerges in the line graph becomes very intriguing, as the schoolwide data team notices ups and downs for different groups at different times of the year. They are also surprised that they do *not* see a discrepancy in the pattern for attendance for African American students, even though comments that this group of students "isn't learning because they don't bother to come" have been part of numerous conversations. They are curious about how the rest of the staff will react when (if) they notice this variation from their current thinking.

It becomes a real challenge for the schoolwide data team to dig for behavior data that will go deeper than the state-required report of overall number of suspensions and expulsions. Since the district has not developed a database that includes the entry of behavior referrals, the data team find themselves sorting folders of pink slips that assistant principals amassed the previous year. To display this behavior data, the data team decides to use Pareto charts that sequence the bars according to frequency (see fig. 4.4).

This will make it easy for faculty members to see the types and distribution of discipline referrals and how they differ from grade to grade. It will become very clear that seventh graders have the fewest referrals and that the most common causes are very different for sixth and eighth graders. Purchase of a one-size-fits-all behavior management plan will not be a solution that matches the details in the data.

Discussing Objective Nonacademic Data

If time allows, a two-stage process for discussing this type of data can be very revealing. The first stage would be predicting—asking participants what they think they will see in the data. This creates interest and provides an opportunity to surface assumptions that may be challenged in the actual data.

The second, and always essential, stage in the discussion of objective data can follow a protocol based on the traditional questions from journalism—five *W*s and *H*:

- What patterns do we see?
- Who are the students predominately represented in the patterns we see?
- When are those patterns more evident?
- Where do incidents most frequently take place?
- Why do we think these patterns have emerged?
- How should we confirm our interpretations, and how might we react if we're right?

The *who*, *when*, and *where* questions in this sequence lead to a deeper analysis of specific patterns in the data. The *why* and *how* questions allow for preliminary discussions of strategy but require that additional attention be paid to confirming interpretations. This necessary step of identifying root causes will be critical for deeper understanding of the problem. The school improvement/leadership team will check alignment of proposed strategies with the specific and actual needs that have been revealed in the data.

Deciding on Action From the Objective Nonacademic Data

As they gather and display the objective portion of the nonacademic student data, Mode Middle School's data team anticipates some of the discussion that will take place in the future when the whole-staff data review takes place and the school improvement/leadership team follows up with action planning. They are certain that there will be discussions about appropriate actions to take in response to the midyear absences of Hispanic students and the late starts and early departures of their Native American students. Discipline problems in the sixth and eighth grades will definitely come up, and the data team hopes that staff will assume collective responsibility for solutions and not just point fingers at certain teachers in those grades.

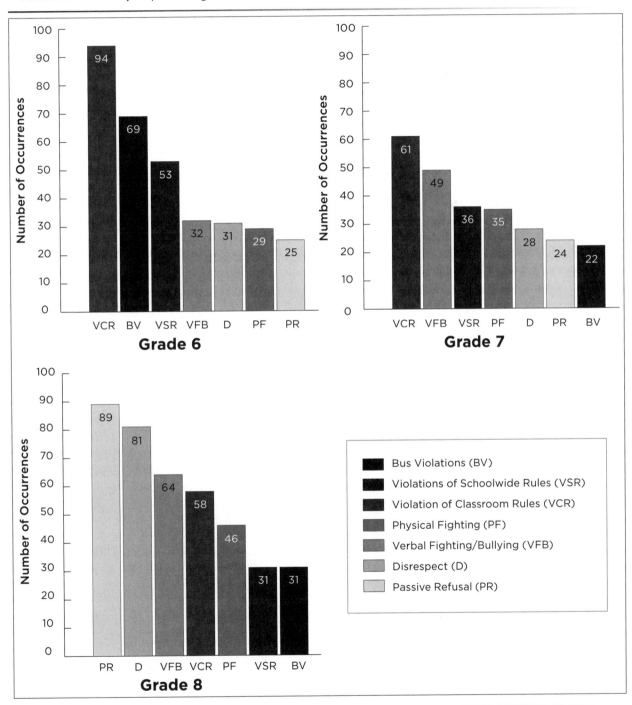

Figure 4.4: Mode Middle School discipline.

Subjective Nonacademic Student Data

A school's use of data should include the regular collection of perceptual data from students through surveys or focus groups. It is useful to remember that a high school senior has observed teaching and school leadership conducted in multiple ways over a span of twelve to thirteen years—which may provide him or her with a more comprehensive view than most educators can acquire from the proximity of their immediate and perennial positions. Views are certainly influenced by experiences, and that is why the data are termed "subjective."

The student voice is even more necessary in situations when students' out-of-school experiences differ greatly from the school environment. Few of us know what it's like to be a child or teenager in this decade in society. In schools where demographics have shifted, few adults have experienced the cultures of race or poverty that are the daily lives of their students. It is certainly and tragically true that teachers encounter apathy and hostility among students daily. But we must not assume we know what they're thinking and feeling without checking directly with them to hear their side of the story. One principal aired her frustration eloquently: "It has always amazed me that adults can sit around and talk about what to do with or to the kids, as if kids don't have minds or opinions or been living it for nine to ten years already."

A study of black and Latino students in a low-performing high school points out the gap between our perceptions and theirs (Thompson, 2008). Ninety-seven percent of the teachers agreed with the statement "I care about my students' academic and personal welfare both inside and outside of school." But students did not perceive this the same way. Only 56 percent of the black students and 57 percent of the Latino students stated that their teachers cared about them.

Some children come to school academically behind—but when they enter our doors, they don't know that. Kindergarteners think they're OK and are fired up to be in school. But they

> quickly learn that they are a liability to the schools that they attend, that they do not have the "right stuff," and that schools are about winners and losers . . . Instead of developing a healthy work ethic, many of these students develop despair, disengage themselves from schoolwork, and leave school before they graduate. An emphasis on test scores as the predominant way to demonstrate school success has been found to increase dropout rates. (Berliner, 2010, p. 136)

We should, at the very least, ask our struggling students what would keep them in school.

Gathering Subjective Nonacademic Data

Voices of students can be heard in many ways—both formal and informal. In the ideal situation, a culture has been developed in which students and teachers have regular discussions, one-on-one and in small groups such as advisories. They talk about issues in the students' lives and incidents that arise in school life. Adults ask for their reactions and suggestions for addressing problems. This culture is more to-be-created than currently present in most schools, especially at the secondary level. The listening can begin "safely" and anonymously, with regular use of a brief survey given to all students, which consists of items reviewed in advance by teachers.

Conversations

Or the listening can begin more personally. Generate two or three questions and urge teachers to ask them in one-on-one conversations with a designated number of students with whom they are comfortable—initially. The "stretch" is when they interact with some students with whom they have not yet formed bonds. This approach is similar to the vignette in *The Blind Side* (Netter & Hancock, 2009), when Mrs. Tuohy asks, "Well, what's one thing I should know about you?" The answer, "I don't like to be called 'Big Mike,'" was specific and actionable. "Then from now on, you are Michael."

Surveys

The downside of a survey is that the responses are often multiple choice and, therefore, somewhat canned, leading, or limited. Open-ended questions yield richer answers. These generic questions can be adapted to most settings and used as a starting point:

- When you are in class and really learning, what is happening?
- When you are in class and having trouble, what is happening?
- What is one thing that would really help you learn?
- If you could change one thing about our school, what would it be?
- What is one thing the teachers should know about you?

Focus Groups

Focus groups provide a structure for hearing individual voices in small-group settings. Stratified random sampling can be used to generate groups with specific characteristics (Holcomb, 2010). The composition of the groups and the design of the questions should reflect the purpose of the study. Everyone who will be affected by changes based on the findings of the study needs to be represented in the data gathering.

The focus group methodology can also be used with specific subgroups of students and very specific questions. For example, each year at Cinco Ranch High School in suburban Houston, the administration and counselors identify thirty freshmen who continue to experience difficulty and invite them to a pizza party during the students' lunch hour. These "students complete a survey about their likes and dislikes regarding the school and offer their perspectives on why they are experiencing difficulty. The administration shares the results with department chairs and uses the findings to develop strategies for meeting the needs of individual students and [to] assess the possibility of revising or adding programs to better serve students" (DuFour et al., 2010, p. 124).

Shadowing

An alternative approach to employ in a setting where teachers actively resist receiving feedback about instruction in the voices of students is to have the teachers simulate the experience of a student. Provide coverage for one day for a teacher chosen by his or her peers who agrees to these minimal conditions: observe both the teachers and the students, try to stay mentally engaged at all times, and be honest in recording and sharing the experiences. Have the teacher choose a student's name at random from your pool of struggling students—and then follow that student's schedule and sit through the entire day of classes. Even if you have to pay a substitute teacher, the observations that are shared will be worth the cost.

Displaying Subjective Nonacademic Data

Because surveys are typically designed in multiple-choice format, they can yield quantitative information by categories and individual items. If a student survey is used as part of a package of instruments for administrators, staff, students, and parents, it is very important that the results can be accessed item by item. Students sometimes draw interesting inferences from the way adults word questions, so it's necessary to see the actual item and even ask some students what they thought it meant.

Figure 4.5 is a display of student data from focus groups, which use only open-ended questions. The analysis of the data can be laborious, first identifying themes, then coding responses by category and counting to find the most frequent responses. However, it is well worth the effort on a periodic basis, as even this brief summary of most frequently mentioned themes illustrates.

Question 1: When you are in class and really learning, what is happening?

- Teacher is explaining, not lecturing.
- Students are listening and asking questions.
- Teacher shows knowledge of students (for example, in tune with kids' lives, knows something good about each student, knows students on a personal level).
- Classroom is quiet and focused.
- Teacher uses hands-on activities, calculators, and computers.

Illustrative quotes:
- You do better in classes where you get along with the teachers.
- One teacher has a good personality. It's easier. You really want to answer his questions.
- The teacher wants to be there and understands where students are coming from.

Question 2: When you are in class and having trouble, what is happening?

- Other students are distracting, walking around, throwing things.
- Everyone is talking over everyone else.
- The teacher gives information but does not explain or break it into steps.
- Teacher gives assignment you don't understand, no help or explanation, just "read and figure it out."

Illustrative quotes:
- When I fool around, I get caught quickly...but American students get away with it. Feels like I'm picked on. Some students pick on me because of my accent. My teacher says, "Sorry I can't do anything about it. You come from a different place."
- Don't yell, stay calm, and lay the law down. Like "sit down and be quiet." Have class rules for behavior and stick by them.

Question 3: What is the one thing that would really help you?

- Teachers who are helpful if you go to them, stay after school to help, and give positive encouragement.
- Sports and activities I can belong to.
- Teachers make class fun, take time to explain and discuss worksheets, not just give them out.

Illustrative quotes:

- Teacher motivating me by telling us what he did to get by in school. Tell the stories, talk the truth about how the world is today and how we need education to be successful.
- ESL teacher and Latino club – when I'm there I don't feel discrimination.
- Teachers who care so much about us call the house, even if it is just because we are not working our best.
- Some teachers care . . . having a relationship with them helps a lot; they have your back.

Question 4: If you could change one thing about our school, what would it be?

- More time between classes and for lunch.
- Rules; for example, dress, cell/texting, detention, food and drinks in class, ten-day suspension.
- Make lessons more engaging; for example, interactive, group discussions, hands-on.

Illustrative quotes:

- Teachers do not all respect the kids . . . they talk the talk but don't have relationships with us.
- All the teachers should grade the same.

Question 5: What is one thing the teachers should know about you?

- Have relationships with students; don't prejudge, don't favor students who learn faster, care about all of us.
- We want help with problems in class, after school, explain a different way; know when we are and aren't learning and respond.
- We need interaction; for example, group activity, discussions, peer help.
- Get to know students' learning styles, strengths, and weaknesses.
- Get to know me personally, my home life, or at least know my name properly.

Illustrative quotes:

- Know and respond when we are learning or not learning.
- If teachers connect to you more, you learn better and pay better attention.
- It's hard for teachers to know every student, but those having problems should be pretty noticeable; have a conversation to understand the situation more.
- Know how we live, know our whole background, understand the problems we have at home.
- If a teacher wants to help me, they pull me to the side and tell me that I'm failing and that they will help me and stay after with me . . . that shows they care.

Figure 4.5: Mode Middle School student perceptions.

Discussing Subjective Nonacademic Data

Perceptual data are always open to multiple interpretations, and adults in schools are sensitive. The greatest value of the findings arises from thorough discussion and thoughtful reflection among the administration and staff of the school. Do *not* print copies of the findings and distribute them in staff mailboxes. Do *not* create a PowerPoint and deliver the findings as a presentation. Staff members need to be able to interact and construct meaning themselves. Here are some suggestions for staff processing of student input in a professional development setting:

- **Create readiness**. Acknowledge that this is "soft" research and may have multiple interpretations. Offer an opportunity for staff to read the raw data and do their own analysis if they wish. Acknowledge that they may find some particular student statement inaccurate or unfair. Encourage them to seek first to understand.

- **Examine the findings**. Conduct a jigsaw-type activity (Holcomb, 2009) with home groups of six to eight staff members. Present the focus group questions, and have the groups predict what they think students would say. Do not have groups report at this time. Show them the demographic groupings and ask them to look at their predictions. Do they think any of the predictions would be different for different groups? Which predictions? Different in what ways? From their home groups, have staff move to expert groups to look at specific parts of the findings. Each expert group might take the findings from all groups on one focus group question or might take all the responses from one grade level or student group. Expert groups discuss things they expected, look for surprises and variations among the different groups, and prepare to give a synopsis to their home groups.

- **Compare to predictions**. Members of expert groups return to share their observations with their home groups. An opportunity to report surprises and overall observations may be provided.

- **Make commitments**. Challenge groups with the question: what are you willing to accept from these students' voices as actionable input? What schoolwide issues will be incorporated for collective action through the school improvement plan? For these, how will specific action plans be developed? What issues will be further addressed in small groups, such as grade-level teams or professional learning groups? What issues will prompt them to set individual goals?

- **Follow up with students**. Students need to know that they were heard, and staff need to acknowledge that they have learned something and will be responding individually and schoolwide. Teachers may choose a question to ask in their own classes to gain more understanding. For example, "We have heard that students want more explaining and less lecturing. Help me understand what you mean by that." Teachers can share their individual goal with a class or small group of students and ask the students for progress reports. This is a powerful way to build relationships and mutual respect and model lifelong learning and openness to change.

Deciding on Action From the Subjective Nonacademic Data

Mode Middle School's data team creates its own summary of observations from the objective and subjective data of nonacademic student data sources. They use their observations to shape the content and process of data review they will use to engage all staff (see table 4.1).

Inevitably, they also speculate on action that might be taken: maybe a late bus so students will take advantage of academic help or participate more in co-curricular activities, perhaps a mentoring program with parent role models from the minority community, and certainly a review of discipline procedures. But they steadfastly resist the temptation to deliver either their findings or recommendations as done deals. They realize that would have a chilling effect on the authentic participation of staff in their own set of discussions.

Table 4.1: Summary of Mode Middle School's Nonacademic Student Data

Category	Celebrations	Concerns
Demographics	+ Overall enrollment is stable.	− The school has been previously unaware of increasing proportion of Hispanic students.
Attendance	+ African American students now resemble overall trend. + Efforts to improve attendance during testing month (April) seem to be paying off.	− Native American students are not in school a full year. − Hispanic students miss a lot of school midyear.
Discipline	+ Seventh-grade students have relatively few discipline problems.	− The top three sources of discipline for sixth graders are violations of classroom rules, bus violations, and violations of schoolwide rules. − The top three sources of discipline for eighth graders are passive refusal, disrespect, and verbal fighting/bullying.
Perceptions	+ Students value classroom discipline. + Students want to learn, and they recognize good teaching.	− Teacher-student relationships are not as strong as students wish. − Staff are unaware that relationships matter as much to the students as teaching methods.

At Bellingham High School in Bellingham, Washington, staff members reviewed data about student participation in school activities, knowing that the students don't always (ever?) come to school *just* to learn their academic skills. They realized that the traditional student council version of student leadership left many subgroups unrepresented and worked with students to add another component to student leadership in the school. But official student council composition and functions are governed by the national association and have benefits that are important to maintain. Their solution was modeled after the combination of Senate and House that make up the Congress of the United States. Regarding the formal student council as similar to the Senate, they added a student House of Representatives, which has a larger scope and size and more fluid membership. Any candidate who generated thirty signatures on his or her petition earned a seat in the House. Individual students could only sign one such petition, so they had to choose candidates and issues carefully. The House is truly representative of the current concerns and composition of the student body.

New clubs could also be added. If students wanted to start a club, they set up a sign-up table. If they obtained at least thirty signatures of support, the school allocated a stipend to the club and they were asked to generate a constitution and help find an adviser.

Future Nonacademic Data Needs

The Mode Middle School data team is creating two sets of next steps. In the short term, they are making plans that will engage staff to develop schoolwide awareness of the data and build commitment to identify and implement responses to the shared concerns. They also have a to-do list for their own role in support of data use. It already has items on it related to needs for more frequent and authentic assessment practices. Now they add needs for future data warehousing, like a better way to archive discipline referrals for easier retrieval and a way to document student participation in clubs and activities.

Elementary Exceptions

Elementary schools have and can use similar objective nonacademic data sources, such as demographics of enrollment, attendance, and behavior. Gathering the subjective data of student perceptions can be modified to fit the ages of the students. Survey questions can be written in student language, and primary students can respond by marking a range of facial expressions (for example, smiley faces, frowns, puzzled looks, sad faces) when an adult reads the items. An elementary version of focus groups can be conducted during class meetings, when teachers agree to ask a few questions in all classrooms and make notes of the answers they hear. Their notes are provided to the schoolwide data team, which compiles them and looks for common themes.

High School Highlights

Disaggregating student data by socioeconomic status can be a challenge at the high school level, since many students do not apply for free or reduced-price lunches—either from pride or because open campus policies provide alternatives. The support of the district can be useful in identifying younger siblings from the same households, which often increases the high school's awareness of the number of students in poverty that they serve. Some states have also implemented a "direct certification" process whereby families who are receiving assistance do not have to go through a separate application process in order to receive breakfast and lunch meals. As a result, at least in some states, data on socioeconomic status have become more accessible and accurate at the secondary level. Of course, it remains a highly protected field under federal privacy law, so it is difficult for schools to disaggregate local assessment data. On the other hand, we have already pointed out that students should be selected for instructional support based on evidence of their skill gaps, not on the basis of the subgroup they populate for AYP reports.

High schools also face the reality that it's easy to lose touch with their graduates after the ceremony has taken place. A practice that may be useful is to include a card in their graduation materials that asks them for the names and addresses of two people who meet these criteria: they will know where you are in a year or two, and they will be willing to receive communication from the school so it will know where you went. This would enable follow-up such as that in a scenario described by Bernhardt (2004): A small California district conducted a telephone survey of students, asking why they had stopped attending college. The nearly unanimous response "They made me write and I can't write!" (p. 4) was a wake-up call that changed the focus and engaged all departments in a schoolwide effort.

Subjective data from high school students are particularly revealing about instructional practices. More than 81,000 students responded to the High School Survey of Student Engagement administered in 110 high schools across twenty-six states (Yazzie-Mintz, 2007). One of the most significant findings was that students are bored. Two out of three students report being bored every day, while 17 percent say they are bored in every class. They say they are bored in class because they dislike the material and experience inadequate teacher interaction. But just knowing they are bored may not be helpful, as discussions of such data tend to focus on the students as the problem. Asking students what *would* engage them is far more productive.

Drawing on data from the same High School Survey of Student Engagement, Amy Azzam (2008) noted student responses to what methods of teaching and learning would excite them in school. They favored discussion and debate, group projects, role playing, and art and drama activities. Nearly one-half indicated that they were "not at all excited" by teacher lectures. It's time we began to listen, because Azzam (2008) also found that "in general, grades, course failure rates, and absence rates were better in schools characterized by supportive relationships between teachers and students and a perception among students that their coursework was preparing them for the future" (p. 94).

Students realize that there are certain things they must learn and that they can't just choose topics they are interested in, but they can provide specific suggestions about how teaching and learning take place. In focus groups I've conducted with ninth graders, it's apparent that they know they need to be active. Participants have stated: "Tell them to use hands-on materials and projects and group activities." "The teacher should be active and be with the class." "Teach us the way we understand—use objects like blocks, basketballs, visuals, etc."

Students on opposite sides of the United States provided the same themes about quality instruction and relationships when I asked what helps them learn. Specifically related to math instruction, their top two suggestions were: (1) breaking it down, step by step, going into detail, and (2) going to the board to work problems so you get a check on if you know it right away. Regardless of whether they were struggling students or successful students, they reinforced the tenets of chunking instruction and providing immediate feedback (Marzano, 2007).

When asked about times when they have trouble learning, the most common responses I've encountered in student focus groups were fear of asking questions, lack of teacher explanation, and the teacher rushing instruction. In one school, a group of students defended their teachers, saying that they realized the teachers didn't have the option of slowing down and helping them because the state test made them keep going.

A revealing comparison emerged from the responses of students in "basic" algebra and those in "standard" algebra classes. When asked for advice about improving math teaching, two of the three top responses from both groups were the same: explanations and examples, and individual help and patience. The first-place response for the struggling students was teacher relationships with students. As one student phrased it, "I am not always a good student or a bad student. I've been both—it depends on who is teaching me." Or in the words of a struggling student receiving extra help, "The teacher in Algebra Support is more understanding and gives us more individual attention. She can do it, but regular teachers can't—why?"

More general comments about classroom instruction make it even clearer that students have a grasp of instructional methodology:

- "Teachers should try to help each student with where they're at instead of trying to teach all students one thing."

- "Teach, don't lecture. It's not the same. Lecturing is when you just sit and go on and on and maybe ask a question now and then, but in teaching you break things down, make sure everyone is getting it; if even one misses, you deal with it and break it down some more."

- "Lecturing is just spitting out information. When you're teaching, you're getting into it and you're really giving an understanding of it and what it is so [students] can actually pull it into their brains and use it."

- "Teachers need to learn different ways of teaching it; different methods because people learn different ways."

Andy Hargreaves (2009) sums up the picture of students as active, responsible partners in their school experiences. He describes students as "partners in change . . . highly knowledgeable about the things that help them learn, such as teachers who know their material, care for them, have a sense of humor, and never give up on them . . ." He reminds us that "students must be a central part of any theory-in-action of educational change . . . [since] they make up the biggest group in education, and their voices matter a lot." He agrees that they should be "involved in school and district decision-making . . . contributing to design of new behavior codes . . . being part of school-improvement planning, professional development days that focus on school change, and the appointment of leaders in their schools" and that they can "foster change in their peers by being involved in programs where they read to younger children, mentor struggling students, or stand up for children who are bullied" (pp. 26–27).

These are the things we want students to do in our schools. If we ask them, and listen, they will tell us how to make it happen. And when they believe we mean it, they will help be part of the change. Isn't that the goal of public education? To develop productive citizens who will contribute to their community?

Conclusion

I saw him sitting in, yet not in, the group of ninth-grade students. He was at the far end of the conference table, with his chair pushed back as far as it would go, so I had to lean forward to make eye contact. When I did, I saw deep, sullen eyes, facial hair, tattoos, and piercings. I saw the strong, mature body of a hostile man, though I knew he was barely fifteen. Through the thirty minutes of short focus group questions, he passed on responding to every one, signaling his option with a sideways jerk of his head on to the next person. The last question was "What is one thing you think would make this school better?" Stalling until he was last to leave the room, he uttered his only response as he crossed behind my chair, "The least you could do is find someone who wants to *teach* us. But I'll be gone by then." As he walked out the door, my mental image of this young man's angry eyes blurred into a vision of the sad eyes of a rejected boy.

Perhaps we've focused too much on what we as professional adults believed should be done to and for our students—and neglected to tap their insights and involvement, while complaining at the same time that they aren't engaged. We need the voices of students and their power to help shape schoolwide decisions, provide teachers with instructional feedback, and participate as partners in their own learning and assessment.

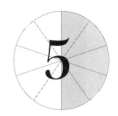

Using Staff Data

The Mode Middle School data team has gathered and prepared data on student achievement and on nonacademic factors that impact students' opportunity to learn and their success. The team knows there will be teachers making the claim that some of those nonacademic factors are outside their control. They will respond to that reaction by turning the focus to the factors that are within the school's control. The most powerful in-school factor affecting student learning is the quality of instruction, and that certainly falls within the purview of the school. The school improvement/leadership team will need data that are related to developing teacher capacity and responding to teacher needs. Their search for that data begins.

Fundamental Concepts for Use of Staff Data

The purpose of using data is to make the best possible decisions regarding how to increase student learning. Actions that need to be addressed on a schoolwide basis are addressed through the school improvement plan. Actions that relate directly to instruction and assessment in specific grade levels, courses, and classrooms are carried out through teacher teams. Data on staff preparation and practice inform the analysis of current practice, help plan and coordinate professional development for new practices, and identify ways to help support staff through change.

Preparation Data Reveal Teacher Needs

The connection between the preparation of teachers for their current assignments and their students' success is both intuitive and well-documented. Charles Clotfelter, Helen Ladd, and Jacob Vigdor (2007) conducted a large-scale study of high school teachers in North Carolina. They found that when teachers are certified in their subject, have higher scores on licensing tests, have more than two years' experience, and are National Board–certified, the combined effects of these qualifications on student achievement exceed the effects of race and parent education.

Basic data about teacher preparation that should be available include the degrees a teacher has been awarded and state licenses that are current. Critical data about preparation also include majors and minors within those degrees. Teachers cannot teach what they don't know, and as Richard Ingersoll (2008) reported, out-of-field teaching has a disproportionate effect on high-poverty schools. In core academic classes nationally, 17.2 percent of teachers in grades 7–12 and 42 percent of teachers in grades 5–8 were teaching out-of-field. For all grade levels combined, 27.1 percent of teachers in high-poverty schools were teaching out-of-field, compared to 13.9 percent in low-poverty schools.

Without knowing colleagues well, leaders may make assumptions that limit effectiveness or, worse, create conflict and confusion. Whenever a teacher changes schools, changes grade levels or course assignments, or encounters a newly adopted curriculum approach, information about prior education and experience is critical to providing appropriate support—neither assuming the teacher is already prepared nor automatically assigning the teacher to a one-size-fits-all orientation training.

Professional Development Data Allow Customization

In typical settings, the district and/or school has offered opportunities through venues such as in-service days, workshops, and stipends or salary increases for graduate work. When asked for data about participation in these offerings, districts may have total numbers who attended, and for a given training initiative, they may produce attendance lists. It is unusual for this information to be compiled teacher by teacher as a record of continued learning beyond initial preparation. Yet these data are critical for diagnosing the needs of teachers and planning for their support. A statement like "All staff were trained in . . ." must be followed by questions like:

- When was that?
- Are all those staff still here?
- Who has joined us since that training, and did they have the training somewhere else, or is it a missing piece?
- What were they teaching then?
- Would anyone need help applying this training if he or she were in a different setting now?

Without considering these questions, assumptions are frequently made that place teachers in the same situation too often faced by students: setting expectations, assuming they have all the prerequisites, and omitting provisions for extra help where needed.

Perceptual Data Guide Teacher Support

The impact of external mandates and changes in student population on teachers' confidence and stress levels may not be obvious in research, but these factors are clear in conversations with teachers. Today's teachers are under incredible pressure to serve more complicated students, cover more curricula, and ensure student mastery. Yet in the interest of saving time and money, less attention is being paid to gathering perceptual data from teachers and other staff in the school. Perhaps the "convenience" of having preset AYP goals and choices of research-based strategies to implement has made it seem less important to draw directly upon teacher input. Challenging targets are good, and information about proven practices is essential, but whether those targets are internalized and whether those practices are embraced and fully implemented depends on the hearts and minds of teachers.

Objective Staff Data

The Mode Middle School data team has some intense conversations about staff data. They know that recent developments like the teacher evaluation component in the state's Race to the Top application have made teachers even more nervous about the *D* word. So they decide to start with three characteristics of the Mode Middle School staff: demographics, education, and experience. They are confident that they can explain to the staff why those areas are of interest. Now that they've seen demographic shifts in the student population, they are more aware of the need to look at the makeup of the teaching staff and see what the students see. And since they have heard many complaints about past professional development experiences, they will explain that understanding the previous education and experience of staff will help them shape teacher support in more personalized and productive ways.

Gathering Objective Staff Data

NCLB included an emphasis on highly qualified staff, which created more accountability for staff data, but this was mainly addressed at the district level and may not have been a source of information or interest at the school level. Figure 5.1 provides a list of useful staff data.

Demographics • Gender • Race/ethnicity **Years of experience** **Areas of certification** **Graduate degrees** **Major in teaching assignment** **Perceptual data** • Surveys • Focus groups	**Locations of experience** • Other schools • Other districts • Other states **Years since completed undergrad** **Professional development participation and specialties** **Days absent per year** • Family, health • Professional involvement

Figure 5.1: Sources of staff data.

In most cases, data related to teachers' education and experience are maintained in the human resources department at the district level. Licensure information is readily available by going directly to the websites of state departments of education. However, these searches can be time consuming, especially in a large school. An alternative is to create a simple questionnaire that can be administered quickly and collected at a regular faculty meeting.

Displaying Objective Staff Data

Student achievement data and nonacademic student data have been displayed in a variety of graphs. The type of graph was chosen deliberately to highlight significant aspects of the data. The staff data being used at Mode Middle School are more straightforward and can be displayed in a simple table, as shown in table 5.1. The differences in demographics among staff groups and students are clear. The range of education and experience is easily read, and a possible challenge for math instruction is evident.

Table 5.1: Mode Middle School Staff Data

Demographics					
Certificated Staff		Classified Staff		Students	
Caucasian 91%	Minority 9%	Caucasian 30%	Minority 70%	Caucasian 44%	Minority 56%
Education					
Certificated Staff Education		BA/BS 34.3%	BA/BS + 30 12.9%	Master's 28.5%	MS + 30 24.3%
Major in Teaching Assignment	English 94%	Math 63%	Science 83%	Social Studies 85%	Electives 100%
Experience					
0–5 years 17.1%	6–10 years 11.4%	11–15 years 8.6%	16–20 years 15.7%	21–25 years 25.7%	26–30 years 21.5%

Discussing Objective Staff Data

Confidence had been building as the data work progressed, but Mode Middle School's data team is getting nervous again. Various voices arise in a chorus of concern.

"Ooh. This could get a little touchy. I can hear it already. Some teachers are going to say it doesn't matter what color we are or what color the students are. We're just here to do our jobs."

"Well, those conversations need to come out. But we definitely need to think about how we will set up the conversations so they are in small groups."

"Yes, and we should make sure we include classified staff when we do that. We'll need to encourage them to share what students may be feeling and how we can build relationships that are authentic but not 'color-blind.' This is one of those areas where we might not even know what we don't know."

"I agree. We can work our way through that. But I do really wonder if we should lay out the data about majors in the full-school conversation. Maybe we should hold that back for when we work specifically on the math part of the school improvement plan."

"Good idea. I'm one of the math teachers myself, and I came here from a high school, so I had a major and a master's in math. I've been wondering at some of the questions that come up in department meetings. Now that I think about it, most of the math teachers came from the elementary level when we started the middle school concept, and I'll bet they had K–8 certification. They may be feeling overwhelmed with these rigorous math standards. I'll work with Mr. Good, and we'll have a more private conversation about their background and needs. Maybe they haven't felt safe to say that they're not sure they have a good grasp on the content knowledge they have to teach now."

Mode Middle School's data team is being courageous in its intention to skillfully surface conversations that need to occur about cultural differences and may lead to a need for cultural competence as a goal of school improvement. They are also being compassionate as they consider their colleagues' experiences and choose the best method for using data that provide important clues for instructional improvement in a specific area. The five *W*s and *H* questions outlined in chapter 4 can also be used effectively with staff data.

Deciding on Action From Objective Staff Data

The use of data related to teacher education and experience is *not* for the purpose of evaluation, but for the purpose of planning. Professional development to strengthen the quality of instruction can take one of two directions. It can be designed on the assumption that everybody needs the *same* thing and one-size-fits-all will work just fine. That's too often been the case. The alternative is to plan professional development based on an assumption that everybody can improve but people have *different* needs—in which case, you don't do one-size-fits-all; you need information about what the needs are.

Learning Forward (previously National Staff Development Council [NSDC]) is an international organization focused on building teacher capacity and the improvement of instruction. Executive Director Stephanie Hirsh (2009b) stated that Learning Forward's theory of change

> stands on the assumption that students achieve more when teams of educators within a school and across a district engage in continuous cycles of improvement that focus their attention on their learning needs, as defined by student learning needs, refining their practice and accessing district and external assistance providers to support their efforts. (p. 5)

Since student learning needs are not all the same, teacher learning needs are not going to be the same or occur at the same time, so it becomes abundantly clear that one-size-fits-all professional development is not only insulting, it is a poor use of scarce resources that should be more strategically directed.

Four aspects of professional development should be differentiated: (1) what, (2) how much, (3) what kind, and (4) where/when. The topics (what) of professional development will change as student performance data identify skills of greatest need and teacher preparation data identify gaps in education and experience to meet those needs. Some teachers are already experts and don't need more professional development, except in the sense of developing others. The amount or degree of professional development (how much) varies by experiential factors such as how long it's been, if ever, since a teacher taught that content—and how much the academic rigor of the relevant standards may have changed in the meantime. The type or level (what kind) of professional development needed depends on whether the knowledge or skill is brand new and the teacher needs to start with the introductory theory, research, and examples, or whether the concepts are familiar and it's time to engage in practice with feedback through peer observation or coaching. Decisions about the most effective setting and timing (where/when) will emerge once the need and goal have been established through the earlier discussions.

This is a quantum leap from the traditional practice of identifying this year's new thing, sitting everyone down for three hours on the first day back from summer vacation, baptizing them in the perspiration of a hot gymnasium, and anointing them to "go forth and implement." But to differentiate in so many directions (what, how much, what kind, where/when), leaders would need either blind faith that all teachers will choose what they really need or diagnostic information to guide choices and to collaboratively develop goal-oriented individual and team plans. After using student performance data to identify their greatest learning needs, leaders would need to collect data on teachers' related learning needs including self-assessments, peer assessments, and student assessments.

A far cry from the traditional "pick one from column A and one from column B" menu of workshops, self-assessment is based on clearly defined expectations and descriptors for the particular content knowledge or teaching strategy. Innovation Configuration (IC) Maps (Hall & Hord, 2001; Holcomb, 2009) are useful tools that present various levels of implementation and enable a teacher or team to identify where they are now and what should come next in their skill building. An IC Map identifies key components for the successful implementation of a new strategy or approach. Various configurations (versions or levels) of implementation are described in cells across a row for each component. The first cell includes the descriptors of full implementation, with partial to no implementation described in the cells moving to the right. (Chapter 7 includes an IC Map for six-trait writing, and the appendix provides an IC Map related to data dynamics.) Without having clear descriptions of what full implementation entails, without various levels of development laid out so teachers know what should be different from their current practice, they have sincerely assumed "we're already doing it," resented any implication to the contrary, and resisted attempts to invite them into a coaching relationship.

In a collaborative culture, colleagues can use the same criteria to support each other through peer assessment. They can affirm what each individual already does well and can more gently help a friend identify what to work on, especially as it is precisely related to the content area, age of students, and school context.

Student assessment or feedback can be powerful in goal identification, even without being as specific as or linked to a set of documented expectations. The open-ended questions "What's one thing I could do *more of* that would help you learn?" and "What's one thing I should do *less of* that would help you learn?" provide fascinating and surprisingly useful information. Seeking feedback models lifelong learning for students, and when teachers share their growth goal with students, they often receive unexpected encouragement and reinforcement for their efforts.

One-size-fits-all professional development wastes time, energy, and resources. The need to help teachers accurately identify what they already do well is not just to help master teachers avoid the boring experience of sitting through the same workshop for the nth time. It is even more important for the positive purpose of identifying internal expertise that should be intentionally deployed to differentiate for someone else by providing a mentor. Questions that should arise in professional development planning include:

- Who are our resident experts?

- Who needs basic training versus advanced review?

- In what areas do we need external assistance and support?

- How will we maximize use of our opportunities (for example, district events, internal experts, time, and money)?

- What will we *not* do this year to make space for customized collaborative learning?

Subjective Staff Data

The schoolwide data team continues its discussions about staff data. Team members barely remember to take turns as they all speak up.

"If we are going to show data *about* staff, we'd better balance it by showing that we listen to information *from* staff also."

"You're absolutely right. We can't have this look like it's all one direction, aimed toward them. But we don't have time to do a new survey at the start of the year like this, and people got pretty surveyed out last year."

"Yeah. I remember wondering why every little grant we got had to do their own survey. One of the surveys was kind of interesting, though. It had forms for administrators, staff, and parents, so there might be some comparisons that would be helpful. Did we ever get results back from that? I'll ask around and see if I can dig it up."

Gathering Subjective Staff Data

Mode Middle School's data team discussion brings out some interesting points about gathering subjective data. First, doing surveys too often decreases the value of the responses because respondents get tired of doing them and invest less time and thought. Second, if the results don't come back and get discussed and used, there is even less perceived value. Third, instruments or items that gather responses from more than one stakeholder group provide opportunities to compare perspectives. This can surface underlying misunderstandings or miscommunication and provide an opportunity to improve relationships and strengthen the culture of the school.

Another powerful way to gather subjective data is through focus groups, which were discussed in terms of student input in chapter 4. Focus groups can also be used effectively with teachers, especially for the purpose of checking implementation of a new program and determining the questions and obstacles that teachers are facing *after* the initial training. The "Elementary Exceptions" section of this chapter provides an example.

Displaying Subjective Staff Data

Surveys are often designed based on a set of variables or characteristics identified through research as being related to high performance (for example, the correlates of effective schools). Multiple items for each characteristic may be clustered together or scattered throughout the survey. Graphic data displays usually show the combined results for all the items related to a characteristic, as seen in figure 5.2.

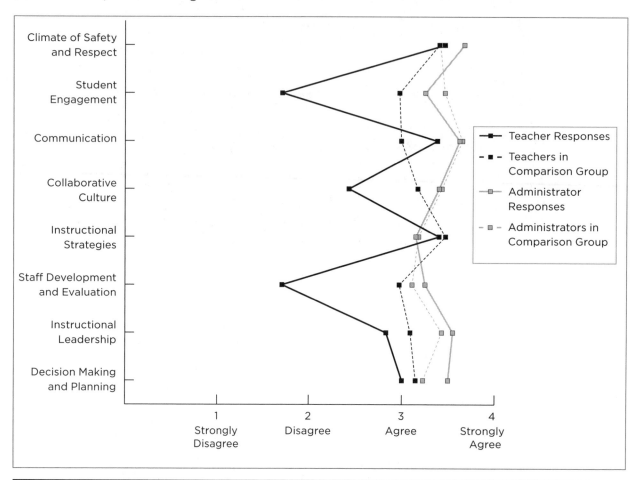

Figure 5.2: Mode Middle School survey profile—teachers and administrators.

This graph includes the responses of two staff groups and two comparison groups. The input from Mode Middle School's teachers and administrators is shown with solid lines. The dotted lines of the same shade display the mean responses from a set of schools with similar demographics that are designated as successful based on state report card criteria.

Discussing Subjective Staff Data

The graph in figure 5.2 provides information by category or characteristic. This condensed information helps the viewer spot general areas with higher and lower agreement (satisfaction). It also communicates areas where the responses of different groups are similar or widely different. It's easy to see at a glance that teachers at Mode Middle School have negative feelings about student engagement and staff development and evaluation, and that these perceptions differ greatly from the perceptions of teachers in the comparison group and from the perceptions of administrators in their own school and others. Where patterns of interest and concern like this are observed, the individual items in the survey must be identified and read carefully. For example, looking at the actual items about staff development and evaluation that were combined into one category may yield a realization that teachers are actually quite satisfied with the professional development they are receiving but very nervous and upset about changes in the evaluation process being considered by the district.

A general protocol for discussion of survey data includes steps that may be done in any sequence but should all be included:

- Identify the overall highs and lows for each group of respondents. (Since this chapter is about staff data, begin with teacher responses.)
  - What were the top three categories of highest agreement from teachers?
  - What were the lowest three categories of agreement by teachers?
- Compare the school's responses to any comparison groups that are provided (for example, benchmark schools, district averages, state averages).
  - What were the top three categories for teachers in the comparison schools?
  - What were the lowest three categories for teachers in the comparison schools?
  - Which categories did our teachers rate similarly?
  - Which categories did our teachers rate differently?
  - Within the categories of disagreement, what were the specific items? Which of those specific items contributed to lower/higher responses?
- Compare responses among groups within the school.
  - What were the top three categories of agreement among administrators?
  - What were the lowest three categories of agreement among administrators?
  - Which categories showed the highest agreement between the teacher responses and administrator responses?
  - Which categories represented the greatest discrepancy between teacher responses and administrator responses?
  - Which specific items in those categories had disparate responses?
- Identify the areas for celebration.
  - Which categories had the highest ratings by all groups?
  - Which categories had the highest levels of agreement? (Even if the high level of agreement related to negative responses, the cause for celebration is that participants have the same perception and there is a foundation for action.)
- Identify areas of greatest concern/urgency for attention in planning.
  - Which categories had the lowest ratings?
  - Which categories had the greatest disagreement between/among groups?

Table 5.2 provides a summary of Mode Middle School's objective and subjective staff data. Responses to specific survey items from the categories of concern will be needed and can be included in coming discussions about current practice and root causes.

Table 5.2: Summary of Mode Middle School's Staff Data

Category	Celebrations	Concerns
Demographics	**+** Classified staff add diversity and better resemble student demographics.	**−** Certified staff may be less aware of students' lives outside school.
Education and Experience	**+** Certified staff are highly qualified.	**−** Math department has lowest percentage of teachers with majors. **−** Nearly half of teachers are nearing retirement. **−** Many teachers are in the early stage of their career.
Perceptions	**+** Strongest responses were for climate, communication, and instructional strategies. **+** Teacher responses were higher than those of the comparison group in climate and communication. **+** Administrators also gave the highest ratings to climate and communication. **+** Administrator responses were also high for instructional leadership and decision making and planning. **+** Administrator ratings were above those of the comparison group for climate, staff development and evaluation, instructional leadership, and decision making and planning. **+** Teachers and administrators had closest agreement on climate, communication, and instructional strategies.	**−** Lowest responses for teachers were student engagement and staff development and evaluation. **−** Teacher responses were below those of the comparison group in student engagement, collaborative culture, instructional strategies, staff development and evaluation, instructional leadership, and decision making and planning. **−** Administrator responses were below those of the comparison group in student engagement. **−** The largest gaps between administrator and teacher responses were in student engagement and staff development and evaluation.

Deciding on Action From the Subjective Staff Data

Objective staff data revealed clues for future professional development planning. Responses from the subjective data should also be included in professional development planning. In addition, input from teachers is essential for developing plans to support implementation and respond to concerns about change. Like all human beings, teachers need support through the changes occurring around them, especially changes over which they have—or feel they have—little to no control.

The Concerns-Based Adoption Model (CBAM) is based on research studies of teachers reacting to various innovations of practice. One component of the model identifies a sequence of stages through which people move as they accept and adjust to new practices. Shirley Hord, Gene Hall, and colleagues (Hall & Hord, 2001; Hord, Rutherford, Huling-Austin, & Hall, 1987; Hord & Sommer, 2008) describe the progression of concerns as: awareness, information, personal, management, consequence, collaboration, and refocusing. When individuals in an organization become *aware* of an impending or developing change, their first concerns revolve around wanting more *information* about it and how they will be affected *personally*. As their questions are answered and they become willing to attempt the new practice, their concerns relate to how they will *manage* such logistics as time, materials, and record keeping. When these concerns of self and the task are addressed, teachers become more interested in the *consequence*—how their use of a new practice is affecting students. More advanced stages of concern relate to sharing their new efforts in *collaboration* with colleagues and using their own ideas to modify and improve (*refocus*) the innovation.

Other components of the CBAM include levels of use aligned with the stages, written and informal tools for diagnosing an individual's stage of concern, and compiling profiles of the concerns within a school. When a leadership team has a better understanding of the range and frequency of concerns being experienced by staff, they can choose appropriate ways to provide support and move all members further along through the change process. The "Elementary Exceptions" section provides an example of gathering subjective data from teachers aligned with stages of concern, so that next-step plans for building teacher capacity can respond to their needs.

Future Staff Data Needs

The Mode Middle School data team gathered data that represented characteristics of the staff: preparation, professional development, and so on. These data provide valuable information about factors that impact student learning, such as the awareness that many math teachers did not have a full major in their teaching assignment.

The focus of the future will be more on the actual results of teacher performance in terms of student learning. In the United States, use of staff data is being explored in various ways with links to student learning as part of teacher evaluations. It is essential that districts and schools define expectations and exercise accountability for quality instruction and assessment practices and fully implement strategies that are collaboratively chosen schoolwide commitments. This will increase student learning. Implementation of a balanced assessment system that provides formative and growth assessment data from every content area will be needed to fairly utilize data about student learning connected to individual teachers.

Elementary Exceptions

This section provides an example of staff data at the elementary level and illustrates how the stages of concern can inform support for implementation. A midsize urban school district in the South Puget Sound region of Washington State was in the second year of using *Investigations* as its core math program, but teachers were expressing frustration, and principals and instructional coaches were noting wide variations in implementation. Focus groups were set up by grade level, and several sessions for each grade level were scheduled after school in various geographical areas of the district to increase opportunities for teachers to attend. The questions asked in the focus groups included one multiple-choice item for which responses were recorded on sticky notes and collected. The multiple-choice answers matched the stages of concern and levels of use as shown in table 5.3. Participants were asked to sign their responses so groups could be formed for customized assistance.

Table 5.3: Response Items Reflecting Stages of Concern

Stages of Concern/ Levels of Use	Focus Group Responses
Awareness/Nonuse	a. I really don't know about *Investigations* yet.
Information/Orientation	b. I'm learning more about *Investigations* but don't know enough to really use it yet.
Personal/Preparation	c. I'm getting ready—my thoughts, materials, classrooms, and so on.
Management/Mechanical	d. I'm using some parts but still struggling to implement all the components.
	e. I use *Investigations* as I should, but it feels awkward, and I really have to work at it on a day-to-day basis.
Management/Routine	f. I'm using *Investigations* as I should, and it feels stable and routine now.
Consequence/Refinement	g. I'm fully implementing all components of *Investigations* and feel comfortable differentiating to match my students' needs.
Impact/Collaboration	h. I'm fully implementing all components of *Investigations*, and my colleagues and I work together to refine our practice and adjust to student needs.
Impact/Refocusing	i. Based on my experiences, I'd like to be a leader in next steps to refine our math instruction in the district.

The responses to open-ended questions were entered on a laptop without identification of the speaker. These questions included:

- From your perspective, what is the biggest difference between *Investigations* and the way you have taught math in the past?

- What aspects of implementing *Investigations* are going well or best for you?

- What do you observe about your students' experiences/reactions with math *Investigations*?

- In general, what are your biggest concerns about using *Investigations* right now?

- What specific aspects of implementing *Investigations* are problematic for you at this time?

- What kind of help do you need to continue to be more effective in your use of *Investigations*? What would "support" look like?

Stages of concern and levels of use varied between grade levels. Kindergarten teachers showed the lowest levels of use, and the open-ended questions provided the explanation; they requested specific help with adjusting pacing guides as they were in schools with only half-day sessions. Primary teachers (grades 1–3) were clustered at the management/routine level and indicated the least concern about the hands-on, exploratory approach used in the program. Teachers from grades 4–5 were clustered more at the management/mechanical level, and they indicated concerns about a lack of workbooks/worksheets for computation practice.

The results identified some further professional development needs that were common to all grade levels. For example, all teachers indicated that the process skills of making connections were difficult to implement and often omitted due to lack of time. Other results provided instructional coaches with specific focus areas for lesson modeling: number sense at third grade; geometric sense and algebraic sense at fourth grade; probability and statistics at fifth grade. As next steps are planned for training and support, the teachers who identified themselves at the collaboration and refocusing levels can be tapped and developed as teacher leaders.

High School Highlights

Use of staff data to guide plans for professional development and support has special challenges at the high school level. Teacher focus groups at the elementary level showed very different needs from grade level to grade level. A high school with grade-level differences and content-area differences needs to be even more systematic and differentiated in its approach to improving instruction.

In their *Learning From Leadership* study, Louis et al. (2010) revealed that teachers at the high school level do not see their principals actively engaged in instructional leadership and asked the question:

> If teachers do not look to principals as instructional leaders, where will they get feedback about their instruction? Our findings indicate that discussions about teaching and learning occur informally between colleagues and peers; they occur less frequently in the context of structured team meetings, content-area meetings, or [other leadership] channels. Infrequent provision of instructional leadership by principals, especially at the secondary school level, leaves little room for dialogue about teaching and learning between leaders and followers. Consistent with Supovitz's (2007) findings, our

research indicates that under current secondary school structures, author-ity relationships tend to discourage candor about problems that secondary school teachers may be having. (p. 91)

Louis et al. (2010) conclude that secondary schools appear to "suffer from a double whammy—low professional growth climate, and few actions taken to support classroom instruction, which appear to be indicators of lower student performance" (p. 93).

If authority structures discourage candor about teacher needs, there is an even greater need for teacher representatives on the school improvement/leadership team and schoolwide data team to help gather, communicate, and use subjective data from teachers.

Conclusion

The data team at Mode Middle School is beset by mixed emotions. They are proud of their progress in gathering student achievement data; nonacademic data related to student learning and student perceptions; information about staff demographics, education, and experience; and survey responses from teachers and administrators. They can see how valuable this information can be. They're also feeling a little overwhelmed and know there is one more source of information they need to tap—the families and community members who provide the home environments of their students.

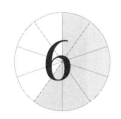

Using Parent/Community Data

Models of school improvement typically require plans to be signed by representatives from within the school community, such as parents within race/language communities, president(s) of parent and community organizations, business partners, or other citizen volunteers. These signatures are meant to convey participation in the entire process of data analysis and decision making and commitment to support implementation. The actual presence of parent/family and community representatives on a school improvement/leadership team is less common and should be seriously considered. Because of the confidential nature of student learning data, the schoolwide data team will not include parent/community representatives on a regular basis. However, it is imperative that two-way communication channels be active and effective. The schoolwide data team must be open to the idea of inviting parents into conversations on an ad hoc basis to help interpret some types of data. As Fullan (2005) states:

> Under conditions of power asymmetry with poor parents, vulnerable and unconfident in their relationship to schools, it is incumbent on principals and teachers to reach out, be empathetic, and create possibilities for parent involvement. When they do . . . greater connection is made with parents and students, and achievement goes up. (p. 61)

Fundamental Concepts for Use of Parent/Community Data

When the Mode Middle School data team acknowledged that perhaps the staff do not know what they do not know, they realized that there is knowledge and wisdom outside the school that need to be tapped.

Parent involvement is often regarded as attending school meetings and conferences, volunteering in classrooms, supporting school discipline policies, and ensuring that students complete homework. Those tasks are vitally important, but they leave parents/guardians in one-way roles in service to the schools, without an active chance to shape the school itself.

Incorporating data about and from families and communities is an ethical necessity. It is also a legal requirement for schools receiving Title I funds. A written parental involvement policy and compact must be developed that include the role of parents in the process of school review and improvement. Activities that engage parents to improve student academic achievement and school performance must be planned and provided. Districts must specifically communicate results of an annual review of each school, including the effectiveness of activities that are being carried out with respect to parental involvement, the instructional program, and professional development. Communications and scheduling must remove barriers of non-English home languages and parent work schedules. Parents must be notified if a school is identified for improvement, corrective action, or restructuring, including information about how parents may be part of the improvement efforts and how to request that their child be transferred.

Fortunately, this involvement of families and communities is not only for compliance with the law in certain settings. It has documented benefits for the bottom line of improving student achievement. The *Learning From Leadership* study (Louis et al., 2010) documented implications for policy and practice related to parents/community. It concluded:

> In their efforts to improve student achievement, school- and district-level leaders should, as a matter of policy and practice, extend significant decisional influence to others in the school community. Compared with lower-achieving schools, higher-achieving schools provided all stakeholders with greater influence on decisions. The higher performance of these schools might be explained as a consequence of the greater access they have to collective knowledge and wisdom embedded within their communities. (p. 35)

Louis et al. (2010) also noted:

> Superintendents and principals working to extend influence to others should not be unduly concerned about losing their own influence. Results reported here show that higher-performing schools awarded greater influence to most stakeholders; at the same time, little changed in these schools' overall hierarchical structure. (p. 35)

In other words, parent/community input is associated with better decisions that can improve student learning—and the internal school structure is not threatened by their inclusion.

Objective Parent/Community Data

The data team at Mode Middle School continues its conversation about data for its school portfolio and whole-school review. Team members chime in with a range of observations.

"Whew. One more big data source to investigate. It's a good thing you unearthed that survey from last spring that had a form for parents. Otherwise, we wouldn't have any information at all from them."

"That's for sure. But as for data *about* them, I guess we've just assumed that all we need to know is that they are the parents of our students. When I stop and think about it, I know a few students who don't even live with their parents. They're actually with an aunt or grandparents."

"I think the EL department at the district has some information about the primary language being spoken at home. But that doesn't tell us what we would need to know—we need to know who's the nearest adult that *does* speak English, so we can figure out a way to get in touch with them."

"There's a lot we could learn about the families that would be helpful, isn't there?"

Gathering Objective Parent/Community Data

Information about families and households in the community is not always readily available at the school level. By law, districts limit access to the socioeconomic information in free/reduced-price lunch applications. English learner information is sometimes available, but schools may not be aware that it can be helpful for purposes other than placing students in programs.

Students are not all the same, so we disaggregate information about them. Staff members are not all the same, so we (should) customize professional development approaches for them. Families and communities are not all the same, so we (should) avoid developing single-focus plans for parent involvement. As the time crunch becomes ever tighter and the pressures increase, we lose focus on outreach and involvement with portions of our community who do not have children in school. The school's data portfolio needs to include information about neighborhoods, races, languages, and ages of its constituents, and service organizations, agencies, and centers that serve them. These data can guide efforts to improve communications, publicize the school, gather input, and increase volunteerism.

As noted in figure 6.1, central office departments beyond Curriculum and Instruction can also be helpful. For example, the transportation department probably has bus route maps that show all of the stops. Where there are no bus stops, there are either no children of school age or the children attend private schools. Community organizations such as the Chamber of Commerce and Realtors' Association also keep information about neighborhoods that can inform school awareness and planning.

Demographics
- Race/ethnicity
- Age
- Households with school-aged children
- Households with children at this school

Perceptual data
- Interviews
- Focus groups
- Surveys

Attendance at parent-teacher conferences
Neighborhood concentrations
- Chamber of Commerce
- Census Bureau
- Realtors' Association

Participation as volunteers
District transportation department

Figure 6.1: Sources of parent/community data.

When asked about stakeholder input, the answer too frequently is, "Well, yes, we used to give a survey to community, staff, and students so we could get their opinions and compare their perceptions, but we haven't done that in quite a while. We've had to really focus on just getting our state scores up." Both parents and nonparents have deeper concerns and broader visions for their schools than making AYP. In order to communicate with and engage a community, it's critical to hear from them. The information on subgroups mentioned previously will help to shape a multipronged set of methods and venues for connecting with the full range of stakeholders. Town hall meetings and focus groups in a variety of settings (and sometimes with interpreters) may need to replace pencil-and-paper surveys that were used in the past. Fullan (2005) emphasizes that "districts need to take the pulse of student engagement, principal and teacher ownership and morale, parent and community satisfaction, and so on" (p. 71).

Displaying Objective Parent/Community Data

As was the case with objective staff data, the information about families and the community may be limited and straightforward. As a start, a simple table will be sufficient to display the available data (see table 6.1). The Mode Middle School data team accessed external data sources to learn about households in the community. An assistant principal's files yielded checklists from teachers about attendance at the previous spring conferences.

Table 6.1: Mode Middle School Parent/Community Data

Community Connection to the School		
% of households with school-aged children	% of households with children at Mode M.S.	% of households with primary language not English
67%	26%	47%
Parents Attending Conferences Last Year		
Grade 6	Grade 7	Grade 8
Fall: 88%	Fall: 80%	Fall: 70%
Spring: 80%	Spring: 75%	Spring: 61%

Discussing Objective Parent/Community Data

Available data about families and neighborhoods can vary greatly in amount and content, so a protocol for discussion relies on a set of generic questions that can apply to all types of data:

- **What do the data seem to tell us?** The word *seem* in this question acknowledges that staff are making inferences about information that is used least frequently in schools and is less familiar.

- **What do the data not tell us? What else do we need to know?** This query prompts the need for deeper understanding and may identify follow-up steps for clarification.

- **What good news can we celebrate from the data?** The tendency to rush toward the negative is strong, and this question prompts attention to any good news that may be drawn from the data.

- **What needs for school improvement might arise from the data?** The word *might* is a reminder that these are tentative conclusions and ideas to be noted for further discussion as the school improvement/leadership team and teacher teams consider next steps.

Deciding on Action From Objective Parent/Community Data

The use of the generic questions in the previous section will provide ideas for future action in several ways. Some ideas will become strategies to be included in the school improvement plan. Some ideas will be referred for further consideration by classroom teachers and teams. Other ideas will prompt the need to look for more data now or design better ways to capture data in the future.

For example, the most recent spring conference attendance across all three grades averaged about 70 percent. The student demographic data displayed in chapter 4 show that 31 percent of the students are Hispanic. Discussion should prompt follow-up data work to determine whether the students who did not have parents or guardians attend conferences were primarily Hispanic students. If so, additional action would include a study of ways to span the language or culture barrier and better connect with the families of these students.

For Title I schools, strategies for action will include activities mandated in the law, such as: workshops on state academic standards, state and local assessments, and how to monitor children's progress; family literacy classes and training in how to use the Internet to communicate with students' teachers and track homework assignments; and opportunities to volunteer and observe in classrooms.

Subjective Parent/Community Data

The Mode Middle School data team has tapped into results from a climate survey that included formats for teachers, administrators, and parents. As they discuss the information they have (and don't have), team members contribute ideas about gaps and needs for clarity.

"We have these results, but we don't know if the parents who responded are representative of all parts of our community."

"And we need to read the specific items on this survey to see how they were asked. I'm not sure some of the terms that are used would mean the same to us as they do to parents."

"And what about the households that don't have children in our school? They vote, they pay taxes, and they probably talk about what's going on here. I wonder what they think about middle school kids. We're going to have to learn a lot more if we want to connect with our whole community."

Gathering Subjective Parent/Community Data

The schoolwide data team has raised some issues about parent/community surveys that affect the value of the data. In the future, they will want to use a coding system for different groups or parts of the neighborhood so they can determine whether the responses they receive are representative of all groups of parents/guardians. They may decide on strategies to gather perceptual data through group meetings at community centers, rather than by mail or email. If they receive Title I support, some funds can be used for transportation and child care, so meetings and conferences can be scheduled at a variety of times, and language interpreters can be provided. Households without children in the school might be randomly identified for mail surveys or telephone interviews. Tips for creating good questionnaires for noneducators (Bernhardt, 2004) include:

- State a strong purpose for participants to complete the questions.

- Keep the questions short and to the point—items and questions twenty words or less.

- Include questions that everyone can understand in the same way; eliminate all jargon.

- Start with more general questions and lead to more specific items.

- Ask all questions in the positive; avoid double negatives.

- Make sure that phrasing does not suggest a particular response.

Displaying Subjective Parent/Community Data

In the previous chapter, figure 5.2 (page 82) displayed the survey responses of teachers and administrators. Figure 6.2 adds the responses of parents, indicated by a solid line. The dotted line indicates how parents in the set of comparison schools responded.

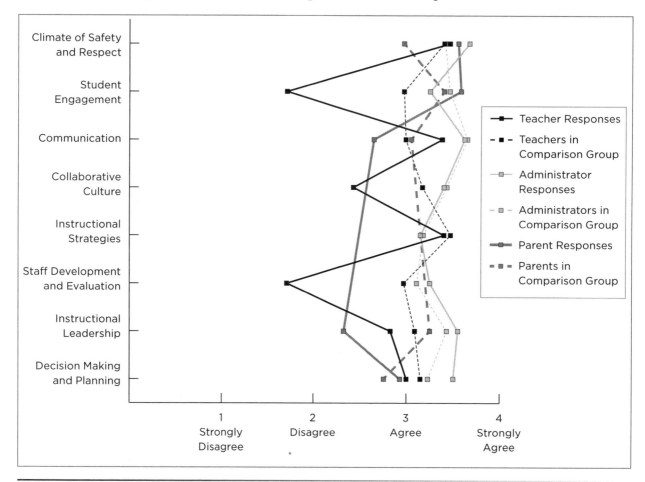

Figure 6.2: Mode Middle School survey profile—including parents.

Note that the graph shows how parents perceived five of the eight categories of the survey. The parent form of the survey did not include questions about teacher collaboration, instructional strategies, or staff development and evaluation.

Discussing Subjective Parent/Community Data

Discussion of the parent/community survey data can follow the same protocol as outlined in detail in the discussion of staff data in chapter 5. Another approach is to invite parents to discuss their responses to the survey, explaining what they thought about the questions.

A follow-up activity that can actively engage small groups of family and community members in problem solving is a cause-and-effect exercise (Holcomb, 2009). A problem is identified with a carefully phrased question that generates the factors participants perceive to be associated with that problem. Sessions can be scheduled for subgroups in the community so that they can all be represented in problem-solving groups and the range of perspectives can be noted. The comfort level and participation increase when the activity is facilitated by a member of the same group (for example, race, language, neighborhood). The opportunity to raise all ideas without judgment (similar in this way to brainstorming) encourages openness, and the responses help school leaders better understand the problem from a diverse range of perspectives. Often solutions become apparent as contributing factors are explored. These aha moments led one group to say, "When you take time to step back and look at it from different angles, it's pretty clear what we need to do. It's not rocket science."

Others have said that it's just common sense to engage all stakeholder groups in solution seeking and even that the solutions themselves are sometimes common sense. For example, a with-it senior citizen once pointed out, "Well, if the cars are coming through the turnaround too fast when kids are walking across it, just figure out a different route for one or the other: the kids or the cars. It's what these teenagers call 'a major *du-uh!*'"

Table 6.2 (page 96) represents the data team's summary of Mode Middle School's parent/community data.

Deciding on Action From the Subjective Parent/Community Data

Concerns have surfaced about communication, conference attendance, and several areas of the survey data. As staff review and react to these data, ideas for action will be generated. But the best ideas will come from the respondents themselves, if they can be engaged in follow-up discussions as described previously.

Future Parent/Community Data Needs

As noted in the earlier discussion of the Mode Middle School data team, information about and from families and the school community is limited. When staff engage in discussion of the data, there will be lots of responses related to the question of "What do the data *not* tell us? What else do we need to know?" This will enable the team to use the snowball approach to data gathering—start small and keep on rolling, adding more data as questions arise and information is sought in response to authentic queries.

Table 6.2: Summary of Mode Middle School's Parent/Community Data

Category	Celebrations	Concerns
Demographics		– About ¾ of households will not receive communication via material sent home with students. – Nearly half of households may not understand communication in English.
Involvement	+ Attendance at conferences is good for sixth grade.	– Conference attendance declines throughout middle school. – Data collection regarding parents and community has been very limited.
Perceptions	+ Parents give highest ratings (above comparison group) for climate and student engagement. + Parents agree with high teacher and administrator ratings on climate.	– Parent responses are lower and below comparison group for communication and instructional leadership. – Parent responses on student engagement are lower than those of teachers. – Parent responses on communication are lower than those of both teachers and administrators.

Elementary Exceptions

Elementary schools tend to have higher parent involvement and interest, so their schoolwide data teams have a somewhat easier task with this category of data gathering. However, the nonschool households in the community should not be forgotten—and may yield not only input, but rich resources. One day as an elementary principal provided extra supervision on the playground, he noted that the seniors who came for lunch at the senior center down the block paused by their cars to watch the children at play. The next day, he made it a point to take a short stroll and engage them in conversation—and ended up tapping an entire corps of volunteers to read with children after lunch each day.

High School Highlights

High schools, on the other hand, may find it very difficult to engage parents/guardians. Joyce Epstein's work (1995; Epstein et al., 2002) on family and community partnerships describes variations in parent involvement and communication as students progress from elementary to middle school and on to high school. Suggestions for high-school-appropriate parent activities (Agronick, Clark, O'Donnell, & Steuve, 2009; Ferguson & Rodriguez, 2005) include:

- Open house with concurrent sessions for students and parents. Parent sessions focus on touring the school, meeting teachers, clarifying expectations, and understanding extracurricular opportunities for students and volunteer opportunities for families.

- Parent academic nights that focus on the curriculum and provide timely responses to questions and concerns.

- School councils and advisory councils for specific programs, such as career, technical, and agricultural advisory boards.

- Career field focus nights. For example, parents and community members who work in health-related fields present wellness information and give career information for a range of positions and qualifications.

- College and career preparation assistance. Minority and ESL parents especially value assistance with the process of applying for college admission and financial aid.

- Planning agendas that include the student handbook and require a parent signature to verify that they have received and read the information.

- Spring parent meetings related to students' course selection for the following year. These may be connected to college- and career-readiness plans.

- Curriculum-based projects that include interviewing family and community members as primary sources.

- Workshops on brain research and learning strategies, including applications to adult work and life as well as student learning.

- Workshops on communication and advocacy, including role-play practice of how to be an advocate for the child.

High schools also have unique needs in connecting with the nonschool householders in their communities, especially the neighborhoods close to the school. These taxpayers may be impacted by student drivers, clusters of roaming or loitering students, noise from athletic events, and such. Providing opportunities for them to give positive and constructive input for school planning can build relationships that help them understand and overlook the normal and natural results of large populations of adolescents in their midst.

Conclusion

The Mode Middle School data team is ecstatic! They have built a data set that includes information about student achievement, nonacademic student characteristics, staff, parents, and community, and perceptions of staff, students, and parents. They are ready to facilitate staff engagement during a review of the data and can't wait to hear the questions and reactions that occur. They've discussed the data themselves and generated their own summaries and some tentative conclusions and recommendations, but they've steadfastly maintained that they'll hold their input to embed in collegial discussions.

The schoolwide data team will be able to breathe a short sigh of relief as the school improvement/leadership team incorporates staff-generated, data-guided strategies into the school improvement plan. But their respite will be short. They still have data needs they want to pursue; they'll be involved in continuing to help track the data to show evidence of improvement; and they've already begun a list of the things they want to discuss with the assessment and accountability department at the central office.

Using Data for School Improvement

Mode Middle School's data team has collected needed information and prepared it for staff review and discussion. Now the school improvement/leadership team will lead staff as they make decisions about how to move the school forward, addressing the concerns that have emerged. The data must be put to use to increase the success and satisfaction of staff and students.

Useful data are actionable, and the school improvement plan is the tool that communicates what actions will be taken in response to the data. Figure 7.1 (page 100) captures the key components of strategic district plans and school improvement plans that have survived the tests of time—from effective school plans in the 1980s to total quality management plans in the '90s and on into the 21st century of templates required of schools designated as failing (Holcomb, 2009). The purpose of this organizer is to create a framework for this chapter's discussion and a generic basis for assessment of the specific plan and process in use in any given setting.

The oval *mission* represents the statement an organization makes to articulate its desired future, its core values, and its ideals. Other terms like *vision* and *belief statements* are associated with this component.

The rectangle *school portfolio* represents the collection of data that is gathered initially, updated regularly, and used frequently to guide decision making. The four bullet points in this box are reminders of the four types of data to incorporate: student achievement data, nonacademic student data, staff data, and parent/community data.

Arrows within the figure demonstrate both sequence and relationships. For example, there is a two-way vertical arrow connecting the mission of the organization to the assembled data of the school portfolio. One serves as a test of the other. The data reflect whether the organization truly walks its talk, including how that is perceived by the stakeholders whose support is so coveted by school leaders. The purpose of disaggregated student achievement data is to check whether the stated ideal of "all students learning to high levels" is actually being realized.

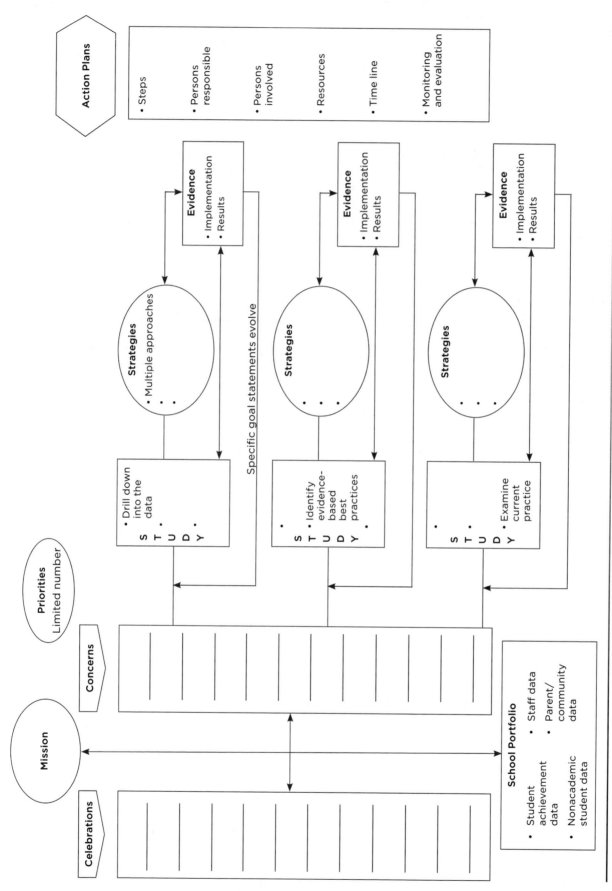

Figure 7.1: School improvement—the context for data use.

Source: Adapted from Holcomb, 2009.

The horizontal two-way arrow represents how the analysis of the data generates two sets of reactions: celebrations and concerns. In an era when accountability for school performance is based on a deficit model, identifying concerns is a reflex as automatic as a knee hit with a hammer. Concerted attention must be given to balance that reaction with a focus on what is positive and what is progress.

An oval is used again for the heading *priorities* above three lines that can be filled in with the areas of focus for improvement planning. This limit of three lines conveys the critical message that an organization must zero in on a limited number of targets. Otherwise, as the saying goes, "when everything's a priority, then nothing's a priority."

For each priority, goal, or focus, there are three related components that communicate the need for more thorough *study* (box), selection of *strategies* for change (oval), and identification of *evidence* (rectangle) that will demonstrate progress. Bullet points within the study box remind school leadership teams to (1) conduct a *deeper analysis of the data* for more specific information and a better understanding of the problem, (2) study the literature and research on *best practices* and network with others making gains, and (3) courageously discuss *current practices* at the classroom, school, and district levels. The in-depth study represented by these steps is sometimes referred to as *root-cause analysis*. All three aspects of *study* must be utilized for every priority area.

In this context, the term *strategies* is used in a broad sense to encompass instructional and organizational changes. It does not refer to a specific list of teaching behaviors. Strategy bullet points do not have the same type of specific definitions as the study bullet points but represent the reality that there are no magic potions that provide a single cure. Ignore the clever marketing of programs that purport to cover all standards and cure all ills. If it were that simple, we would have solved all student performance problems long ago. The deeper analysis of challenges (study box, first bullet) will reveal several points of leverage, and a variety of strategies will be needed to address each of these factors.

In the *evidence* rectangle, the two bullet points represent indicators that will be identified to monitor *implementation* and *results* in student learning. Evidence of implementation answers the question "Did we faithfully carry out the plans we committed to?" Evidence of results in student learning responds to the question "Did we make a difference in student outcomes?"

This sequence of studying the situation to identify strategies and indicators must occur for each priority/goal area. However, it is not a one-time, straightforward, linear process. As the arrows among these components indicate, it is a cyclical inquiry process. Collection of evidence may indicate that a strategy is working and will be sustained or that more study is needed to seek additional solutions. The evidence may even suggest going back to priorities to shift the focus or revise goals.

The presence of *action plans* at the right is not tightly linked to any/all of the *strategies*. Some changes are fairly simple, and there is no need to overcomplicate them with the listing of multiple steps. Some changes, such as restructuring the master schedule and staffing a high school, are very complex with many implications. For these strategies, a thorough task analysis is critical, and an action plan would be developed to describe the concrete details: what the specific steps are, who's responsible, who's involved, what funding will support the work, what the time frames are, and what evidence will be gathered to document progress. When there are multiple action plans, dates from the time-frame sections can be compiled to generate a calendar that will guide the school improvement/leadership team in its responsibilities of coordinating professional development, gathering evidence to support implementation, and monitoring results.

Data at Decision Points

Data use is ubiquitous in the context of school and district improvement. Figure 7.2 illustrates the use of data to ask questions and take action at critical decision points in the process.

Developing a mission statement involves asking, "What do we value, regardless of external mandates?" and necessitates action to gather data and use it to hold all members of the organization accountable to upholding and striving for the mission. As the data team assembles the school portfolio, they ask, "What data do we have, and what data do we still need?" They then assemble available data and identify needs for future data work. The school improvement/leadership team will facilitate staff comparison of the available data with the lofty ideals of the mission statement. As they ask for evidence of what's working, they act to continue those gains by sustaining momentum around the strategies that led to success. Where the data fall short of the mission, the question of what's not working will lead to action as priorities are set for immediate action.

Further data use occurs in the study stage. An ad hoc study group is formed for each priority area, made up of staff and others most directly affected by the concerns raised. These ad hoc groups will drill deeper into the data to answer the question "What are the specific skills, and who are the specific students who need attention?" During their study process, these teams also seek information about the most effective strategies, as documented by data proving their effectiveness. The most courageous analysis occurs in response to the question "What are the gaps between best practices and our practices?" Answering the question honestly involves looking at what the school's data show (and do not show) and identifying additional data that are needed to verify what happens in classrooms throughout the school.

Data that answer the questions of the study phase result in recommendations from the study groups about the actions that should be taken as strategies in the school improvement plan. Gathering data to prove that the strategies are implemented and that they benefit students is action taken by the school improvement/leadership team to cycle back to assessment of the school's status and progress.

All-Staff Data Review

All staff should be engaged in the interpretation of the schoolwide data so they can react to it and generate ideas. The schoolwide data team may facilitate a protocol that engages staff in data discussion, empowers them to interpret what the data mean, and allows them to express reservations about its use. (See fig. 7.3, page 104.)

The materials to be prepared for this protocol include the data displays that are the graphs and tables prepared by the schoolwide data team (chapters 3–6), enlarged to poster size so they can be displayed on the walls of the lunchroom or gym and discussed in small groups.

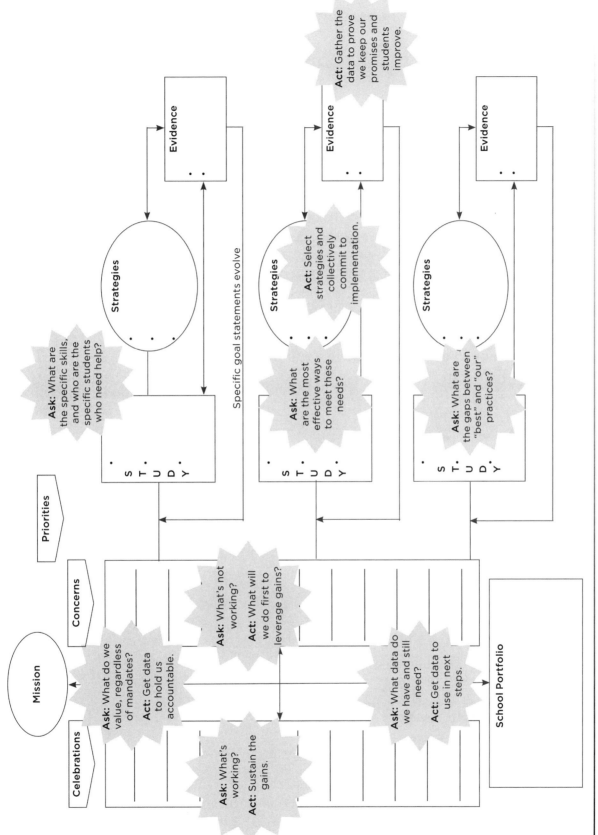

Figure 7.2: Data at decision points in school improvement.

Preparing the Materials
• Enlarged copies of the data displays • Questions for discussion on flip chart paper • Colored markers • Data displays and questions posted at stations around a large room with blank wall space
Preparing the Participants
• Structure groups of 5 to 11 that cross department or grade-level boundaries. • Have groups designate a facilitator and recorder; the colored marker travels with the recorder. • Read and respond to previous entries, then add.
Questions for Discussion
1. What do these data seem to tell us? 2. What do they not tell us? What else do we need to know? 3. What good news is here to celebrate? 4. What needs for school improvement might arise from these data?
Use of Results

Question 1
  • Refined into schoolwide data summary
  • Used in focusing on priority goals
 	
Question 2
  • Guides study phase—drill deeper, further analysis
  • Identifies indicators—evidence of implementation and results
 	
Question 3
  • Reinforces effort
  • Generates ongoing effort
 	
Question 4
  • Used in focusing on priority goals
  • Stimulates search for strategies

Figure 7.3: All-staff data review.

Source: Adapted from Holcomb, 2004.

To prepare the participants, groups should be structured before the event to help cross the boundaries of grade levels or departments that people naturally drift into. Grouping can be very straightforward, by providing a handout of groups and the station where each will begin, or done in a more lighthearted way, such as colored dots on name tags or numbers on the sticks of lollipops. Members of the school improvement/leadership team and data team will introduce the activity, and two or three will observe/facilitate, but most of the team members should be sprinkled among the groups. They should participate, not lead, but redirect to the purpose when necessary. They will also make mental notes of comments and dynamics for debriefing with the team later.

The Questions for Discussion will be provided on four sheets of chart paper posted next to each data display. Groups will record their observations as described in the following steps. These comments will be summarized and used (Use of Results) to complete the data summary, refine goals, sustain successful efforts, and identify new strategies.

This activity takes one and a half to two hours, so it fits well within a late start or early release time frame. Take the first fifteen minutes to explain the purpose of the activity and the reasons the participants have been placed in groups. The purpose is to give everyone an opportunity to view all the data that have been prepared for the school portfolio. The participants are being asked to contribute to the interpretation of the data and provide input to complete the data displays. The groups are a way of encouraging discussions among people who may not often see each other and sharing various perspectives. The activity is modeling the collaborative culture that looks at the big picture of the whole school (rather than how the specific grade or department is doing) and the collective responsibility that a school staff should share.

A staff of fifty with fifteen data displays to consider would be divided into fifteen groups of three to four in each group. There would be fifteen stations to visit. At a *minimum* of five minutes per station, the data review would take seventy-five minutes.

Variations can be made for a group of one hundred. One such variation is to have groups of seven or eight people. Another is to have two sets of graphs and operate two sets of stations. Another is to have larger groups and cluster several related data displays at each station.

The numbers or color codes of the groups will help participants find the other members of their group and the station where they will start. Give them a few minutes to get located and to choose the facilitator and recorder for each group. The group will have a designated time at that station. Their task is to discuss the data that are shown and react to each of the questions. The group should review what other groups have already noted and add a *star* by those they agree with, a *question mark* by any they don't understand, and a *"no" sign* (circle with diagonal) where they disagree. Then the recorder will add their group's new comments. After the designated time, at a signal determined in advance, each group moves to the next station to review another type of data.

A somewhat less effective alternative is to have groups seated at tables and provide each table with one set of all the data displays for discussion. Each group has a timekeeper and chart paper on which to record their reactions to each set of data. At the end of the activity, charts from each group are posted in clusters and everyone does a gallery walk to see the total results.

Overall Data Findings for Mode Middle School

The data team at Mode Middle School has gathered and displayed important data and prepared and facilitated an activity to engage the entire staff. When they debrief and compile the responses from the charts, they are a little disappointed—but not surprised—to find some snide comments about using data and some negative insinuations about students and parents.

They include everything that was said as they create a master summary for further reference. They are also thrilled to discover that the staff identified the same celebrations and concerns they had noted. Their data summary (see table 7.1) will guide ongoing work of the school improvement/ leadership team and staff study groups as they select priorities, set goals, identify strategies, and implement and monitor changes needed to improve the school as a whole and increase student achievement.

Table 7.1: Mode Middle School's Data Summary

Student Achievement Data		
Category	Celebrations	Concerns
Reading	✚ Over 80% of students are proficient. ✚ Each grade level is showing gains. ✚ All cohorts increase percent proficient as they move through grades (for example, 60.1% to 80.4%). ✚ Strategies to support African American, Hispanic, and economically disadvantaged students are paying off. ✚ Gains are being made in all strands of reading assessment.	– Gaps still remain. – Largest gap is special education, then EL. – Proficiency with informational text is lower than with narrative. – In general, reading proficiency is lowest for all grade levels in vocabulary and in critical thinking related to informational text.
Math	✚ Each grade level is showing gains.	– Only 67% overall meet proficiency. – Proficiency is lowest in the algebraic sense strand.
Writing (no separate state test)		– Constructed responses are lower than multiple-choice items in all tested areas.
Science (state test only used in one grade)		– Constructed responses are lower than multiple-choice items.
Social Studies (no state test)		– Teachers observe that reports submitted by students are loosely connected links of quotes from the Internet. – There is a lack of critical thinking and organization.
Electives (no state test)		– Teachers are concerned about how to assist with academics and still honor their own curriculum.

Nonacademic Student Data		
Category	Celebrations	Concerns
Demographics	+ Overall enrollment is stable.	− The school has been previously unaware of increasing proportion of Hispanic students.
Attendance	+ African American students now resemble overall trend. + Efforts to improve attendance during testing month (April) seem to be paying off.	− Native American students are not in school a full year. − Hispanic students miss a lot of school midyear.
Discipline	+ Seventh-grade students have relatively few discipline problems.	− The top three sources of discipline for sixth graders are violations of classroom rules, bus violations, and violations of schoolwide rules. − The top three sources of discipline for eighth graders are passive refusal, disrespect, and verbal fighting/bullying.
Perceptions	+ Students value classroom discipline. + Students want to learn and recognize good teaching.	− Teacher-student relationships are not as strong as students wish. − Staff are unaware that relationships matter as much as teaching.
Staff Data		
Category	Celebrations	Concerns
Demographics	+ Classified staff add diversity and better resemble student demographics.	− Certified staff may be less aware of students' lives outside school.
Education and Experience	+ Certified staff are highly qualified.	− Math department has lowest percentage of teachers with majors. − Nearly half of teachers are nearing retirement. − Many teachers are in the early stage of their career.
Perceptions	+ The strongest responses were for climate, communication, and instructional strategies. + Teacher responses were higher than those of the comparison group in climate and communication. + Administrators gave highest ratings to climate and communication.	− The lowest responses for teachers were in the categories of student engagement and staff development and evaluation. − Teacher responses were below those of the comparison group in student engagement, collaborative culture, instructional strategies, staff development and evaluation, instructional leadership, and decision making and planning.

continued →

Category	Celebrations	Concerns
Perceptions (continued)	**+** Administrator responses were also high for instructional leadership and decision making and planning. **+** Administrator ratings were above those of the comparison group for climate, staff development and evaluation, instructional leadership, and decision making and planning. **+** Teachers and administrators had the closest agreement on climate, communication, and instructional strategies.	**–** Administrator responses were below those of the comparison group in student engagement. **–** The largest gaps between administrator and teacher responses were in student engagement and staff development and evaluation.
Parent/Community Data		
Category	Celebrations	Concerns
Demographics		**–** About ¾ of households will not receive communication via material sent home with students. **–** Nearly half of households may not understand communication in English.
Involvement	**+** Attendance at conferences is good for sixth grade.	**–** Conference attendance declines throughout middle school. **–** Data collection regarding parents and community has been very limited.
Perceptions	**+** Parents give highest ratings (above comparison group) for climate and student engagement. **+** Parents agree with high teacher and administrator ratings on climate.	**–** Parent responses are lower and below those of the comparison group for communication and instructional leadership. **–** Parent responses on student engagement are lower than those of teachers. **–** Parent responses on communication are lower than those of both teachers and administrators.

Setting Authentic Goals

A rule of thumb in school improvement tradition has been: no more than five goals, which *must* include two to three with an academic focus and *may* also address concerns related to other organizational factors such as character, climate, and communication. This translates into guidance that if your total change efforts won't fit on two graphic organizers (see fig. 7.1, page 100), you are trying to do too much and will achieve little.

A first step of the school improvement/leadership team is to review all the concerns generated and, based on the data reviewed, select priorities for focus.

Figure 7.1 indicates that *specific goal statements evolve* through the process of studying and selecting research-based strategies and identifying evidence that will document progress. Prior to the era of mandated targets, students, staff, and stakeholders identified areas for priority attention by reviewing data from both academic and perceptual sources and discussing their mission and desired future for their school. This authentic participation in goal setting has been somewhat overshadowed by NCLB. Reading and math are plugged in as automatic priorities, and the targeted level of performance is set at the mandated amount of adequate yearly progress.

Reading and math are fundamental skills and should be included, but the opportunity to address other areas of concern to the school is available. If schools use two visual organizers (fig. 7.1), one can be used to summarize the main components of the mandated school improvement template provided by the state, and the other can include the areas that must also receive attention, as determined by the school's purpose and stakeholder concerns and priorities.

The use of AYP targets should not replace the authentic goal setting of school improvement as illustrated in two well-respected practices. One is the use of SMART goals by schools, teams, professional learning communities, and individual teachers. The other is couched in Michael Fullan's many years of research and insight.

SMART goals (O'Neill & Conzemius, 2006) refer to goals written with specific criteria in mind. They are both specific and strategic (S). They focus on specific skills and learning targets and narrow that focus to a vital few skills for which learning gaps are largest and represent the greatest potential gains. Such goals are measurable (M) and specifically identify multiple measures that will be used at the school and classroom levels. The goals are attainable (A) but not easy, "almost but not quite within reach" (O'Neill & Conzemius, 2006, p. 15). SMART goals are results based (R) and time bound (T), setting specific time frames for action and evidence of impact from those actions. Jan O'Neill and Anne Conzemius (2006) state that attainability is related to "how large that gap is we want to close and how much focus, energy, time, and resources we are prepared to put into attaining the goal" (p. 16). Where the gaps are largest, teacher motivation and energy are most critical. Most teachers feel they are doing all they know to do or can, given their constraints of time and resources. If they view the goals as impossible or do not see adequate support aligned with their efforts, it will be very difficult to maintain a positive culture of collective responsibility.

From his international perspective, Fullan (2005) has not been shy in his description of NCLB in the United States:

> NCLB requires all states to have an achievement-driven system in which "annual yearly progress" in student achievement is documented and reported publicly for every school in each state, with a sequence of escalating consequences for those schools not improving. There is little investment in capacity building and it places people in a high-alert dependency mode, jumping

from one solution to another in a desperate attempt to comply. Any minor
gains are bound to be outweighed by a system that guarantees superficial-
ity, temporary solutions, and cynicism in the face of impossible goals. (p. 11)

His thinking about goals (2009) is presented as part of a Theory of Action for System Change (TASC). One component in the TASC model includes two aspects: an inspirational overall vision and a small number of goals publicly stated. The overall vision is a picture of the purpose, nature, and rationale of the reform, and its essence is nonnegotiable. He does not question the essence of higher achievement for all and closing achievement gaps. But Fullan goes on to assert that the most important elements in any target are to be able to assess how well you are doing relative to your starting point, to keep track of this on an annual basis, and to determine progress on a three-year rolling cycle. He recommends that schools compare themselves (1) to themselves, (2) to other schools in similar circumstances, and (3) to an absolute or external standard—not to obsess over the target, but rather keep it as a focus of inspiration.

Conducting the Study Phase

The earlier discussion of figure 7.1 (page 100) identified the three bullet points in the study phase as drilling down into the data, identifying evidence-based best practices, and examining current practice in comparison to the research. If a school sets five priority areas, five ad hoc study teams would be formed to gather this information. It is essential that study teams related to reading and mathematics *not* include *only* teachers from those departments.

Drilling Deeper Into the Data

The data discussions in chapters 3–6 included several examples of drilling deeper into the data. It was recommended that specific item analyses from large-scale assessments occur within smaller teacher teams for their specific content areas. The detailed analysis is like peeling off the layers of an onion—revealing that within reading, for example, comprehension is a need area; that within comprehension, nonfiction is the specific need area; and that within comprehension of nonfiction, supporting conclusions with details is a priority for focused attention.

In the discussion of survey data, emphasis was placed on examining the specific questions that were asked in connection with categories of low satisfaction ratings or large discrepancies between responding groups. Responses to the question "What else do we need to know?" add new lines of inquiry to investigate before decisions are made about changes in programs and practice.

Another way to delve deeper into a concern to gain better understanding is root-cause analysis. The previous item analysis that led to a focus on conclusions and supporting details in reading does not address the question of *why* students may not be learning and using inference skills. Answers to the why question may include lack of material in the curriculum, lack of time in the instructional period/day/year, or uncertainty about how to explicitly teach and model that set of skills.

Paul Preuss (2003) writes in detail about root-cause analysis and five ways it can be helpful to an organization: root-cause analysis (1) helps reveal the problem, not just the symptom; (2) eliminates mere patching and wasted effort; (3) conserves scarce resources; (4) induces discussion and reflection; and (5) provides a rationale for choices of strategies. Chapter 6 referred to the use of a root-cause analysis tool, the cause-and-effect diagram, for generating stakeholder perceptions about problems in the school. A cause-and-effect diagram combines information from both objective and subjective data—and raises theories that need to be confirmed or contradicted with *additional* data.

Depending on the focus of the cause-and-effect exercise, the climate, and the perceptions of participants, an additional step may be needed before the root-cause analysis is considered complete. Some groups get caught up in or detoured by comments like "We can't do anything about that" or "It's not within the scope of our plan." Assure them that this reality will be acknowledged, and continue pursuing causes and related factors. At the end of the exercise, review what's been generated and let participants address the issues that are outside their influence. If the whole group agrees that they can't do anything about it, put an X or check mark by that item. Then challenge the group to also identify the factors over which they have the most direct influence, and circle those. The root-cause factors that are circled will be the starting point for the discussion of actions to be taken, having already met the test of whether they are the school's responsibility.

At Mode Middle School, math performance is identified as an area of concern, and a study group is formed to pursue the topic in-depth, study recommendations from math experts, and examine current practice. As part of their inquiry, they focus on low scores in algebraic sense and create the cause-and-effect (fishbone) diagram seen in figure 7.4 to analyze the concern.

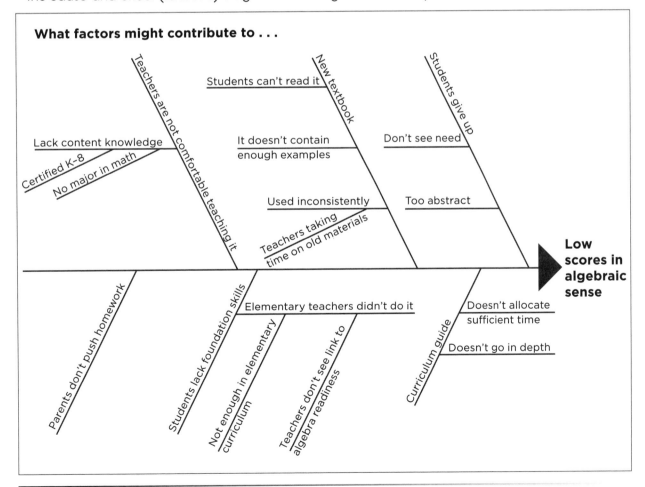

Figure 7.4: Root-cause analysis in Mode Middle School math.

The activity begins with the stem "What factors might contribute to . . . ," and the concern is stated as a noun phrase at the head of the fish. During the discussion, the facilitator continues to ask questions like "And why might that be?" or "What else might be related to that?" or "Where did that start?" The prompting either raises a new factor to be placed on the fishbone or adds more details (the barbs) to a factor that's already been noted. The entries on the fishbone are theories that will be pursued by checking for related data in the research literature and collecting data about current practice.

As the study team surfaces the possibility that "teachers are not comfortable teaching it," the data held back in chapter 5 about majors in teaching assignments will confirm the need for professional development that includes content knowledge and pedagogy for teachers of this specific skill area. The fishbone diagram will be a reference point as the study team continues its work.

Meanwhile, other study groups are conducting root-cause analyses related to more general schoolwide concerns, like factors that might be contributing to eighth-grade discipline problems and parent concerns about the communication of student progress.

Identifying Evidence-Based Best Practices

Drilling deeper into the data and completing a root-cause analysis can also focus the study of research and best practices through literature searches, surfing "what works" websites, and visiting comparison schools with similar students and higher achievement. Mode Middle School's search is not for generic recommendations about middle school discipline or reading in general but for a specific understanding of the concerns that were raised, such as the pseudo-senioritis of eighth graders, the use of conclusions and supporting details in reading, and nonfiction writing in all content areas.

Examining Current Practice

The most difficult and courageous aspect of the study phase is the honest and rigorous examination of current practices in the school. In the context of school improvement, these would be practices that cross content areas. Teacher teams would also engage in candid conversation about daily practice in their classrooms.

Reeves (2006) describes this type of inquiry as:

> the degree to which leaders correctly analyze the underlying causes of deficiencies and successes in student achievement and equity. Successful inquiry attributes the causes to adults in the educational system—teachers, school leaders, and policy makers. Unsuccessful inquiry attributes causes to students . . . [and this] "blame the victim" is not only morally reprehensible but statistically untrue. (p. xxiii)

He goes on to quote his study of more than 300 schools with more than 300,000 students, in which the researchers reviewed data on student gains compared to teachers' responses about causes of student achievement:

> In schools where teachers examined the evidence of the impact of teaching effectiveness on student achievement and regarded their professional practices as the primary cause of student achievement, the gains in student

achievement were three times higher than in those schools where the faculty and leader attributed the causes to factors beyond their control. (p. 246)

Dennis Shirley (2009) wrote in a similar vein:

> We have to move beyond du jour compliance, flavor-of-the-month change strategies, and educational tourism that seeks the "next big thing." If we really look at ourselves and our cultures, we cannot circumvent deep personal introspection in companionship with one's colleagues, and the most painful and poignant of all questions: when things go wrong in my school or in my system, could it have something to do with how I am acting, but also perhaps even with my deepest presuppositions and biases? (p. 143)

Before new strategies are selected, grade-level and department discussions need to be carefully planned and skillfully facilitated to identify how critical skills are taught, with what materials, and how much time is allocated. These discussions can lead to savings in time and money, as they identify specific skills that need more time or earlier introduction, needs for supplemental materials for specific topics, or the need for collaborative support in planning how to teach difficult concepts. These solutions are more strategic, more cost effective, and can be applied more quickly than the whole-scale adoption of a complete new program or intervention. As Reeves (2006) points out, "The question is not 'What have we done wrong and how do we fix it?' but rather 'What do our results tell us about our most effective professional practices, and how can we identify and replicate those practices?'" (p. 90).

Selecting Sensible Strategies

In schools with an existing school improvement plan, the discussion of strategies should begin with questions like "What have we already been working on? What strategies did we put in place to address our needs?" Review of the data will provide a reality check with further queries: "What improvements did we see in the areas we've been working on? To what do we attribute those changes? How will we celebrate those successes and sustain those efforts?"

Then the conversation can turn to consideration of whether and what new strategies should be added. Key questions include:

- What did we attempt that doesn't seem to have been effective yet?
- Do we have evidence that we fully implemented those changes?
- Do we need more common work, more time, more training—or do we need to seek a new set of strategies?

NCLB has made a positive impact by emphasizing the use of approaches that have already been demonstrated as effective and making that information more accessible. But is it possible for strategies to be research-based and yet "wrong"? The strategy is wrong if it doesn't match the underlying need or root cause. It is wrong for the school if resources are inadequate to implement it with fidelity. And it is wrong if there is a lack of understanding and commitment for it. Selecting the right strategies is more complex than "pick one from the pull-down menu of 'what works.'" School improvement/leadership teams must rigorously query the evidence in support of a recommended strategy, with questions like:

- What evidence shows that this program or strategy was effective?

- Were the findings based on quality research standards?

- Are the validation studies done only by the program's developers, or have they been replicated by other researchers?

- Is the population in the research studies similar to our school/district population?

- What professional development is needed, and do we have resources to provide it?

- What are the critical factors involved in implementation fidelity so that the results in the research can accrue in our setting? Do we have the commitment to ensure those critical factors are consistently implemented?

A reality of this stage of selecting strategies is that the school does not always (or even usually) have full autonomy. Some strategies or programs may be designated by the district for implementation at all schools. The involvement of school staff members on district teams is critical. Representatives from the site level must be able to raise these same questions *before* systemwide decisions are made and financial resources are committed. Once such decisions are made, the district-mandated strategies must be listed on the school improvement plan so that all the expectations are clear in one big picture. And just as Mode Middle School's data team will consider how it will provide evidence of implementation and results, the district central office department creating the mandate will have to decide how it will evaluate its initiatives and have data by which to make adjustments when needed.

The recommendations of the study groups are combined with mandated strategies and considered carefully by the school improvement/leadership team. Some strategies from the past are affirmed for continuation, and new ones are selected to match each priority area. The synthesized work will look similar to Mode Middle School's school improvement plan (fig. 7.5).

The Mode Middle School leadership team has captured its work so far on a graphic organizer (fig. 7.5) so that staff and stakeholders have a big-picture view of the alignment between the celebrations and concerns from the data, the priority areas, the study phase, and the strategies identified for implementation. The deeper look at the data surfaced further concern about students' background knowledge and academic vocabulary. Some strategies are content-area specific (for example, professional development on algebraic sense). Others drive change in every classroom: a schoolwide approach to writing, explicit instruction in essential vocabulary, and exploration of co-teaching as a model that may improve learning for special education students and English learners. Schoolwide actions will also be taken in the area of relationships and student engagement. Drilling deeper into the data and having follow-up discussions with students revealed that sixth graders feel overwhelmed and confused with a variety of different classroom rules, so teachers made a commitment to reach agreement on one set of expectations and include better explanation, role playing, and examples during orientation. They also learned that eighth graders are convinced this year doesn't really matter and that they will pass no matter what. Eighth-grade teachers, counselors, and one assistant principal will work with counterparts at the high school to make plans for transition and accountability. They anticipate developing four-year high school plans in the fall of eighth grade, reviewing academic histories with students, setting goals, and pointing out the prospect of summer and Saturday school if the students are not prepared when they come to the high school.

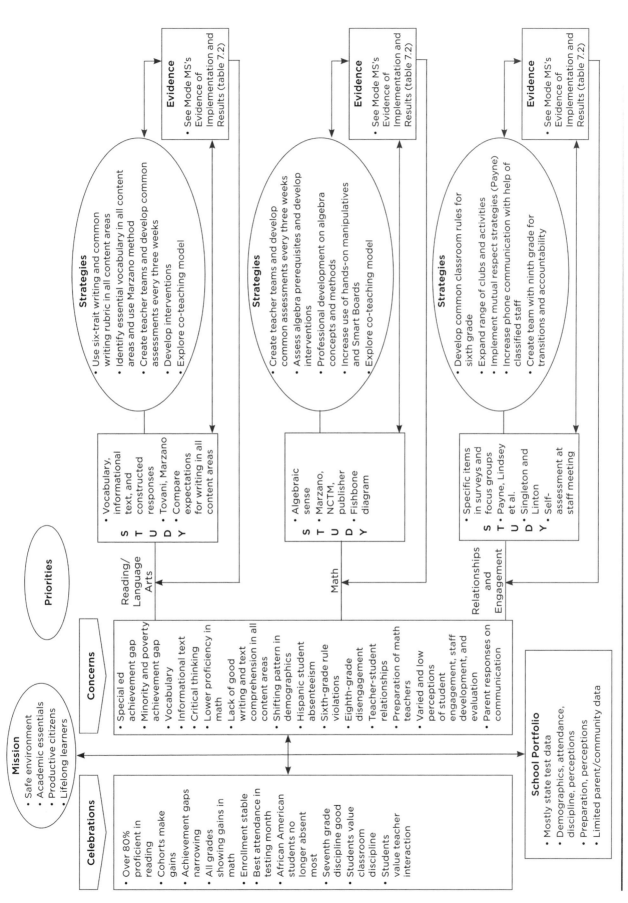

Figure 7.5: Mode Middle School's improvement plan.

The graphic organizer helps Mode Middle School's school improvement/leadership team view all of its strategies in one place. They will engage staff in a holistic analysis of what they have planned. Before asking staff to affirm their commitment, the team will discuss these questions to make sure they are presenting a powerful package of recommendations:

- Will the combined set of strategies raise achievement for all students?

- Will the combined set of strategies also directly address disparate learning needs and narrow achievement gaps?

- Will the combined set of strategies involve every adult in the school? Does every staff member see his or her contribution and the expectation it sets for him or her?

- Is the overall school improvement plan an ambitious stretch but manageable and necessary? What support will staff need?

The remaining steps for Mode Middle School are to determine how they will ensure that the changes are being put in place, to coordinate the support teachers need, and to verify that student learning is improving as a result. The commitment to work in teacher teams and develop common formative assessments is a major strategy that will affect all teachers, depend on the development of shared knowledge and skills, and require collaboration time. It will also provide evidence of results, as teachers will have a way to monitor progress in student learning throughout the year.

Evidence of Implementation

The last two critical steps in the school improvement process are monitoring implementation and reviewing results. With accountability expectations, evidence must be provided that staff have implemented a strategy. To do so, the indicators of implementation must be articulated in advance and plans must be made about how data will be gathered and reported. Evidence must also be reported to show that the time, energy, and money invested in the new strategies were worth it. The planning process must also identify what assessments will document short-term and ongoing evidence of results in student learning.

The process of monitoring evidence of implementation is simply ensuring that we do what we say we will do. School improvement plans represent a set of commitments, and school leaders—teachers and administrators—need to make sure the planned actions happen. As Reeves (2006) notes:

> The "Foolproof Reading System" worked in some schools, but did not in others. The "Can't-Miss Math Program" succeeded one month and fell flat the next. The source of such inconsistencies is hardly a mystery, as the cause of success in improving student achievement is not the brand name of the product but the degree of implementation by the teacher. (p. 78)

He also declares that "plans without monitoring are little better than wishes upon stars" (p. xxiv). Sources of evidence must be identified that will provide data to demonstrate use of the schoolwide and classroom changes designed into the plan.

Four-Step Process for Evidence of Implementation

Gathering evidence should be an ongoing process so the information is readily available, unlike the experiences of some schools that reach the end of a year or planning cycle and frantically look backward, trying to retrieve and recapture documentation for reports and next rounds of grant applications.

The four-step process outlined in figure 7.6 helps ensure that expectations are clear to all and that evidence of implementation can be produced. These steps should also be followed at the district level, when programs are adopted with the expectation of implementation in every school.

Priority/Goal:
Strategy:
Step 1: Identify the indicators.
Step 2: Develop tools with which to gather the evidence (for example, files for artifacts, meeting logs, walkthrough forms).
Step 3: Design the gathering process (who, how, when).
Step 4: Draft possible reporting statements.

Figure 7.6: Planning to monitor implementation.

The first step is to identify the indicators to ensure that everyone has a shared image of what the innovation looks like in practice. Clarification discussions will address these questions:

- What will implementation of (name the strategy) *look* like?

- What will teachers be doing? How will that be different from what we do now? What will we do more often, more consistently, more rigorously?

- What will teachers not be doing or doing less? What are we leaving behind to make room for more powerful strategies?

- What will students be doing that is different, more consistent, more rigorous?

- What artifacts will be observable in the school/classroom (for example, materials, manipulatives, student work samples)?

- What will (the strategy) *sound* like? What terminology and phrases should all teachers be using?

- Will the classroom be quiet or filled with productive noise? What will students be saying and talking about?

Curriculum designers and program publishers often include criteria or checklists for implementation. Helpful items from these resources should be connected to the specific, authentic questions listed previously.

The next two steps outlined in figure 7.6 are designing the tools with which to document the evidence of implementation and the process by which that documentation can occur. Teacher involvement in this planning is essential so there is a clear distinction between ensuring the success of the school improvement plan and formally evaluating individual teachers.

A typical method of gathering implementation data is the school and classroom walkthrough, in which administrators, teacher leaders, and colleagues make note of the specific indicators and record the frequency of occurrence. However, Reeves (2006) suggests that "effective monitoring include not only frequency but also the specification of levels of implementation" (p. 78). He defines *implementation* as "the degree to which the specific elements of school improvement processes are implemented at the student and classroom levels" and describes effective implementation, not as just present or absent, but as "a continuous variable . . . [with] degrees of successful implementation that are subject to quantitative and narrative description" (p. 78).

Innovation Configuration Maps (Hall & Hord, 2001; Holcomb, 2009; Hord & Sommers, 2008) address the need to describe various levels of implementation. Figure 7.7 is an IC Map that presents four components of six-trait writing, one of Mode Middle School's chosen strategies, and lays out a progression of stages of implementation from the *lowest* level on the *right* to the most complete and sophisticated use as level 1 on the *left*. When this developmental sequence is provided, teachers can more accurately self-assess their own current skill level, see what their next steps of progress will look like, and identify needs for support or clarification.

The fourth step in preparing to monitor implementation is to draft possible reporting statements. This makes future communication much easier. It also creates a test of whether the indicators, tools, and process (steps 1–3) will provide the type of evidence that the school wants to be able to report for internal and external purposes. Some evidence of implementation will simply verify that concrete tasks were accomplished, such as "Common rules identified and shared by teachers and mentors." Other forms of evidence of implementation include reporting statements that show an increased use of a new practice: "Walkthroughs show increasing use of (name the strategy) with evidence of indicators present in 20 percent of settings in September and 78 percent in January," or "Student attendance at help periods increased from an average of twelve students per session in September to twenty-seven students per session in November."

Component 1: Teacher demonstrates a thorough understanding of the six-trait writing approach.			
Level 1 (Best)	Level 2	Level 3	Level 4
• Articulates rationale for the value and importance of six-trait writing through advocacy and support of colleagues • Uses a variety of instructional strategies that are appropriate to each of the six traits • Integrates the language of six-trait writing into all curricular areas	• States rationale for the value and importance of six-trait writing • Uses a variety of instructional strategies that are appropriate to several of the six traits • Integrates the language of six-trait writing into at least one other curricular area	• Expresses an emerging awareness of the value and importance of the six-trait writing approach • Recognizes and accepts the six-trait writing approach as a schoolwide initiative • Uses the language of six-trait writing only in the context of a writing lesson	• Recognizes and accepts the six-trait writing approach as a schoolwide initiative • Uses six-trait language only in the context of writing

Component 2: Teacher uses effective instructional strategies to implement six-trait writing in his or her classroom.				
Level 1 (Best)	Level 2	Level 3	Level 4	Level 5
• Seeks and uses examples of writing to model the traits from traditional and current sources (textbooks, basals, teacher writing, news media, literature) • Embeds writing activities across many areas of the curriculum • Uses six-trait writing rubrics regularly to establish expectations and provide exemplars	• Seeks and uses examples of writing to model the traits from traditional sources (textbooks, basals, teacher writing) • Embeds writing activities across some areas of the curriculum • Uses six-trait writing rubrics occasionally to establish expectations	• Uses limited examples of writing to model some of the traits (computer-generated lessons, teacher's lessons/ideas) • Utilizes writing activities primarily during language arts • Experiments with six-trait writing rubrics when required to provide example	• Uses limited examples of writing to model some of the traits (computer-generated lessons, other teachers' lessons/ideas) • Utilizes writing activities only during designated language arts period	• Assigns required writing to students, but the six traits are not actively modeled or explicitly taught

Figure 7.7: Innovation Configuration Map for six-trait writing. continued →

Component 3: Teacher evaluates student work to monitor progress and revises classroom lessons to improve students' writing.			
Level 1 (Best)	**Level 2**	**Level 3**	**Level 4**
• Consistently uses formal and informal assessments based on the six traits to document student improvement in writing and identify areas for growth • Consistently creates and revises lessons relevant to student writing needs • Regularly differentiates and works with individuals and small groups based on their work • Engages students in analysis and assessment of own writing and peer editing	• Frequently uses formal and informal assessments based on the six traits to document student improvement in writing and identify areas for growth • Occasionally creates and revises lessons and reteaches based on student writing needs • Engages students in analysis and assessment of their own writing	• Periodically uses formal and informal assessments based on the six traits to document student improvement in writing • Selects and prioritizes lessons from the curriculum that match one or more of the six traits	• Uses formal and informal assessments based on the six traits only when required to provide evidence • Creates lessons based only on the curriculum

Component 4: Teacher collaborates with colleagues to refine common practice using the six-trait writing approach.			
Level 1 (Best)	**Level 2**	**Level 3**	**Level 4**
• Initiates conversations with colleagues about the components of six-trait writing • Seeks input on lessons and reactions to student work • Offers lesson plan ideas • Willingly tries new ideas, offers, and listens to constructive criticism on how to improve writing instruction	• Meets regularly with colleagues to discuss components of six-trait writing • Shares examples of student work as part of protocol in collaboration time • Listens to, but may not employ, new ideas or take into account constructive criticism about effective writing instruction	• Meets with colleagues to discuss components of six-trait writing when scheduled • Shares examples of student work only at required staff meetings • Resists trying new ideas and has difficulty accepting constructive criticism	• Discusses components of six-trait writing only as required at staff meetings • Listens to contributions of others

Source: Adapted from Holcomb, 2009.

When evidence of implementation is collected, it should be reported for purposes of celebration and communication. Fullan (2009) lists communication as one of six components of systems change and points out:

> Policies and strategies require many more times the communication than you might rationally feel is sufficient . . . When you articulate strategies along with progress or lack thereof, you become more clear, you monitor and spur implementation, and you continually link to people's ongoing new experiences. Communicate often, but be sure you have something specific to communicate about. (p. 291)

Another component in Fullan's framework for systems change reinforces the norm of continuous evaluation and inquiry. He recommends the questions "Are we implementing the strategy effectively? Is it working? Are there any surprises? What are we learning?" and emphasizes that "assessment of implementation is a must to determine what is working and where, as well as what is not working and why" (2009, p. 288).

The need to monitor implementation is more than just the need to ensure that schools deliver on their promises. It is also a necessity to discover which implementers are most successful so they can help others and which implementers need further encouragement, specific help, or a reminder of expectations. Before a school determines that it should give up on a new initiative and go looking for the next new thing, honesty demands verification of whether it was really put into use. If not, teachers must be asked the follow-up questions of why not and what they need.

Professional Development Planning

When evidence of implementation is clearly outlined and teacher needs are expressed, a new focus emerges for the school improvement/leadership team. They must plan and coordinate the content and formats of professional development to ensure that every staff member has the knowledge and skills to implement the strategies.

This professional development must be *differentiated*, based on teachers' prior knowledge and experience. Some teachers may have had little or no exposure to the new strategies, while some could and should be designated as mentors or coaches. One-size-fits-all professional development is demoralizing to teachers and wastes time, energy, and money.

Professional development for implementation must include the levels of follow-through necessary to result in classroom application. Overview-level training during the rush of August in-service days is useful to create momentum and signal the focus of the year but is not sufficient to ensure that students throughout the school benefit from the new strategies. Professional development must be ongoing and include multiple exposures with content-specific examples and practice with feedback through arrangements such as use of video, coaching, or professional learning communities.

Marzano (2010a) asserts that "school systems can develop expert teachers if they are willing to devise comprehensive models of effective teaching and provide time for teachers to engage in deliberate practice relative to the skills articulated in the comprehensive model" (p. 3). A five-year landmark study conducted in California (Bush, 1984) examined data on the impact of various approaches to professional development, based on whether or not teachers used the new teaching practices. Researchers found that when teachers were given only a description of new instructional skills, 10 percent used the skills in the classroom. When modeling, practice, and feedback were added to the training, teachers' implementation of the teaching practices increased by 2 percent to 3 percent each time. When coaching was added to the staff development, however, approximately 95 percent of the teachers implemented the new skills in their classrooms.

When schools select strategies for school improvement, the planning for professional development should include these steps:

- Identify all the possible venues for professional learning. The phrase *professional learning* is used intentionally, because it opens up a broader range of possibilities. Use of the term *professional development* tends to limit thinking to the designated professional development day(s) in the school calendar. The possible venues include all opportunities (times and places) that are already available—for example, staff meetings, common planning times, grade/department meetings, early/late dismissals.

- Decide which of the possible times and places best fit the purpose of introducing new knowledge (training) and which opportunities make it possible to coordinate the practice with feedback and coaching. For example, a twenty-minute segment of a staff meeting can accommodate a mini-lesson or video clip of a concept or teaching behavior. But for coaching to occur, students should be in session and the coach or observer must be available.

- Double-check the overall professional development plan for the year to ensure that more time is dedicated to practice with feedback than just initial training.

Traditional professional development schedules may be effective for establishing the fundamental knowledge and skills associated with an innovation in curriculum or instruction. But more in-depth experiences will be needed to ensure implementation and transform practice.

When Louis et al. (2010) examined specific leadership practices that were perceived to help improve instruction, a large proportion of both principals and teachers agreed on the importance of these specific practices:

- Focusing the school on goals and expectations for student achievement (100% principals, 66.7% teachers).

- Keeping track of teachers' professional development needs (100% principals, 84% teachers). Although professional development was often prescribed, designed, and delivered at the district level, principals were involved in managing teachers' attendance at workshops offered outside the school, as well as planning for, and sometimes providing, onsite professional development.

- Creating structures and opportunities for teachers to collaborate (91.7% principals, 66.7% teachers). Principals supported collaboration among teachers by scheduling times for teachers to meet and discuss how they were working through the curriculum. (p. 71)

Chapter 8 will focus on the collaboration of teacher teams as they implement the school improvement plan and strengthen their instructional and assessment practices.

Evidence of Results in Student Learning

The desired impacts on students are both academic and affective. Some evidence of affective results will show up as the schoolwide data team checks the nonacademic student data (for example, attendance and behavior referrals) on an ongoing basis. Evidence of results on student learning will require the use of frequent academic data, which may not yet be available. This is why Mode Middle School decided to create teacher teams and develop and use formative assessment practices. (See *Strategies*, fig. 7.5, page 115)

The movement toward frequent and formative assessment has been almost a revolution to counter the misuses of large-scale, standardized tests. Fullan (2005) refers to assessment *for* learning as "one of the most high yield strategies to come on the scene" and describes it as high yield "in the sense that it represents a powerful strategy for changing teaching and learning, and is learnable within reasonable time frames" (p. 54). He then summarizes the research of Black, Wiliam, and associates (Black, Harrison, Lee, Marshall, & Wiliam, 2003), which addressed four areas of classroom teaching and learning: questioning, feedback through grades, peer- and self-assessment by students, and the formative use of summative tests. Black et al. (2003) stated that the improvements documented for most participating teachers were of such significance that "if replicated across the whole school they would raise the performance of a school at the 25th percentile of achievement nationally into the upper half" (p. 29).

The challenge is twofold: to develop good formative assessments that align with the local curriculum and to ensure that they are used in formative ways. "Formativeness" is not just a function of how long or short the instrument is or how often it is given. Formative use of assessment information means that the teacher uses it to understand how students are *form*ing new concepts and skills, to in*form* instructional plans for the following day/week, and to *form* flexible groups for additional help.

In response to the concern that the addition of formative assessments will cause over-testing, Reeves (2006) counters:

> Schools are, indeed, over-tested if we define tests as summative, evaluative, provided at the end of the year, and accompanied by feedback that is woefully late and inherently useless. But schools are under-*assessed* [italics mine]. Assessments in contrast to tests, are formative, provided during the year, designed to improve teaching and learning, and accompanied by immediate feedback . . . [Referring to the Broad Prize–winning district of Norfolk, Virginia:] never less frequent than quarterly, often every other week . . . feedback typically provided the day after the assessment, sometimes the same day . . . results include not only the scores for each student but a detailed item and cluster analysis, used for planning instruction the following week. (p. 86)

Mode Middle School's school improvement/leadership team and data team are now poised to track progress on the school improvement plan. As shown in the first column of table 7.2, they listed the strategies for schoolwide action that were summarized in figure 7.5 (page 115). Then they worked through the four-step process in figure 7.6 (page 117) to identify evidence of implementation and results, and to anticipate the progress reports they will be providing.

Table 7.2: Mode Middle School's Evidence of Implementation and Results

School Improvement Strategies (What we promised to do)	Indicators That Will Provide Evidence of Implementation (Proof we are doing what we said)	Indicators That Will Provide Evidence of Results (Proof that our work is helping students)
Use six-trait writing process and common writing rubric in all content areas.	Rubric developed (attach) All staff trained (dates and sign-in sheets) Include indicators on walkthrough form Frequency seen in Sept. _____, Oct. _____, Nov. _____, Dec. _____, Jan. _____, Feb. _____, Mar. _____, Apr. _____, May _____	Analysis of student work using common assessments (prompts and rubric) shows increases Percent proficient: Sept. _____, Oct. _____, Nov. _____, Dec. _____, Jan. _____, Feb. _____, Mar. _____, Apr. _____, May _____ Percent proficient on state test from _____ to _____
Create teacher teams, and develop common assessments for use every three weeks.	Agenda/report template adopted (attach) Schedule of meetings developed (attach) File of meeting reports from each teacher team File of common assessments developed by each teacher team	Results of common assessments show increasing proficiency for all students Percent proficient: Sept. _____, Oct. _____, Nov. _____, Dec. _____, Jan. _____, Feb. _____, Mar. _____, Apr. _____, May _____
Identify essential vocabulary, and use Marzano method in all content areas.	Lists of essential academic vocabulary developed (attach) Vocabulary notebook format created (attach) Include indicators on walkthrough form	Percent proficient on state test from _____ to _____
Identify essential vocabulary, and use Marzano method in all content areas. (continued)	Frequency seen in Sept. _____, Oct. _____, Nov. _____, Dec. _____, Jan. _____, Feb. _____, Mar. _____, Apr. _____, May _____	

School Improvement Strategies (What we promised to do)	Indicators That Will Provide Evidence of Implementation (Proof we are doing what we said)	Indicators That Will Provide Evidence of Results (Proof that our work is helping students)
Develop interventions for most critical skills.	Most critical skills identified in each content area (attach) Plans for interventions developed (attach, date) Records of students served	Results of common assessments show increasing proficiency for served students Percent proficient: Sept. _____, Oct. _____, Nov. _____, Dec. _____, Jan. _____, Feb. _____, Mar. _____ Percent proficient on state test from _____ to _____, Apr. _____, May _____
Explore co-teaching model.	Study team formed including general education, special education, and EL staff (list of members) Study process and time line planned (attach) Updates to all staff Recommendations for next year implementation presented	
Assess algebra prerequisites and develop interventions.	Diagnostic test chosen/developed and administered (dates)	Diagnostic test as baseline: _____ Results of common assessments show increasing proficiency Percent proficient: Sept. _____, Oct. _____, Nov. _____, Dec. _____, Jan. _____, Feb. _____, Mar. _____, Apr. _____, May _____ Percent proficient on state test from _____ to _____
Provide professional development on algebra concepts and methods.	Individual PD plans filed by math teachers Common/best lesson plans for critical algebra concepts on file and used	Results of common assessments show increasing proficiency Percent proficient: Sept. _____, Oct. _____, Nov. _____, Dec. _____, Jan. _____, Feb. _____, Mar. _____, Apr. _____, May _____

continued →

School Improvement Strategies (What we promised to do)	Indicators That Will Provide Evidence of Implementation (Proof we are doing what we said)	Indicators That Will Provide Evidence of Results (Proof that our work is helping students)
Increase use of hands-on manipulatives and Smart Boards.	Include indicators on walkthrough form Frequency seen in Sept. _____, Oct. _____, Nov. _____, Dec. _____, Jan. _____, Feb. _____, Mar. _____, Apr. _____, May _____	
Develop common classroom rules for sixth grade.	Rules developed (attach) Orientation provided to students (plan, dates) Communication provided to parents (plan, dates)	Decreased number of referrals for violations of classroom rules, bus rules, school rules: Sept. _____, Oct. _____, Nov. _____, Dec. _____, Jan. _____, Feb. _____, Mar. _____, Apr. _____, May _____
Expand range of clubs and activities.	Interest survey conducted (dates, results, recommendations) New opportunities provided	Increase in percent of students participating in nonacademic school activities: Sept. _____, Oct. _____, Nov. _____, Dec. _____, Jan. _____, Feb. _____, Mar. _____, Apr. _____, May _____
Implement mutual respect strategies.	Review of previous PD content with emphasis on application (dates) Include indicators on walkthrough form Frequency seen in Sept. _____, Oct. _____, Nov. _____, Dec. _____, Jan. _____, Feb. _____, Mar. _____, Apr. _____, May _____	Develop and administer short survey on relationship/respect. Results: Fall _____, Winter _____, Spring _____

School Improvement Strategies (What we promised to do)	Indicators That Will Provide Evidence of Implementation (Proof we are doing what we said)	Indicators That Will Provide Evidence of Results (Proof that our work is helping students)
Increase phone communication with help of classified staff.	Plan developed (attach) Log of phone communications	Decrease in Hispanic absenteeism Decrease in eighth-grade passive refusal and disrespect: Sept. _____, Oct. _____, Nov. _____, Dec. _____, Jan. _____, Feb. _____, Mar. _____, Apr. _____, May _____ Increase in parent attendance at conferences
Create team with ninth grade for transitions and accountability during eighth grade.	Study team formed (list of members) Study process and time line planned (attach) Updates to all staff Recommendations presented for implementation second semester	Decrease in eighth-grade passive refusal and disrespect: Sept. _____, Oct. _____, Nov. _____, Dec. _____, Jan. _____, Feb. _____, Mar. _____, Apr. _____, May _____ Results of eighth-grade common assessments show increasing proficiency Percent proficient: Sept. _____, Oct. _____, Nov. _____, Dec. _____, Jan. _____, Feb. _____, Mar. _____, Apr. _____, May _____ Percent proficient on state test from _____ to _____

Elementary Exceptions

Table 7.3 (page 128) provides an elementary example of a chart for gathering and reporting evidence of implementation and results. The school has already analyzed and reported the data for Evidence of Implementation. Under Evidence of Results, they have named the assessments that will be used and are working with the district assessment department to obtain their numbers. The importance of support from the district level to provide timely, user-friendly information directly to the school is further explored in chapter 9.

Table 7.3: Elementary Evidence

Reading		
Strategies	Evidence of Implementation	Evidence of Results
Implement Harcourt Brace core reading program.	Classroom walkthroughs: Jan.—have conducted 120 walkthroughs. All teachers using core components, except . . .	Terra Nova GRADE 4Sight K–2 common classroom assessments For each grade level by standard categories: Phonics—50% proficient in Sept.; 55% in Jan. Comprehension (fiction)—49% proficient in Sept.; 65% in Jan. Comprehension (nonfiction)—35% proficient in Sept.; 50% in Jan.
Use common assessments across grade levels and district.	Assessments developed: on hold for district time line Assessments in use Teachers using assessments to plan groups: logs of grade-level meetings	
Use guided reading groups within classrooms based on instructional level.	Classroom walkthroughs: Jan.—saw guided reading groups on 80% of walkthroughs held during reading time; two teachers need additional help	
Assign intervention tutor to work with students in basic and below-basic levels.	Log of tutor groups with students and meetings with teachers; sharing data with faculty: Jan.—reviewed logs, main issues . . .	
Hold workshops for parental involvement to build reading skills.	Development of materials: folders on file in parent resource center Log of parent attendance: 40% of invited parents attended first meeting; 60% attended second meeting Report form of minutes reading: Jan.—received reports from 20% of parents, average ten minutes per evening	
Create word walls to include critical vocabulary for ELs.	Classroom walkthroughs: Jan.—only observed in K–2, none in grades 3–5	Assessment of English language development: Jan.—_____% of students increased two levels

Math		
Strategies	Evidence of Implementation	Evidence of Results
Create word walls to include critical math vocabulary.	Classroom walkthroughs: Jan.—120 walkthroughs, 50% included math vocabulary	GMADE 4Sight For each grade level by standard categories: _____% proficient in _____; now _____
Use Elmo to engage students in analyzing errors.	Classroom walkthroughs: Jan.—50 walkthroughs during math, 10 using Elmo (20%)	
School Climate		
Strategies	Evidence of Implementation	Evidence of Results
Display successful work samples for all students.	Classroom walkthroughs: Jan.—120 walkthroughs, 30% show evidence	Student survey: will administer in May; item(s) such as, "My teacher values my work. I am proud of my work."

High School Highlights

At Coatesville Area Senior High in Pennsylvania, the leadership team aligned professional development plans with their school improvement plan and created a walkthrough tool to gather evidence of implementation (fig. 7.8, page 130). Their report of progress (fig. 7.9, pages 131–134) is outlined, and they have begun to populate it with large-scale test data and baseline data from local assessments.

Conclusion

This chapter has linked the use of data to decision points in the school improvement process—from initial analysis of starting points, to data about practice that charts the course, to data that will be gathered to keep things on course and capture proof of progress toward the goal. Fullan (2005) summarizes the challenge ahead:

> Work at all levels to infuse the system with excellent data . . . and ensure that school and district staff have the capacity to use the data so that everyone knows what effect the staff's actions are having on student learning. (p. 93)

This is the essence of data use for school improvement. The next two chapters will reinforce Fullan's admonition to "work at all levels," from classroom-level teacher teams to the central office administrators and teams that must guide and support their efforts.

Coatesville Area High School Classroom Walkthrough Form

Date: _____ Period: _____ Time: _____

Teacher: _____ Observer: _____

Classroom Environment	Activities in Progress
Daily objective(s) posted	Lecture
Student work displayed	Teacher demonstration
Print-rich environment	Discussion
Room appears neat and organized	Cooperative activity / group work
Effective classroom management	Independent seat work

Instructional Strategies	Relational Behaviors
BDA: "Before reading" (establishes purpose—anticipation guide, active reading)	Teacher uses courtesies
	Students use courtesies with teacher and peers
"During reading" (what students do as they read—active reading, text structure)	Teacher calls on all students
	Teacher is in proximity of all students
"After reading" (check for understanding—CSQT, text structure, anticipation guide)	Teacher greets students at the door
Teacher use of chunking (processing, checking for understanding)	Teacher smiles at students
	Classroom has a businesslike atmosphere
BDA terms used by teacher and students	Students are given tools to assess/evaluate their own work
Teacher modeling	
Journaling	Student questions are used as part of instruction
Higher-order questioning	Grading/scoring is clear and easily understood
Partner work	Students may ask for and receive extra help from teacher

Student Responses to Questions
What BDA strategy was used in this lesson?
What did the teacher do that helped you learn today?

Figure 7.8: Coatesville Area High School classroom walkthrough form.

Source: Created from information provided by Coatesville Area High School, Coatesville, Pennsylvania.

Coatesville Area High School's Summary of School Improvement Plan for Monitoring and Reporting Progress

Priority Area: Reading comprehension of nonfiction text		
Action Plans / Strategies	Indicators to Provide Evidence of Implementation	Indicators to Provide Evidence of Impact/Effectiveness
Compile teacher needs based on self-assessment of familiarity with before-during-after (BDA) strategies.	Data from needs assessment survey in November Repeat in February and at end of year	Classroom walkthroughs show students utilizing strategies independently; random questions of students Anecdotal observations of student discussions (Development of new walkthrough form; see attached) **4Sight Reading, Grade 9** Sept. 9 (baseline) / Jan. 10: Advanced—4% / 5% Proficient—44% / 43% Basic—21% / 23% Below—32% / 30%
Identify and implement "before reading" strategy, "during reading," and "after reading" in all classrooms. CSQT format Anticipation guide Text structures Active reading	Teacher daily lesson plans viewed during walkthroughs Increased teacher use of chunking (processing and checking for understanding) strategies from 10% to 60% of walkthroughs	**Reading, Grade 10** Sept. 9 (baseline) / Jan. 10: Advanced—3% / 11% Proficient—56% / 56% Basic—23% / 20% Below—18% / 13%
Step 1: All teachers receive overview training with the exception of mathematics and foreign language teachers (Nov. 25). Step 2: Teachers process how these strategies would appear in lessons in that content area (Feb. 5).	Attendance Creation of lesson plans and resources needed to implement strategies; lesson plans viewed during walkthroughs	**Reading, Grade 11** Sept. 9 (baseline) / Jan. 10: Advanced—13% / 16% Proficient—61% / 57% Basic—13% / 14% Below—12% / 13%
Step 3: Use department meetings to collaborate and reflect on implementation of BDA strategies.	Meeting minutes and outcomes Exit tickets at the end of Nov. 25 and future meetings (Feb. 5 and TBD)	**Reading, Grade 11, by Percent Subscale** Comprehension and reading skills—65% to 68% Interpretation/analysis of fiction/nonfiction—78% to 75%
Develop common language—the terminology of the BDA strategies used by both teachers and students.	Meeting minutes Walkthroughs Questions of students at end of walkthrough	**Reading independently—68% to 70%** Reading critically—67% to 67% Reading/analysis/interpretation of literature—80% to 78% Open-ended—72% to 77% **MAP Scores for Targeted Students** 58% of grade 11 English seminar students have shown growth 46% of grade 10 English seminar students have shown growth 62% of grade 9 English seminar students have shown growth

Figure 7.9: Coatesville Area High School evidence collection.

continued →

Priority Area: Reading comprehension of nonfiction text (continued)		
Action Plans / Strategies	Indicators to Provide Evidence of Implementation	Indicators to Provide Evidence of Impact/Effectiveness
Implement interventions (support/safety nets) for struggling students. Grade 9: "Failure Is Not an Option" Grade 9: Title I push-in tutoring Grades 9–11: After-school program Grades 9–11: Reading seminar classes Fast ForWord reading program	Attendance records for after-school programs Title I students being serviced within ninth-grade reading seminar	Formative common assessment **English Midterm, Grade 9** Advanced—29% Proficient—50% Basic—12% Below—9% **English Midterm, Grade 10** Advanced—4% Proficient—36% Basic—31% Below—30% **English Midterm, Grade 11** Advanced—21% Proficient—58% Basic—14% Below—7%

Priority Area: Math; school below target, improve instructional practices in all math classes		
Action Plans / Strategies	Indicators to Provide Evidence of Implementation	Indicators to Provide Evidence of Impact/Effectiveness
Provide more opportunities for the department to collaborate and share instructional practices utilizing PLC design. Overview of school improvement plan to math department on Feb. 5.	Department collection of teacher samples of best practices beginning in late Feb. after technology training Attendance sheets from department meetings—60% to 100% Increase the use of teacher modeling, evident in walkthroughs: from 9% to 30% Implement the use of journaling, higher-order questioning, and partner work: 0% (Sept.) to 10%, observed in walkthroughs	Classroom walkthroughs show students utilizing strategies independently; random questions of students Anecdotal observations of student discussions (Development of new walkthrough form; see attached) **4Sight Math, Grade 9** Sept. 9 (baseline) / Jan. 10: Advanced—0.003% / 0.03% Proficient—20% / 23% Basic—41% / 42% Below—39% / 32%
Monthly meetings are led by department head to share instructional practices by subject.	Meeting minutes by beginning of March	

Priority Area: Math; school below target, improve instructional practices in all math classes (continued)		
Action Plans / Strategies	Indicators to Provide Evidence of Implementation	Indicators to Provide Evidence of Impact/Effectiveness
Textbook publisher and other resources provide in-service trainings for full use of instructional resources available.	Walkthroughs Student survey of teaching strategies collected during walkthroughs	**Math, Grade 10** Sept. 9 (baseline) / Jan. 10: Advanced—9% / 16% Proficient—37% / 35% Basic—34% / 32% Below—20% / 16%
Identify key competencies for algebra comprehension. Implement interventions (support/safety nets) for struggling students Grade 9: "Failure Is Not an Option" Grades 9–11: After-school program Grades 9–11: Reading seminar classes Grade 11: Tutoring pull-out Grade 11: Peer-to-peer tutoring	Department time to reflect on quarterly assessments as they relate to core algebra competencies	**Math, Grade 11** Sept. 9 (baseline) / Jan. 10: Advanced—31% / 32% Proficient—39% / 39% Basic—18% / 16% Below—12% / 13% **Math, Grade 11, by Percent Subscale** Numbers and operations—66% to 64% Measurement—57% to 58% Geometry—50% to 46% Algebra concepts—55% to 56% Data analysis/probability—46% to 51% **MAP Results for Students in Math Seminar** 63% of grade 11 math seminar students have shown growth 62.7% of grade 10 math seminar students have shown growth 64% of grade 9 math seminar students have shown growth

Priority Area: Math, conceptual understanding of basic algebraic concepts		
Action Plans / Strategies	Indicators to Provide Evidence of Implementation	Indicators to Provide Evidence of Impact/Effectiveness
Identify key competencies for algebra comprehension.		Baseline data from grade 8 basic skills assessment and MAP 4Sight Quarterly math assessments
Identify and refine the assessment of core algebra competencies within the common assessments.		

continued →

Priority Area: Math, conceptual understanding of basic algebraic concepts (continued)		
Action Plans / Strategies	Indicators to Provide Evidence of Implementation	Indicators to Provide Evidence of Impact/Effectiveness
Allow department time to reflect on quarterly assessments as they relate to core algebra competencies.	Attendance sheets from department meetings—60% to 100% participation Meeting minutes	MAP results for students in seminar Study Island
Use anticipatory set activities as review and formative assessment of core algebra concepts in all math classes.	Daily teacher lesson plans	Improved results on quarterly math assessments
Pre/posttest on algebra concepts developed by department and administered as formative assessment with cohorts of teachers and students.	Developed	
Implement interventions (support/safety nets) for struggling students Grade 9: "Failure Is Not an Option" Grades 9–11: After-school program Grades 9–11: Reading seminar classes Grade 11: Tutoring pull-out Grade 11: Peer-to-peer tutoring		

Source: Created from information provided by Coatesville Area High School, Coatesville, Pennsylvania.

Using Data in Classrooms and Teacher Teams

Congratulations to Mode Middle School! They have used data in a variety of ways to complete a school improvement plan, committed themselves to a set of strategies, and identified the evidence they will gather to monitor implementation by staff and outcomes for students. One new strategy is the creation of teacher teams to develop common assessments. Although teachers have already worked in various configurations and roles throughout the process, openly and continuously sharing their practices of instruction and assessment and finding a comfortable commonality is a whole new endeavor. This chapter provides the help they will be seeking as they forge ahead into new territories of even deeper data discussions, the dilemma of autonomy versus common practice, pacing and planning instruction, analyzing student work, keeping track of student proficiency, and engaging their students directly with their own data work to set goals and monitor progress.

The work of teacher teams in collaboration is more than a structure. Hargreaves (2009) describes how such teams

> have sharpened collaborative cultures by adding a clear school focus and providing performance data to guide teachers' joint reflections, discussions, and decisions, and to connect them to student achievement . . . They are living communities and lively cultures dedicated to improving the life and learning of students and adults where data inform but do not drive judgments about practice . . . And members of the community care not just about the outcomes of their short-term teams, but about each other as people because they are in a long-term relationship. (p. 31)

Defining Teacher Teams

Teacher teams as described in this book are smaller groups and have more specific tasks and targets than the schoolwide data team. The members of teacher teams all work within the same grade or content area. In large high schools, for example, they all teach the same course. They maintain a tight focus on instruction, assessment, and student intervention as it relates to their teaching assignment. The following list describes some of the configurations of people who could be called teacher teams in schools:

- Grade-level teams

- Department teams

- Multiple departments related to similar content areas (for example, in smaller high schools, all fine arts or all applied arts)

- Co-teaching combinations of general education and special education teachers

- Student support teams (for example, counselor, social worker, dean, psychologist)

- Adviser, homeroom teacher, and counselor

- All teachers of a grade level and the teachers who support them (for example, staff who work with special education students, English learners, and gifted students)

- Grade-level teachers and the media specialist

- Middle school combinations of a math teacher, language arts teacher, and special education teacher to plan interventions

- Interdisciplinary teams focused on developing norms of professional learning

- Grade-level team leaders and union building representatives

- Team leaders with reading and math coaches, counselors, paraprofessionals, and parents

- Cross-district teams of like content, linked by videoconferencing (for example, small rural districts)

- Enrichment teams of classroom teachers joined by an extended learning specialist, a technology integration specialist, and a library media specialist

These could all be referred to as teacher teams. They merit the name if they develop and share norms, conduct effective meetings, focus on student learning, and take action related to their instructional and assessment practices.

Data Teams

In this book, the term *data team* is used to describe a schoolwide group in which membership is based on the representation of all staff. The writings of Wahlstrom (1999), Bernhardt (2004), and Schmoker (2001, 2006) also emphasize the need for staff involvement in the use of data. Love and colleagues (2008) outline the work of "data coaches" who are "teacher-leaders, instructional coaches, building administrators, or district staff." Their role is to guide "data teams," which consist of "four to eight teachers, other school faculty, and ideally, their building administrator, who work together to use data and improve student learning . . . focused on a particular content area, such as mathematics, or on school improvement in general" (p. 20). This definition combines the broader school improvement data work and the more focused content-area work with the same term. As described in chapter 2, I distinguish between the general schoolwide use of data and the instructionally focused content-area work by using two different terms: *schoolwide data team* and *teacher team*, stressing that *both* are dependent upon good data for good decisions. The difference is the breadth or scope of the decisions being made and the changes being implemented.

My definition of *schoolwide data team* differs from the way the term *data team* is used by Douglas Reeves' Leadership and Learning Center. In the center's publication *Data Teams: The Big Picture: Looking at Data Teams Through a Collaborative Lens* (Allison et al., 2010), the term is used to describe

> collaborative teams designed to improve teaching, learning, and leadership . . . groups of educators who teach the same course or grade level, or who have a similar focus . . . [and] can talk about student learning because [they've] also used the same formative assessment to measure student learning. (pp. 1–2)

The second part of the definition would correlate Reeves' data teams to the roles and responsibilities ascribed here to "teacher teams." The Leadership and Learning Center draws parallels between its data teams and professional learning communities.

Professional Learning Communities

The body of research on teacher collaboration goes back over twenty years to the seminal work of Milbrey McLaughlin (McLaughlin & Marsh, 1978), Judith Warren Little (1982), Susan Rosenholtz (1989), Jerry Bamburg and Nancy Isaacson (1992), Linda Darling-Hammond (1990), Tom Sergiovanni (1992), Karen Seashore Louis (Louis & Kruse, 1995), Gene Hall and Shirley Hord (2001), and others.

Hargreaves describes Hord as "the originator, the Archimedean source point, of the triple-headed concept, professional learning community" (Hord & Sommers, 2008, p. x). Based on her extensive portfolio of research and work with practitioners, Hord (2007) reiterates six essential strategies for professional learning. They include:

1. Create an atmosphere and context for change.

2. Develop and articulate a shared vision of the change.

3. Plan and provide resources.

4. Invest in training and professional development.

5. Monitor, check, and assess progress.

6. Provide continual assistance.

Meanwhile, the concept of professional learning communities has also been advanced by Rick DuFour and colleagues, now designated with their specific trademark, "PLC at Work." The four key questions of PLC at Work™ focus on what students should learn, how to assess the learning, how to respond when students don't learn, and how to respond when they are already proficient. This set of powerful questions seemed to overlook the critical element of pedagogy. However, I read a new emphasis in *Raising the Bar and Closing the Gap*; DuFour et al. (2010) state:

> Educators are constantly gathering evidence of student learning to inform and improve *their professional practice*. They use common assessments

and make results from those assessments easily accessible and openly shared among members of the team in order to build on *individual and team strengths.* (p. 8, italics mine)

In descriptions about Boones Mill Elementary, Prairie Star Middle School, and Whittier Union High School District, DuFour et al. refer to comparing teachers' results (p. 74), discussing instructional strategies (p. 95), and learning from each other to promote best instructional practice (p. 146). It appears that these authors would support the additional question I raise: how can we most effectively teach this skill or concept in order to maximize the chances that students will be able to learn it the first time? This question creates a bridge between the PLC at Work focus and the studies of Marzano (2007), Hattie (2009), and others that define the instructional factors most strongly linked with student success.

The bottom line is an affirmation that everything said here regarding teacher teams is congruent with the training and guidance provided by DuFour's group and others. As they tell us:

> No system of interventions will ever compensate for bad teaching. A school that focuses exclusively on responding to students who are having difficulty without also developing the capacity of every administrator and teacher to become more effective will fail . . . The professionals within a school will also be called upon to build a collaborative culture, engage in collective inquiry regarding matters that impact student learning, participate in action research, create continuous improvement processes, and help each other monitor and improve upon results. (DuFour et al., 2010, pp. 42–43)

Louis et al. (2010) point out:

> Supportive interaction among teachers in school-wide professional communities enable them to assume various roles with one another as mentor, mentee, coach, specialist, advisor, facilitator and so on. However, professional community amounts to more than just support; it also includes shared values, a common focus on student learning, collaboration in the development of curriculum and instruction, and the purposeful sharing of practices. (p. 44)

Fullan and Hargreaves (1996) agree on the necessity of discussing instructional practices:

> By examining their practices and by critically reflecting on the reasons for them, teachers (and administrators) push themselves to give good reasons for what they are doing. This in turn prompts them to change their practice when they find it wanting. (p. 70)

The work of teacher teams must be courageously reflective and intellectually rigorous, enhanced by data to focus attention on student needs over adult interests.

Time for Teacher Teams

Schmoker (2006) described the development of professional learning communities at Adlai Stevenson High School and emphasized the need for

> deliberate steps to ensure that standards-based, results-oriented collaboration occurs on a strict schedule throughout the school, for every course, in every department . . . The schedule, frequency, and quality of good team

meetings need continuous care and attention—especially in high schools, where variable schedules and extracurricular duties present a daunting challenge. (p. 11)

The issue of time is one of the critical factors empowering or inhibiting the ability of teacher teams to utilize data for identifying student needs, adjusting instruction, and creating interventions. Hord and Sommers (2008) provide a substantial list of suggestions on how districts and schools can provide time for this teacher collaboration:

- Longer school day four days per week with time "saved" used another day for professionals to meet, study, plan.

- Extend each day of the week by 10 minutes for an early or late start to provide a periodic release day.

- Extend the school day by ½ hour on Monday, Tuesday, Thursday, Friday; on Wednesday . . . staff are involved in professional development and dialogue, and so on from 8 to 10:30. Students arrive at 10:30 for a modified day: thematic work, community activities, field trips, community assistance exchanges.

- Bank time by choosing one hour per week before or after school in study groups—compensated by districtwide professional development days.

- Consider the possibility of gaining time from scheduled lunch periods.

- Add minutes to beginning and end of four days—give ½ day off to students on the fifth day.

- Cut down on passing time to build time available for teachers to meet.

- "School day" becomes "school week" with beginning and ending hours of each day flexible for schools.

- Extend to eight-hour paid workday for teacher, principals, and all others who directly support learning.

- Extend school year to gain days.

- Come an hour early or stay an hour late and document attendance and accomplishments in exchange for attending district-planned professional development or work-day.

- Meet after school or on Saturday and document it as the professional development hours in contract.

- Meet beyond the "contract" day in exchange for being able to leave early on another day.

- Seek waivers from state for instructional contact hours.

- Reconsider the use of scheduled faculty meetings.

- Teachers from one grade level invite students in for "buddy work" with older students while the other grade level teachers meet; exchange the trade another day.

- Use professional development money in grants to hire floating subs that release one grade level/department at a time. (pp. 14, 17, 54, 56–57)

Hord and Sommers (2008) caution that whole-staff meetings should not be abandoned and recommend whole-staff meetings at least once a month to address schoolwide goals and common learning. They point out that

> if the whole school community does not work together, the goals, purposes, and activities of the individual teams may be moving willy-nilly in various and opposite directions . . . The larger PLC [whole school] allows for the smaller team units [teacher teams] to do specific work, but also maintains movement toward common schoolwide goals and mission. (p. 54)

Tools for Teacher Teams

In addition to the prerequisite of time to meet, tools are needed to support communication and accountability for how that precious time is used. Figure 8.1 is a teacher team meeting agenda that provides the instructional focus for a series of two meetings. The next critical student learning goal is identified, and the teacher team discusses what it looks like when a student is proficient and how they will know each student has learned the concept or skill. That discussion leads to development of the common formative assessment. Teachers then explore teaching strategies that may be particularly effective for this skill and agree on some common steps they will all take with their classes (steps 1–3).

After instruction occurs and the assessment is given, the assessment becomes formative when teachers bring the results to the *second* meeting, during which they summarize their students' results (steps 4–6). The assessment results are used formatively, as teachers then decide how to differentiate interventions and enrichment to further ensure mastery of the learning goal.

Drilling Deeper and Discussing the Data

School improvement/leadership teams often start with analysis of large-scale, high-stakes assessment results, then gather additional data about the characteristics of students and staff and the school, home, and community conditions for learning. Their purpose is to identify the schoolwide factors that affect a broad range of staff and student concerns and implications and therefore need to be addressed through schoolwide strategies with consistent implementation. Teacher teams typically start from one or both of two entry points. One sequence is to begin with the more in-depth item analysis and identify the actual assessment items that many students miss and that are consistently problematic. Another approach is to start from the course/grade standards and benchmarks, using the process of setting curricular priorities and moving forward to plan instruction and develop assessments.

Some of the questions addressed in teacher team discussions are outlined by Schmoker (2001) as:

- What specific results do we want our students to achieve, based upon our analysis of all assessment results?
- What evidence will we accept that students achieved these results?
- Which students achieve these results and which do not?
- How will we change instruction to maximize every student's opportunity to achieve our desired academic results? (p. 73)

Teacher Team Meeting   Date _____ Time _____

Members Present

_____   _____   _____

_____   _____   _____

Norms Reviewed

1. Student learning goal(s) for time period beginning ___ and ending ___ :
   (What do we want students to know?)

2a. Common assessment(s) used to determine mastery of goal(s):
   (How will we know they learned it?)

   *Attach copy of assessment/observation sheet

2b. Define mastery:

3a. Possible teaching strategies to ensure learning:
   (Brainstorm and share list of possible strategies.)

3b. Agreed common strategies:

4. Results of assessment:

   _____ 1-# mastered _____ # not mastered _____ # assessed _____ # not assessed

   _____ 2-# mastered _____ # not mastered _____ # assessed _____ # not assessed

   _____ 3-# mastered _____ # not mastered _____ # assessed _____ # not assessed

   _____ 4-# mastered _____ # not mastered _____ # assessed _____ # not assessed

5. Interventions for those students not meeting the standard:
   (What and when?)

6. Interventions for those students meeting the standard:
   (What and when?)

Figure 8.1: Teacher team meeting template.

Source: McAuliffe Elementary, Tulsa Public Schools. Used with permission.

Other critical questions include:

- How will we assess the critical skills in formative ways?
- How will we keep records of student status and progress?
- How and when will we observe each other teach, and share and compare our results in student work?

These questions, especially those concerned with observing each other and comparing student work, raise anxiety and illustrate the dilemma of teacher individuality versus common practice that has been exacerbated by the standards movement and high-stakes assessments and accountability. I understand and agree when educators point out that students are all different and shouldn't be treated the same, and adults are professional and should be trusted.

It brings back the anxiety I felt when Deming's (1986) work on total quality management espoused the need to reduce variation. My students performed very well on the Iowa Tests of Basic Skills, and I was afraid I would risk lowering their scores if I had to do everything the same way the other teachers were doing it. I didn't realize that the application of his principle was to the variability in outcomes—exactly what we now refer to achievement gaps. The principle of reducing variation is more correctly applied to education in terms such as "guaranteed and viable curriculum" (Marzano, 2007) or in reminders that the potential for student growth should not be a result of the random chance that places students in classrooms where teachers vary in effectiveness. In a sense, the purpose of work in teacher teams *is* to reduce variation in effectiveness of teachers and success of students—by raising the performance of all to higher standards.

More recently, Good (2010) states that lack of appropriate, ongoing professional development is definitely one of the major factors related to what he describes as marked variation:

> Typically, classrooms focus on drill and practice, have limited time for conceptual development, focus on basic skills and concepts, and provide limited time for application and even less so for problem solving. The affective climate is generally supportive, and students' answers are typically correct. Most instruction is in whole-class or large-group settings. Students ask few questions, make few choices, and get few, if any, rewards. Yet . . . the results from this basic faire show marked variation, as some teachers working with similar students under similar conditions obtain significantly more achievement from their students than do other teachers. (p. 48)

Variation in results for students is a big problem. For disenfranchised groups, routinely taught by less qualified and experienced teachers, it represents an obstacle over which they have no control. For engaged parents, it represents the challenge of leveraging their children into the classes with the "best" teachers, creating problems of all sorts for the principal and scheduling staff. Lyn Sharratt and Michael Fullan (2009) pose at least one part of the solution to such marked variation as

> weekly after-school meetings, by division or department, focus on individual student's (literacy) achievement by using common assessment tools and exemplars so that same-grade/course teachers can come to common understandings of the expected standards of student work . . . collaborative

> examination of student work by administrators and teachers promotes consistency, ideally across classes within and across schools in a district, ultimately eliminating variation in instruction among classrooms. (p. 18)

The consistency described by Sharratt and Fullan is around expectations, standards, and assessments. Reducing variation is not about scripted, robotic instruction. It's about increasing the assurance that the targets set for student learning, and the criteria for demonstrating that learning, are predictable—and that a student's opportunity to learn is not based on the "luck of the draw" when students are assigned to classroom lists and schedules.

In addition to working on standards and assessment, teacher teams assist each other with pedagogy:

> Innovative leaders provide teachers with opportunities to observe other teachers so they can develop other frames of reference on their teaching. When they are given these opportunities, even excellent teachers report they find valuable new ideas for diversifying their instructional repertoire. (Shirley, 2009, p. 145)

The National Staff Development Council (Harrison & Bryan, 2008) recommends that grade-level or content-area groups meet at least once a month to use data from student performance on classroom and common assessments, discipline records, and student work for discussion of:

- Diagnosis of individual knowledge and skills
- Next steps for students
- Grouping of students for instruction and intervention
- Developing a pyramid of interventions

They suggest meetings at least every six to eight weeks to use data from state assessments, benchmark assessments, common assessments, and unit assessments for analysis of:

- Growth of students
- Patterns in proficiency
- Instructional strategies
- Assessment strategies

These authentic notes from a teacher team meeting at Media Elementary in the Philadelphia area provide a taste of how it sounds when teachers discuss data. The group included the principal, instructional support teacher, reading teachers, and classroom teachers.

> There was discussion about the students on the cusp of proficient and advanced on the PSSA [Pennsylvania System of School Assessment]. Often these students could advance if the open-ended responses were targeted for more instruction and support by the teachers. Often students who are barely proficient do not receive Title 1 services because they are proficient. They do not meet the criteria for support. A suggestion was made to have RD [reading department] work with them or IST [instructional support teacher] could intervene.

Strategies to help the students on the cusp included highlighting directions and reviewing test-taking skills. Another suggestion was to use the reading anthology. This is a great resource. It is good literature, and the skills are interwoven.

What is the area of weakness for these students? Teachers should focus on the subtest where the students are weakest. Then a question was raised about how we bolster EL students' scores. Direct instruction on test-taking was suggested. An example was to create a PSSA test item to share with students. Make sure there is a distracter in answer A. Have students make sure they read all the answer choices before answering. Another idea was to focus on vocabulary; for example, Does the question read least to greatest or greatest to least?

A teacher shared that her class averaged 10 RIT [Rasch Unit] lower in numbers and operations compared to the other categories for the same students: measurements, data, geometry, algebraic concepts. It is also an average 10 RIT lower than the numbers and operations of the students last year, but it's more interesting that the whole group this year came much weaker in that category compared to their preparation in other categories. In the past, the averages were very similar across categories. If other teachers see the same trend, that could mean that *Investigations* may account for the drop. It's a little disturbing because numbers and operations questions form the lion's share of PSSA problems.

Prioritizing, Pacing, and Planning Instruction

The Media Elementary teacher team meeting ended with a recognition of one of the curricular priorities in math, which will necessitate further discussion of how, where, with what, and how much instruction is provided. Although districts often develop pacing guides, teacher teams at the school level must be the final arbiter of whether more time is needed for instruction with all students or whether there are sufficient interventions to assist students and classroom instruction can move on to new targets.

Schmoker (2006) recommends that teachers work together to develop lessons specifically designed to address difficult learning objectives and that teams "keep and catalogue the best lessons and units for the benefit of colleagues and future teachers . . . collect and organize lessons by skill and standard." He reiterates that "the team's effectiveness depends on the system's capacity to reveal those standards and skills where the team is strong or weak and to concentrate its efforts in order to accelerate improvement" (p. 16).

The "sound" of shared instructional planning is captured in this excerpt from the fifth-grade team's meeting notes at Highland Elementary in Montgomery County, Maryland.

Reading Mastery Objectives:

1. Develop and apply comprehension skills through exposure to a variety of text

2. Develop and apply comprehension skills by reading a variety of self-selected and assigned literary texts

Whole-Group Instruction:

Begin historical fiction unit of study, found in MCPS, Q1 Instruction Guide

SWBAT [Students will be able to]:

- Compare characteristics of fiction and nonfiction—use Lesson 1, p. 124
- Identify characteristics of historical fiction—supplement to Lesson 1
- Explore examples of historical facts found in the texts—Lesson 2, p. 126

Small-Group Instruction:

- Continue with the Fountas and Pinnell assessments.
- Below and on grade level: JR formatted groups. All groups will spend September utilizing nonfiction in small groups.
- Above grade level: Alternate weekly between comprehension and vocabulary.
- After the F & P assessments, Words Their Way will be integrated into small-group instruction based on reading levels and students' needs. ESOL Level 1—Book B. Below grade level—Book D. Above grade level—Book E.
- Independent work centers: Reader's Notebooks, Independent Reading, Independent Writing, Words Their Way extension activities, Grammar Practice.

Sharratt and Fullan (2009) provide the corollary for high schools, stating that "at the secondary level, departmental teams [should] establish collections of multilevel resources, including multiple copies of longer texts and genres such as comics, graphic text, newspapers, and magazine articles that relate specifically to a subject area of study" (p. 19). These become shared resources for collaborative instructional planning and differentiation based on reading ability, ensuring that students are not denied access to the concepts and skills of content-area curricula.

Designing Assessments

Schmoker (2010) illustrates the interdependence of instructional planning and formative assessment:

> Good lessons start with a clear, curriculum-based objective and assessment, followed by multiple cycles of instruction, guided practice, checks for understanding (the soul of a good lesson), and ongoing adjustments to instruction. Thanks to the British educator Dylan Wiliam and others, we now know that the consistent delivery of lessons that include multiple checks for understanding may be the most powerful, cost-effective action we can take to ensure learning. Solid research demonstrates that students learn as much as four times as quickly from such lessons.

When priority learning targets have been established and teachers are planning instruction, they should concurrently think about assessment. Teacher teams ask the question "What does it look like when a student really gets it?" and design assessments that will provide the frequent and multiple checks for understanding that are used formatively to guide whole-group instruction and inform small-group work and interventions. Such assessments are referred to as unit assessments and common/classroom formative assessments, interspersed between quarterly benchmark tests that review larger sets of learning targets.

Huebner (2009, citing Lachat & Smith, 2005) states that it is most effective for

> teachers within a school to collaborate on developing common performance-based interim assessments. Such assessments allow teachers to combine and compare data across classrooms and work together to develop appropriate instructional responses. One specific study, which examined five low-performing, high-poverty urban high schools in three districts and their use of data to inform school improvement, concluded that the more school staff worked collaboratively to discuss and analyze student performance, the more likely staff members were to use data to inform curriculum decisions. (p. 86)

These assessments must include a range of items to determine the student's proficiency, not just whether the student completed the task or how many generic points were scored. Marzano (2007, 2010b) recommends a four-point scale in which 4.0 represents the ability to apply the knowledge to a new setting or example not experienced in the teaching, 3.0 represents mastery of the explicitly taught material, and 2.0 represents accomplishment of the simpler portions of the content (for example, vocabulary terms). Larry Ainsworth and Donald Viegut (2006) describe a process in which the learning targets are analyzed by level of Bloom's taxonomy, and assessment items are checked to be sure they require the same level of rigor as the target.

Because of the high stakes attached to annual state testing, debates about them have created a huge emphasis on the use of terms like *validity* and *reliability*. Validity is the degree to which an assessment measures what it is intended to measure, and reliability is the degree of consistency with which repeated testing yields the same results. Reeves (2007) addresses the concern about whether teacher-developed common formative assessments are accurate enough to guide instruction:

> If our purpose is the selection of students for a limited number of places in next fall's Yale Law School class, then a focus on extensive domain sampling and high reliability would be appropriate. But when our purpose is a quick determination of the extent to which students understand skills and concepts and the equally important purpose of adjusting teaching strategies to help students who have not yet mastered those skills and concepts, the practical utility takes precedence over psychometric perfection . . . Suppose the assessment insufficiently samples the domain of "reading comprehension" and the results suggest, incorrectly, that a student needs to do extra work in this domain. Consider what the risk really is. If the teacher makes such an error, the very worst that will happen is that students will receive extra instruction in reading comprehension—hardly the worst error teachers and leaders can make. Moreover, because assessments are frequent, the error will be quickly caught and corrected. If, by contrast, leaders make the mistake of failing to notice a student needs help when in fact, the student desperately needs help, the consequences are far more serious. This typically happens because leaders want psychometric perfection and they make the error of supplanting practical, if imperfect information, with the mythical idea of the perfect test. In such circumstances, leaders may be almost certain that students will never receive meaningful feedback because (1) the assessment may not be administered in the first place; (2) teachers will be intellectually and emotionally detached from the assessments and will telegraph those feelings to students; (3) the feedback will be inscrutable for both teachers and students; and (4) the feedback, even if provided in a clear manner, will be late and voluminous. (pp. 235–236)

The Assessment Reform Group (2006) also addresses the tension between assessments that are scientifically sound and those most useful for teachers and students. Their conclusion is that when teachers' professional judgment regarding the quality of student work is based on the conscientious development and application of consistent criteria, the teacher's judgments are likely to be more valid and reliable than the results of external tests. This supports the importance of collaborative teacher work on common formative assessments. The best way to ensure the quality of formative assessments is to reassure teachers of findings such as these and help them get started. With practice developing the assessments and discussing the results, the quality of the assessments will improve and the time needed to create them will rapidly decrease.

Discussing Assessment Results and Analyzing Student Work

DuFour et al. (2010) describe a scenario that could easily depict the interaction between teacher teams and the schoolwide data team:

> After the assessments are administered to all students in each course or grade level, individual teachers submit results to the designated person in the school (for example, team leader, department chair principal, data coach, or other appropriate individual) who compiles the data for the course or grade-level team and promptly forwards the results to the team members for joint analysis. Each team then works together to analyze the results for all students—skill by skill (and sometimes item by item) and identify areas of celebration and concern.

> Initially teachers may be reluctant to share their results with their colleagues. For that reason, some schools provide each teacher with his or her own data compared to the total group rather than providing each teacher's results to all members of the team. This practice allows teachers to begin sharing results at their discretion when they are comfortable, as opposed to having results exposed by the administration.

> Teachers may also feel anxious that the results will be used against them in the teacher evaluation process. We recommend that the results of common formative assessments be used to help teachers identify their individual strengths and weaknesses, allow teams to identify areas of concern in student achievement in that course or grade level, and identify students who need either additional time and support or enrichment. We do not believe common formative assessments are an effective tool for rating and ranking teachers. . . . We have found that when teachers have acknowledged certain outcomes are essential, helped to create assessments they agree are valid tools for monitoring student proficiency, and then discovered irrefutable evidence that their students are not learning as well as students taught by a colleague, they are motivated to improve without the necessity of rankings or ratings . . . Individual teachers are able to identify problem areas in their teaching, and then call upon teammates for help in addressing those areas. If the entire team is experiencing difficulty in teaching a specific concept, that team should have access to school or district support to receive the professional development members need to address the difficulty. (pp. 31–32)

The focus of this phase of the work of teacher teams is fourfold:

1. To evaluate student work after the teaching
2. To determine whole-class reteaching and flexible-group reteaching
3. To develop further interventions
4. To monitor implementation of the strategies and interventions

Figure 8.2 provides a protocol for teacher teams to use in their discussion of student work—whether it's quantitative data prepared by the schoolwide data team on a more formal interim assessment or artifacts of authentic work they have brought to share.

As noted by Angie Deuel and colleagues (2009), teachers sometimes come to the discussion of student work with an intent to *prove* that their students learned. Teachers should look at student work with an intent to *improve their* practice through reflecting on the data before them. Teachers focused on "proving" hold on to predetermined ideas about students' abilities, assume that high-achieving students understand content even when their work does not reveal understanding, and take for granted that low-achieving students do not understand. They often hold onto and score by rigid ideas about just one way to express understanding, in contrast to the "improving-focused" teachers who try to use students' work to understand student thinking. This second approach yields decisions to add explanation space to multiple-choice items and sharpens thinking about instruction, learning styles, content expectations, and student engagement.

Teacher teams that have trouble opening a discussion about student work may find it helpful to choose one or two of these questions as a prompt:

- Here's what I see as the strengths of my class. How about you?
- Here's what I see as the needs of my students. (This may be stated as the whole class, needs for a small group, or needs of individual students.) What needs do you see?
- What instruction needs to occur to move my class (our students) ahead? As a whole? As small groups? For individual students?
- What patterns are we noticing?
- What commonalities do we see within a class? Our grade level? The whole school?
- What goals can I set for particular students? For the class? For myself?
- What can I do to impact those patterns? Are there lessons to be eliminated, or are there lessons that need to be added?
- How is the reteaching going to be different from the first time I taught it?
- It looks like your students really did well. What did you do (differently) that helped your students succeed where my students did not do so well?
- What can I learn from my colleagues?
- What are the interventions/enrichments that are needed, and how will they stay connected to the classroom?

Date _____

Grade _____   Subject _____   Student Work _____

Attendance	

Assessment of student work:

Number of Students	% Advanced	% Satisfactory	% Limited Knowledge	% Unsatisfactory

Strengths	Explanations

Areas to Improve	Explanations

Possible instructional strategies to use:

How will we know if the strategies are successful?

Figure 8.2: Analysis of student work.

Source: Highland Park Elementary, Oklahoma City. Used with permission.

- What types of intervention and enrichment activities could we provide for our students within the general education classroom setting?

- Discuss use of the assessment. What went well? What was most useful? Are there things we need to revisit about the assessment?

- What teacher learning do I need to make learning happen for my students? Teacher support? Teaching resources?

- What specific steps will we take to offer these specific students (names) help with this specific skill?

For constructed responses, essays, and reports, Gayle Gregory and Lin Kuzmich (2007) propose that collaborative analysis includes questions that focus teachers on higher-level thinking, such as: What was the level of critical thinking students demonstrated? Did it match the standards? Did the prompt and scoring guide clearly push students to higher levels? Did students receive instruction and learning activities at this level of rigor prior to the assessment?

Tracking Student Proficiency

Authentic and collaborative use of formative assessment practices will inevitably lead to discussion of the question "What should we be keeping track of?" Issues of grading and reporting have been explored in depth by many authors (Marzano, Reeves, Stiggins, Guskey, O'Connor, and more). Traditional practice has been to record numbers of points for various activities and assignments and average them together into a letter grade. The natural result is that students focus on how to get more points or how to raise their grade. At the same time, teachers wonder why students aren't intrinsically motivated to learn for learning's sake.

The following section will deal more with engaging students, but at this point, it is critical to say that students can't be intrinsically motivated to learn for learning's sake unless they know exactly what it is that they are supposed to learn and have specific and timely information about how they are doing on those specific skills.

Teacher teams that look at student work and use formative assessments will ask different questions and keep track of student progress in different ways. They will talk about specific students and specific skills. Before determining that the student is not successful, they will ask, "What other data do we have for this student related to these same skills?" Before averaging the student's worst and best performance to assign a mean grade, they will ask, "What is our most recent evidence of his or her level of proficiency?"

Figure 8.3 provides a glimpse of how this looks in a teacher's computer or three-ring binder. The items on the left represent the list of most essential benchmarks for sixth-grade math. Even the short list of most essential benchmarks has been broken down so that students and teachers will know exactly what to work on. For example, the originally stated benchmark indicates that the student will be able to add, subtract, multiply, and divide using decimals. Here the four operations have been separated into separate lines to better target the student's zone of proximal development.

Mode Middle School Sixth Grade Math

Name of Student ____________________

Benchmarks	Most Recent Evidence	Evidence of Progress								
Add decimals	4 1 / 3 2	9/15 Quiz 3								
Subtract decimals	4 1 / 3 2	9/15 Quiz 2								
Multiply decimals	4 1 / 3 2									
Divide decimals	4 1 / 3 2									
Add fractions with like denominators	4 1 / 3 2									
Add fractions with unlike denominators	4 1 / 3 2									

Figure 8.3: Individual academic progress chart.

The circle with four quadrants in the second column represents four proficiency levels, which may be aligned with the state's proficiency levels or may reflect the type of four-point scale recommended by Marzano (2007, 2010b). The column heading "Most Recent Evidence" indicates that this entry will not be a calculated average but will show progress over time as the quadrants in the circle are shaded in based on formative assessments, actual student work, or observation during class. In this case, it is early in the year and the first assessment was a quiz given September 15. The student reached proficiency on adding decimals but missed some of the items related to subtracting decimals. This format provides both *status* and *progress* information. The shaded quadrants in the circle show the student's current status in terms of proficiency level. The series of entries across the row illustrate how many attempts and opportunities have occurred and how the student's performance has changed over time.

In many settings, teacher teams begin by creating their own spreadsheets similar to this layout. The discussions are valuable and support instructional planning and motivating students. Unfortunately, if the district still requires a traditional report card, even the teacher leaders who most value and advocate for standards-based record keeping acknowledge that it is time consuming, and some feel they have to keep two sets of books in order to enter the data the way the district requires and track the information they want for authentic use in planning instruction. They insist that it is worth it but wish they had the kinds of district support described in chapter 9.

Figure 8.3 provides teachers and individual students with specific, accurate, and timely information about the student's status and growth on specific learning targets during the course of the school year. There is also a need to summarize information about students at the end of the year in order to create a profile of incoming students for the next teacher. Figure 8.4 was designed for this purpose and should be revised every year.

The next set of conversations can address the question of how the columns for quarterly grades will be defined—by letter grade or perhaps by the percentage of grade-level expectations accomplished by the end of each quarter. The role of the district surfaces again when teachers debate over what's required, what's realistic, and what's clearest and most accurate in terms of true communication of student learning.

Empowering Students With Personal Data

Teachers have the most direct impact on student learning and the most direct contact and communication with families. As a result, teacher teams are in the best position to engage students with data as they review assessment results and monitor their own progress.

Stiggins (2007) writes about assessment *for* learning as "a series of interlaced experiences that enhance the learning process by keeping students confident and focused on their progress, even in the face of occasional setbacks" (p. 23). He describes characteristics of the process in which teachers enhance, not merely monitor, their students' learning. First, teachers share achievement targets with the students. They provide the benchmarks in student-friendly language and show them examples of high-quality work. Second, they engage students in frequent self-assessments that provide descriptive feedback in small amounts they can digest, related to specific skills. Third, they help students use this feedback to chart their progress

Teacher _____   Grade _____

Name	School attended & Teacher 09-10	Quarterly Grades 1st R/M	2nd R/M	3rd R/M	4th R/M	Benchmarks Comp 1	Comp 2	Comp 3	DIBELS Pre	Mid	Post	Special Services Yes No	Safety Net 10-11 Yes No	ELL Yes No	High Mobility Y-N	Race or Ethnicity	# of Discipline Referrals	Attendance by Quarter 1	2	3	4	Intervention(s) Status RTI - Tier 1/2/3	Comments

Figure 8.4: Student academic profile data.

Source: Angela Houston, Principal, Eisenhower Elementary School, Oklahoma City, Oklahoma, and Rochelle Converse, Principal, Stonegate Elementary School, Oklahoma City, Oklahoma. Used with permission.

and set goals. In turn, "the students' role is to understand what success looks like, to use feedback from each assessment to discover where they are . . . and to determine how to do better next time" (Stiggins, 2007, p. 23).

These practices reflect three factors Marzano (1992) found related to student motivation. Students are more likely to put forth effort when there is task clarity, relevance, and potential for success. Showing students the criteria and exemplars helps them to clearly understand the learning goal and know how it will be evaluated. Feedback directly on specific skills is more relevant than scores from major tests or percents of points. And setting their own goals enhances students' self-efficacy and reinforces their optimism about future success.

After describing the characteristics of assessment *for* learning, Stiggins (2007) goes on to address the impact of high-stakes testing on teachers and the emotional impact of assessment on students. He cautions that "even the most valid and reliable assessment cannot be regarded as high quality if it causes a student to give up" (p. 24). This emotional impact on students is illustrated by comparing the assessment experiences of students on winning streaks with those on losing streaks. Students who receive continual evidence of success feel hopeful and empowered, believe the school holds them in high regard, consider feedback as helpful, and become more likely to seek challenge, practice, and persist in spite of setbacks. Winning streaks lead to the feeling that success is its own reward (learning for the sake of learning) and to resilience and a strong foundation for future success. In contrast, students who are struggling receive continual evidence of failure, feel hopeless and eventually resigned, experience feedback as painful and embarrassing, and become more likely to give up and retreat. Losing streaks lead to stress, frustration, and fear, unbalanced by any success or reward, so that students yield quickly to defeat on the next new challenge and never master foundational skills for future success.

Davies (2007) supports the principle that when students are involved in the assessment process, they "learn more, achieve at higher levels, and are more motivated" (p. 32). She describes the roles of students as "co-constructing" criteria, self-assessing based on the criteria, collecting and presenting evidence of their learning, and reflecting on their strengths and needs to set informed, appropriate learning goals and further improve their learning. As a result, students develop a sense of ownership and commitment to their learning, make choices about what to focus on next in their learning, engage more actively in learning, and experience fewer discipline problems.

Fullan (2009) also takes a broad view of students as self-assessors. Describing their roles in the context of a large-scale literacy initiative in Ontario, he includes:

- Knowing and understanding what they are expected to learn
- Identifying their own strengths, needs, and interests
- Reflecting on their progress and setting goals
- Taking steps to improve their literacy learning
- Writing nonfiction with ease and coherence
- Advocating for themselves

Referencing the students' ability to now write nonfiction with ease and coherence, Fullan emphasizes that he is not talking about just passing a test. The students have accomplished a skill that they can transfer, one that will enable them to be more successful in every content area. As they advocate for themselves, they describe what they need to learn and provide input on how they demonstrate their acquired knowledge and skill. For example, teachers may provide students with green and red cards that represent whether they understand the discussion points or have the correct answer for a problem (green) or they don't. Raising the red flag can become a comfortable way for students to state their own need for further explanation. Exit cards given to the teacher at the end of a class period can be used to identify a key question or point that was missed or simply record a numerical code such as 4 = got it, great; 3 = doing OK; 2 = got parts of it and I'll try; or 1 = really need help before I can go any further. These examples give students opportunities to communicate how well they are learning during or after the introduction of new content.

Students should also be partners in planning for their learning in a broader sense. They should be assisted in learning about themselves in order to be metacognitive and advocate for their own accommodations. There are many models that describe learning styles and tools to identify career interests. In addition to their preferred methods of learning, students should have a toolbox of strategies to use while they are engaged in academic reading, homework, and other tasks—including test taking. Teachers learn, for example, that comparing and contrasting activities (Marzano, 2007) help students master new concepts, so they utilize tools like a Venn diagram in their lesson plans. Students enjoy doing it (as long as it's not the *only* visual organizer they ever use), and it helps them learn the content, but they may not recognize it as a tool they can put into their *own* toolboxes and use independently when they encounter other new material—or even when they are reading a passage on a standardized test. A middle school literacy coach told me recently about a student who asked, "Would it be, like, *cheating* if I used one of these things to help me when I'm having the test?"

In *Formative Assessment and Standards-Based Grading*, Marzano (2010b) lists ways that students can participate in assessment and adds examples of students tracking their own improvement over multiple attempts on a critical skill, evaluated on a scale of four levels of increasing cognitive demand. Looking forward to set goals is important. Looking backward to see evidence that effort has its own rewards is empowering.

The power of goal setting with individual students extends to group goal setting and motivation of the entire class. Table 8.1 (page 156) represents a chart used in a classroom to celebrate increasing proficiency throughout the year. In this classroom, a student gripped my sleeve and pulled me aside to whisper, "We don't put names on there, but I know somebody who's not proficient in math yet, and I'm smart in math and I'm helping him so we can *all* learn this stuff."

As stated by Chappuis (2005), "We know the power of self-reflection to deepen learning for adults. It also works for students. One of the strongest motivators is the opportunity to look back and see progress" (p. 42). Portfolios of student work create this type of momentum as the collection of successful accomplishment expands—whether concrete or electronic. The same thinking is behind the *Breaking Ranks* recommendation in which high school students have four-year plans and portfolios to help them chart their progress toward the finish line—which is only another beginning if they are prepared for it (National Association of Secondary School Principals, 2004).

Table 8.1: Percent of Students on Track to Proficiency

	Quarter 1	Quarter 2	Quarter 3	Quarter 4
Reading				
Writing				
Math				
Science				
Social Studies				

As educators, we often express the wish that students would be intrinsically motivated and would value learning for learning's sake. That wish would come closer to reality if we engaged students, ensured that they knew exactly what they were supposed to learn, and provided specific and timely feedback about how they were doing on those critical skills.

Elementary Exceptions

Even young children can—and do—understand learning expectations and connect with group and individual goals. Figure 8.5 is a simple chart used in an elementary classroom to display the percentage of students reaching proficiency on pretests and unit assessments. It creates motivation for individual effort and peer support in similar fashion to table 8.1.

In its districtwide approach to standards-based practice, Adams County School District 50 in Westminster, Colorado, created the "smiley face" version seen in figure 8.6 (page 158) to help students track their own progress.

High School Highlights

The role of teacher teams using data for instructional decision making is powerfully demonstrated in this account from a large comprehensive high school in the South Puget Sound region of Washington state. Katelyn Hubert, Michele Rennie, and Celeste Blay are teacher leaders who saw a need and envisioned a solution. With an average of less than five years of teaching experience, perhaps they were too new to realize that a system serving over 14,000 students is too big and bureaucratic to influence. They didn't *know* you can't work the system, so they just went ahead and did it—not once, but twice.

The first year that Rennie and Blay joined their high school math department, there were several levels of algebra courses, including a basic track. They noticed that the basic classes were predominately black and Hispanic students, which was a major difference in proportionality from the standard algebra classes. The basic algebra courses were only getting through half of the standards, ensuring that even those who passed would not be properly prepared for any higher-level algebra or algebra-based mathematics. Rennie and Blay led their colleagues to this observation and began the mantra "this must change; it is not OK." Hubert was department chair, and these three teachers talked about equity and access, and proposed getting

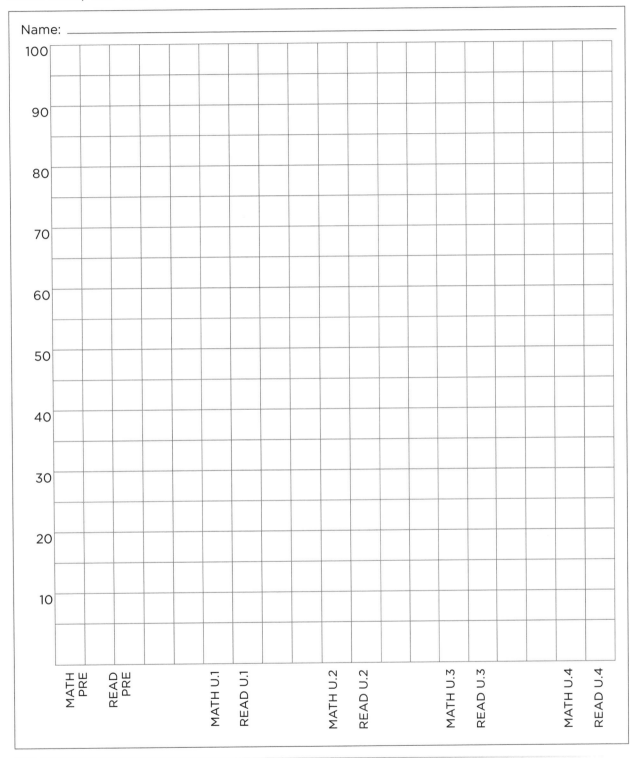

Figure 8.5: Class benchmark tracker—Elementary.

Source: McClure Elementary School, Tulsa, Oklahoma. Used with permission.

Name:	Date Started:				Date Completed:	
Subject:	Level:				Teacher:	
	1	2	3	4		
	Emerging	Partially Proficient	Proficient	Advanced		
	I need help.	I learned the simple parts.	I learned the simple and complex parts.	I can go beyond by showing it in a new way.	What is my evidence?	Teacher Sign-Off and Date
Learning Target: MA.04.02.01.02 Explains and/or models the computation of addition and subtraction of two-digit numbers (using place values) including regrouping (Colorado Math Standard 3.6.1a)						
I can add two-digit numbers without regrouping.						
I can explain how to add two-digit numbers with regrouping.						
I can model how to add two-digit numbers with regrouping.						
I can add two-digit numbers with regrouping.						
I can subtract two-digit numbers without regrouping.						
I can explain how to subtract two-digit numbers with regrouping.						
I can model how to subtract two-digit numbers with regrouping.						
I can subtract two-digit numbers with regrouping.						

Figure 8.6: Student benchmark chart—Elementary.

Source: Adams County School District 50, Westminster, Colorado. Used with permission.

rid of the basic classes and placing all ninth graders in standard algebra. They knew that some kind of additional support would be needed somehow but didn't wait to figure that out. They operated from a thought process that "we are at least giving them an equal chance to be exposed to the content they need. And we knew that we needed to see if the discrepancy in placement and skills was because of reasons outside the students, like the teaching at the elementary and middle schools. We wanted to be able to work with the kids first and give them an equal chance." Hubert went to the principal and explained that half the kids were not getting the content to pass the state test and that his support was needed because the department was split with half against dropping basic but strong evidence in favor of the change.

The principal affirmed support, and the new practice of placing all ninth graders in a standard algebra class was already in place when Hubert, as department head, attended a fall math conference and came back all excited about the idea of an algebra support class. By this time, seven or eight algebra teachers were seeing a large number of students struggling, and there was no basic algebra to move them down to. With no other alternative, the math department supported changing the schedule for second semester and overloading other sections to rearrange the existing staff allotment and create one class of algebra support. The district approved the class using a pilot provision in district policy. The change agents worked with this class themselves, saying, "Let us see them for ourselves, and then we'll have a better chance to see their real skills." The following year, departmental resources were further stretched, in order to provide three sections of algebra support, increasing the number of students served and successful.

Meanwhile, a district strategic plan had raised the issue of below-grade-level courses, and the curriculum director was intrigued by the enthusiasm and success coming from one high school. It was time to reapply for the pilot status, and more resources were needed as the pioneers' energy was spread thin and departmental staffing was stretched to the breaking point. The curriculum director leaped into the fray and helped incorporate another full-time teacher equivalent for each high school math department into a grant application that was being prepared.

Rennie, Blay, and Hubert had identified the initial problem by looking at student data and observing through the equity lens of their own vision. They continued to seek data sources they could use to check on the results of their innovation. By the second year of implementation, *79 percent* of the students in algebra support—almost all previously destined to fail—received passing grades on the regular algebra course criteria, including 22 percent receiving As and Bs.

New benchmark assessments were added (with some acknowledged glitches), and class-by-class results were available. On the benchmark test of solving problems, the standard algebra sections produced a range from 13 percent to 41 percent of the students proficient or above, with an average of *23.8 percent* of students from all sections of standard algebra successful. The algebra support sections ranged from 9 percent to 27 percent of the students achieving proficient or advanced, an average of *18 percent* of all students in those sections successful. On the test related to numbers, expressions, and operations, standard algebra classes ranged from 5 percent to 50 percent of students reaching proficiency, with an average for all sections of *18.9 percent*. Of the students attending algebra support classes, the range between sections was 10 percent to 25 percent achieving proficiency, an overall average of *16.2 percent* of these students being successful on their first benchmark test. It's true that a somewhat smaller percentage of the subset of students receiving help through algebra support attained proficiency. But the overwhelming evidence is that in previous years, similar students would not even have been introduced to the necessary content, and conceivably *none* of them would have been successful.

By this time, the grant supporting the additional staff member was expiring, state budgets were being slashed, and Hubert had moved on. Undaunted, Rennie and Blay, now co-department leaders, confronted the district with a combination of idealism and practicality: their equity goal and evidence of student learning at higher levels. In spite of overall budget cuts, their persuasion won the day, and one additional teacher was provided for each high school math department from the regular budget.

These teacher leaders got involved at the district level and built relationships and learned how the system worked—so they could work it for their kids. In their words, "The more involved you are, the better relationships you build, the more the district sees you and you build credibility just by getting to know people." But the motivation comes from within. "A major part of our work is a belief that these kids actually can succeed in algebra, so we are fighting for them and sometimes fighting against the stream and against other teachers and against what seems to be the logical solution. People think the logical solution is 'If they don't know fractions, go back and teach fractions only until they get it.' We say, 'Have them do algebra anyway—and we know how to help them.'"

Rennie and Blay are not driven by external mandates and AYP benchmarks. Their exceptional performance is a result of their own intrinsic motivation and their ability and willingness to reach out to the bigger system and advocate for their students. The great news is that there are exceptional teachers like Rennie and Blay in many places.

The rest of the story of teacher efficacy involves some characteristics of the culture in which Rennie and Blay confronted the reality of low expectations and student (non-)learning. They were quick to attribute parts of their success to the openness and acceptance of the rest of the faculty that first- and second-year teachers were respected as knowledgeable and their opinions were heard. Their ideas weren't pooh-poohed at the district or principal level. "This is now only our fourth year teaching, and we know if we were at any other school, you would not see fourth-year teachers being co-department heads. We've been on district- and state-level committees, and we were invited and welcomed into opportunities that our college classmates did not get. As a result, we have different ideas about how to bring in new teachers. We've made it a point to incorporate brand-new teachers as full professionals. It depends on the teacher, but we don't believe that sheltering first-year teachers from all aspects of all of the work does them any service. Being involved in everything actually reduces frustration in the classroom because you realize what the reasons are behind things. It gives you the control to be able to go back and say, 'Here's how we need to approach this.' We know that new people usually get the hardest classes, but we believe that all teachers should have one 'subject-difficult' class and one 'management-difficult' class. So as department heads, we make sure nobody gets all the higher-level math classes with the more compliant students."

The culture of the school is not only open to these teacher leaders and supportive of their ideas, but recognizes how they lead within their department. "The school knows we do some formal or informal work and supports that with a common lunch. That gives us the option to do some work during that time instead of before or after school, even though by contract we don't have to work then." With limited space, there are teachers from other departments who share the lunch environment as well and are amazed at the types of conversations that occur. "Why do we give this half a point? How did you teach this? We discovered we taught factoring three different ways but were trying to give and score a common assessment. Our department has an ability to work together. We can have heated philosophical debates, loud and almost angry, very emotional arguments—and still put that and our personal relationships into separate places. We have monthly potlucks at each others' houses. The more we know each other, the easier it is to argue about things . . . You can hear us yell down the hall, but it works for us. We work on nurturing each other as relationships."

Bryk and Schneider (2002) found that organizations with high levels of trust combine respect and personal regard, provide high pressure and high support, and are more aware of the realities that improvement is tough going and disagreement is normal. Collaboration is more than trusting and caring. Its root word conveys its essence—*labor*. Co-*labor* means *work* together. In this culture, the math department is able to get real work done and fulfill Reeves' (2007) expectations for collaboration: "At the very least, teachers must create common assessments, examine the results of those assessments to improve teaching practices, and examine student work" (pp. 241–242).

Conclusion

Increased use of data will generate a push for new assessment practices to increase student engagement and provide them with more accurate knowledge about their progress and the remaining goals ahead of them. Courageous conversations about assessment will inherently raise such grading-related questions as averaging, weighting, bell curve, zeroes, making up work, extra credit, and homework (Marzano, 2010b; O'Connor, 2007; Reeves, 2006). These conversations will ripple beyond the school level to bump up against district policies, and the role of the district will become clear and critical. The math teacher team in the previous section had to interact with the school and district context and found the support they needed. Chapter 9 describes the fine balance that must be struck between district direction and support.

Supporting Data Use From the District Level

The high school teacher team in the previous chapter made changes in practice that led to increased student learning. Their professionalism, intrinsic motivation, and sense of equity generated their initial enthusiasm and exploration. The support of school and district leadership was essential in helping them sustain their effort and work through several obstacles that emerged during their journey. One way they gained district trust and support was by being active and visible on district committees and at district events. These teacher leaders are what Fullan (2005) describes as *systems thinkers*: "leaders at all levels of the system who proactively and naturally take into account and interact with larger parts of the system as they bring about deeper reform and help produce other leaders working on the same issues" (p. x).

These leaders see beyond their own classroom, their own campus, and their own constituency, and contribute to a culture of collective commitment. They both represent and challenge their colleagues, driven by the deep moral purpose Fullan describes in *Leadership and Sustainability* (2005). He emphasizes the need to focus the work of educators at all levels on three dimensions of moral purpose:

> (a) commitment to raising the bar and closing the gaps of student achievement for all individuals and schools; (b) a commitment to treat people ethically—adults and students alike (which does not mean being soft); and (c) a commitment to improving the whole district, not just one's own school. (p. 68)

He goes on to link moral purpose, systems thinking, and sustainability—the desperately needed capacity to persevere, to maintain momentum, to temper knee-jerk reactions, and to stay the course through implementation challenges:

> Moral purpose has a long tradition in education at the level of the individual teacher or principal. It is time to make it a system quality. Moral purpose is the link between system thinking and sustainability. You cannot move substantially toward sustainability in the absence of widely shared moral purpose. The reason is that sustainability depends on the distributed effort of people at all levels of the system, and meeting the goals of moral purpose produces commitment throughout the system. (Fullan, 2005, p. 87)

Such commitment will increase appreciation for and willingness to engage in the practices that Wiggins (2010) advocates. In his view, the K–12 system will only be truly systematic when:

- Teachers of all grades write curriculum together.
- Teachers of all grades score student work together.
- Teachers are required, as team members, to issue team reports each semester to the rest of the K–12 faculty on what worked, what did not, and what will be done to improve learning against goals and standards, mindful of best practice in the building as well as in the education world more generally. (p. 25)

Paul Houston (1998), executive director of the American Association of School Administrators, put it this way:

While top-down reform has its place and bottom-up reform has its merits, something must connect the two, and that something is the system. Education is a living, breathing organism that cannot be taken apart or fixed in pieces, as one might fix a mechanical apparatus. It is organic and must be improved systematically. All the parts must be attended to and that is the role of school systems and school system leaders. (p. 53)

Systems thinking is thinking outside our own box, perceiving the impact and connections of our work beyond the boundaries of our own classroom or office. One of the ongoing dilemmas of public education is establishing the appropriate balance of district leadership for system coherence and school-based planning for each unique situation. This balancing act of schools and the central office is critical because, among other reasons:

- Districts, not schools, set board policy
- Districts, not schools, negotiate collective bargaining agreements
- Districts, not schools, govern access to professional days and times in the district calendar
- Districts, not schools, receive direct communication from state departments of education
- Districts, not schools, receive federal funds and are accountable for using them appropriately

The urgency and scope of work needed to fulfill the ideal of all students succeeding with no achievement gaps linked to subgroups of the student population constitute what Marzano and Waters (2009) describe as second-order change. Such change is very complex, because it is perceived as a break with the past, lies outside existing paradigms, conflicts with prevailing values and norms, requires the acquisition of new knowledge and skills, and requires resources currently not available to those responsible for implementation.

Second-order change, such as developing a collaborative culture of collective responsibility for all students' learning, will almost inevitably bump up against some district policy:

It is possible for a school to become highly collaborative despite the district that it is in, but it is not possible to stay highly collaborative in these circumstances. The district role can foster continuous improvement of schools, or it can take its toll on continuity through neglect or misguided policy actions. (Fullan, 2005, p. 6)

District leadership does affect student achievement. Marzano and Waters (2009) found a .24 correlation between certain district leadership behaviors and student achievement, close on the heels of the .25 correlation between principal leadership and student achievement discovered previously (Marzano, Waters, & McNulty, 2005). (Correlation is a statistical analysis that helps one see the relationship of scores in one distribution to scores in another distribution. Correlation coefficients have a range of –1.0 to +1.0.) The word *nonnegotiables* is used frequently in their report, as they outline five district-level responsibilities:

1. Ensuring collaborative goal setting
2. Establishing nonnegotiable goals for achievement and instruction
3. Creating board alignment with and support of district goals
4. Monitoring achievement and instruction goals
5. Allocating resources to support the goals for achievement and instruction (p. 6)

Figure 9.1 (pages 166–167) summarizes the school improvement work done at Mode Middle School (center) and illustrates how the schoolwide efforts of the data team influenced the work of teacher teams (right) and their interaction with students at the classroom level, and also created implications for action at the district level (left). Maintaining the level of commitment to the changes planned by Mode Middle School staff and implementing them effectively so that results become evident will depend, in large part, on how the district handles the implications that spin off—or bounce up—to the district level.

The District Data Team

Figure 2.1 (page 24) illustrates two kinds of links to the district as a whole. The school's administrative team reports to the district administrative team, and the schoolwide data team should have representation on a district data team that is typically part of curriculum and instruction.

Composition and Characteristics

The district data team is usually part of the instructional division of the district, under an assistant superintendent. In some cases, the Office of Accountability is structured as a stand-alone department that reports directly to the superintendent. A large district may have a director of assessment or accountability that leads the team. But the assistant superintendent of instruction must have an active role. Whoever leads the district data team must sit on the superintendent's cabinet along with the administrators who evaluate principals, in order to ensure that expectations for schools are clear and shared, evaluated, and supported.

The membership of the district data team should balance district curriculum coordinators with school-based teacher leaders so there is a two-way flow of information and input. If the district has a director or coordinator of technology who handles the data system, this individual may be on the district data team but should not lead it. The role of technology is

DISTRICT provides principal with support and coaching

MODE MIDDLE SCHOOL principal diagnoses context after one year

Principal engages staff in reaffirming mission

Principal engages staff in culture-building activities

Principal expands school improvement/ leadership team (SI/LT)

Liaison connections created with district data, assessment, accountability departments

Principal and SI/LT form schoolwide data team

Schoolwide data team identifies initial data available

District assists with staff-related data and parent-community data; finds and funds survey instruments

Schoolwide data team gathers the available data

District staff do *not tell* school what their data show

Schoolwide data team reviews the data to determine priorities for sharing with all; creates draft summary and holds it back

District staff assist with data displays

Schoolwide data team prepares displays for all staff to review

District begins discussing data for non-state-tested content areas

SI/LT and schoolwide data team engage all staff in overview of the data and generate summary of findings

District generates responses to teachers' stages of concern and questions

Ad hoc study groups examine current practice; conduct root-cause analysis and recommend strategies

SI/LT coordinates staff review of strategies, which include structure for teacher teams

District affirms priority of time for teacher teams; waives some district demands

Every staff member identified as part of a teacher team

SI/LT leads work on six-trait writing

TEACHER TEAMS use IC Map to determine status and next steps/needs for six-trait writing

District coordinates vocabulary selection across schools; provides training in instruction for vocabulary

SI/LT leads work on academic vocabulary

Teacher teams identify critical vocabulary for their content

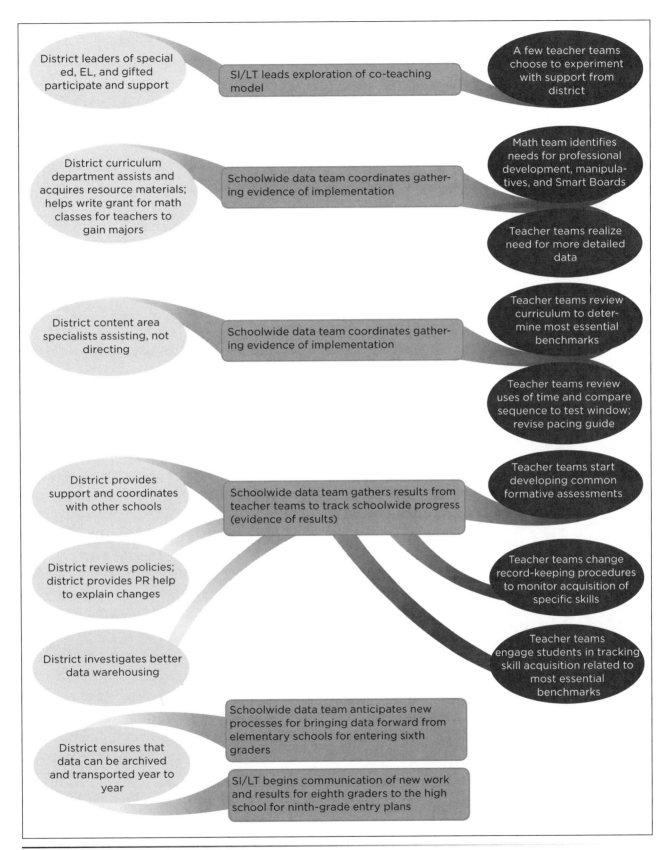

Figure 9.1: The work of Mode Middle School in the district context.

to respond to and serve the needs of students and their teachers, not to dictate how things must be done based on electronic capability.

Roles and Responsibilities

Although DuFour, DuFour, Eaker, and Karhanek have provided visible and compelling descriptions of PLC at Work™ in their earlier work, their focus was primarily on the school level. In *Raising the Bar and Closing the Gap* (2010), they state, "In recent years, we have become much more aware of the critical role the central office can play in building the capacity of staff and students throughout the district" (p. 5). They go on to describe district roles in support of implementation of professional learning communities and include a specific focus on support for use of data:

- Provide training on building high-performing teams with regard to focused school improvement
- Provide professional development support to school staff in the development and/or refinement of strategic plans
- *Provide support to enable school teams to implement collaborative processes for data analysis* and continuous improvement
- Provide focused coaching to schools in order to attain critical student achievement, including achieving adequate yearly progress on state assessments and closing the achievement gap
- *Train principals and school staff on data collection and analysis, interpretation, and strategies for continuous improvement*
- Coach schools to initiate and implement focused improvement models and tools
- Provide support to schools on meeting their performance measures based on identified goals
- Develop measures and evaluate professional development opportunities related to school improvement support
- Support the implementation of the Administrative and Supervisory Professional Growth System (p. 110, italics mine)

Chapters 3–6 described data needed for schoolwide attention. The district data team helps schoolwide data teams find the data they seek, advises them on effective ways to display it, and listens to anticipate future needs. Chapter 7 outlined the strategies chosen by the school, including development of common formative assessments. The district data team might provide training in assessment development and coach teacher teams through their initial efforts. The district data team also helps address issues related to curriculum, pacing, assessment, grading, and record keeping (as outlined in chapter 8). Meanwhile, principals discuss the same issues with their supervisors, adding to the urgency for all departments at the central office to provide similar responses and direction.

The District as a Model

There is a more global need that transcends the district data team and includes all central office leaders. The district as a whole must model the characteristics and teamwork they expect of schools, including monitoring evidence of implementation and results for the strategies they mandate and making adjustments and exceptions as indicated by their data and the evidence from each school:

> Unfortunately, rather than functioning as a well-organized, goal-driven system, too many districts are characterized by a lack of unified direction, a lack of agreement about the central office role in supporting school improvement, and a lack of alignment between goals and strategies. This disjointed arrangement can lead to competing goals, programs, and initiatives; struggles over resources; and a depletion of energy. A central office lacking a systemic, coherent approach cannot give schools the help they need to improve student learning. Instead, it pulls schools in competing directions, leaving them feeling isolated and adrift. (Agullard & Goughnour, 2006, p. 3)

In contrast, Fullan (2009) describes "Supportive Infrastructure and Leadership" as the third component of his Theory of Action for System Change. He refers to effective districts that focus on instruction, model and help with use of data, develop capacity within and across schools, foster leadership, build learning communities, and link all efforts to evidence of their desired results.

As Joellen Killion and Patricia Roy point out (2009), district improvement efforts, including professional development planning, should be informed by the provisions in school improvement plans. The district and schools should actively exchange information and action at each step of the school improvement process. In the case of using data, the district would have a supportive role in managing the data, creating effective visuals for school use, and facilitating interpretation. Each school would present a summary of its data, highlighting celebrations and concerns, so that the central office could identify common patterns and needs between and among schools, provide sources of research and best practices, and facilitate networking among schools with similar challenges.

When multiple schools identify the same strategies for implementation, the district should create economies of scale by coordinating the delivery of initial training (knowledge and comprehension), so that school-based resources can be used for the collaborative job-embedded learning of application and practice with feedback. The central office should synchronize school and district planning time lines so that school-based decision making truly informs broader initiatives. In short, the school improvement plans *are data for district decision making*.

The process for gathering additional data for district decision making should mirror and model what schools do to get input directly from teachers. (District-mandated initiatives should be incorporated among the strategies that are included in the school improvement plan, so there is *one* picture of the expectations.) District leaders model continuous improvement and gather data when they invite teachers to respond to questions like:

- What support do you need with the _____ initiative?

- Which populations of students are most challenging? What would help you better meet the needs of these students?

- Do you know how decisions get made at the district level? Do you participate? What would make this process work better?

Flexibility

Sustained focus on a nonnegotiable goal represents a clear "what" that is appropriately iden-tified at the district level. Sustaining commitment at the school and classroom levels requires some flexibility around the "how." Fullan (2009) refers to flexibility and partnership as he describes a relationship that is "not unidirectional or simply top-down . . . the district gives clear and firm direction as we have seen, but also has a keen sense of partnership with the field, and flexibility according to local needs and variation" (p. 280).

Flexible is an adjective also used by Leithwood (Leithwood, et al., 2009) in his summary of roles for the district:

> Districts contribute most powerfully to principals' sense of efficacy by
>
> * Establishing clear purposes which become widely shared
> * Unambiguously awarding priority to the improvement of instruction
> * Providing flexible, varied, meaningful, and just-in-time professional development for both school administrators and their staffs
> * Creating productive working relationships with all the major stakeholders
> * Assisting schools in the collection, interpretation, and use of data for decision-making (p. 84)

The sequence may intuitively seem to be that the district sets the "what" and the schools then shape the "how." But sometimes the sequence spirals back, in typical chicken-and-egg fashion. As school leaders create action plans for change, they become inspired with ideas that are second-order changes, and those become action items for district attention.

A district in Pennsylvania invited me to work with their principals on their school improve-ment plans. As I visited schools and met with principals and teachers, I asked about their challenges and what kind of support they needed. After several visits, five themes emerged that principals wanted to tackle but correctly identified as beyond the scope of any individual school within a system: a common language of instruction, common elementary assessments, professional development design and delivery, grading policy and practices, and middle-to-high-school transition. In response to this input, the district formed study teams to address those issues. Their actions will, in turn, influence the direction of continuous improvement at the schools.

Balance

The necessary balance of district and school leadership occurs in two ways. First, district mandates focus more heavily on the "what" than being too tightly prescribed on the "how." Second, the proper balance of flexibility on the "how" creates a clear set of criteria for exemp-tions. For example, the strategic plan of a large urban district mandated development of common assessments for critical skills. The central office worked with teacher leaders and teacher teams to create the assessments. Meanwhile, a group of elementary schools had received substantial resources through Reading First grants, with assessment requirements attached. The central office administrator met with representatives from this group and reviewed the information about student learning that could be gleaned from their grant-related assessments. Where assessments provided knowledge of student learning on the same learning objectives, use of the district assessments was waived to avoid over-testing. For the learning objectives not addressed on the grant-related assessments, schools were expected to implement the district common assessments. The balance around the mandate was focused on its end goal: ensuring that all critical skills were assessed for every student.

Implications of Data Use: Curriculum

When teacher teams tackle the development of common assessments to formatively guide instruction and track student proficiency, two issues inevitably surface. The first is the over-stuffed curriculum, and the second is the use of instructional time and pace of instruction. Teacher efforts will sink or swim, depending on the timeliness and nature of district responses.

Most Essential Benchmarks

If districts expect teachers to differentiate according to student needs and bring all students to proficiency, the plethora of standards and benchmarks must be acknowledged and addressed. Ainsworth and Viegut (2006) emphasize the need to set curricular priorities in order to know what should be assessed in formative assessments and to provide the guaranteed and viable (meaning deliverable) curriculum that Marzano (2007) described.

The Leadership and Learning Center (Allison et al., 2010) refers to these instructional priorities as the "power standards," so called because they are characterized by endurance, leverage, and readiness. Endurance refers to the underlying or foundational skills that will have longevity in a lifetime of learning. For example, the ability to read nonfiction text, add whole numbers, understand cause and effect, or classify information by comparing and contrasting will empower lifelong learners throughout school and beyond. Leverage refers to prioritizing skills and concepts that support the learner in other content areas including those not tested on state exams and can be used to create horizontal alignment and interdisciplinary experiences. Readiness implies a vertical alignment of prerequisites. A standard would be prioritized if it is critical to prepare learners for new learning later in a course of study or in future courses.

The Kenosha (Wisconsin) Unified School District chose the term *most essential benchmarks* rather than *power standards* because standards were stated in general K–12 language and did not provide the grade/course specificity needed to guide development of common assessments. Teachers were familiar with the term *benchmarks* as the more finite expectations for their teaching, and "most essential" fit better with that noun. The criteria for prioritizing the most essential benchmarks were based on the characteristics of power standards noted previously, but were described as:

- Limited in number, ideally ten to twelve per subject per year
- Essential for:
  - Success in the next grade/course

- • Success in other content areas
- • Success demonstrating proficiency (on state test and more)
- • Success in life
- • Assessable

Teacher committees worked with curriculum specialists to identify the most essential benchmarks and compare them vertically to ensure articulation. Those benchmarks were then distinguished in all district curriculum documents with bold, italicized print. They were also published for parents and students as the "Success Steps" needed at each grade level, K–8. Figure 9.2 is an example of the Success Steps brochure for sixth grade.

At the high school level, most essential benchmarks were listed in the common syllabus for each course, which is provided to students and is also available on the district website for parent reference.

Pacing of Instruction

Districts frequently develop curriculum maps or pacing guides to illustrate the sequence of instruction and relative amount of time to spend on various concepts and skills, which is closely related to whether they are power standards (most essential benchmarks) or not. One function of a pacing guide is to ensure that topics or units that are heavily tested on large-scale assessments are actually taught before the test is given. Another function is to ensure that teachers don't spend too much time on their favorite unit or topic and overlook or avoid portions of their teaching responsibility they enjoy less or feel less confident about.

Pacing guides are always theoretical and must be tested in practice, so the traditional five- or seven-year cycle for revising curricula and selecting textbooks must be abandoned. The cycle is set for budget purposes, to space out the major purchases of a districtwide textbook adoption. But pacing guides are a function of curriculum revision that must occur at least annually, based on the real experiences—and the data about student learning—that teachers provide. The district must be careful not to circumscribe the sequence and pace of instruction to the point that teachers feel they must move on whether students learned it or not or eliminate active learning and resort to lecturing and passing out assignments in order to save time.

Implications of Data Use: Assessment

Chapter 3 displayed a pattern of assessments that included quarterly benchmark tests, unit tests, and common formative assessments used frequently to check student understanding and adjust instruction. Regarding the district context for this practice, the *Learning From Leadership* study (Louis et al., 2010) found:

> One of the most productive ways for districts to facilitate continual improvement is to develop teachers' capacity to use formative assessments of student progress aligned with district expectations for student learning, and to use formative data in devising and implementing interventions during the school year. (p. 214)

Sixth Grade Success Steps

The mission of Kenosha Unified School District, an education system which values our multicultural heritage, is to empower all students to reach their unique capabilities, contribute to our community and compete in a global society by providing diverse and challenging opportunities to learn through the collaborative efforts of students, families, community and staff.

This mission statement declares our belief that students learn the most and grow the best when we all work as partners.

The district establishes standards and benchmarks to describe what students should know and be able to do in each content area and grade level. This brochure highlights **essential skills** that students need to develop by the end of sixth grade. The complete standards and benchmarks can be found at **www.kusd.edu** under Departments and then Curriculum and Instructional Services.

This brochure also provides specific tips for **"Parents as Partners."** Thank you for the time and attention you devote to helping your child take these success steps this year.

August 2008

Based on Middle School Program of Study
Adopted December 2006

PARENTS AS PARTNERS

- Review assignments with child each night.
- With your child, go to *www.kusd.edu* and click on **Middle School Library Online Subscription** for research and other educational opportunities. For passwords or questions, contact the school library media specialist.
- Parents may support their child in mathematics by visiting the following online resources: online book—*www.my.hrw.com* (user name and password required and provided by teacher)—or additional resources— *www.go.hrw.com/gopages/ma/msm1_07.html* (no registration required).
- Visit Kenosha Unified's Web site: choose departments and then Instructional Technology for online touch keyboarding resources.
- Visit *www.atomiclearning.com* (user id: trolley, password: kenosha) for training on Microsoft Word.
- Discuss technology used around the home and career skills of parents/guardians.
- Ask your child to teach you words from other languages.
- Discuss the importance of learning about other cultures and the values of knowing about other languages and customs.
- Discuss current science issues with your child, and encourage him/her to ask good questions. Be sure to help him/her search for evidence to back up the answers.
- Encourage children by discussing how they succeeded in elementary school, and remind them that they can continue to use strategies that helped them in the past.

CONTACT INFORMATION

Reading/Language Arts	(262) 653-7730
Mathematics	(262) 653-6311
Science	(262) 653-6314
Social Studies	(262) 653-7730
World Languages	(262) 653-6314
Health & Physical Education	(262) 653-6386
Art	(262) 653-7399
Music	(262) 653-6388
Career & Technical Education	(262) 653-6304

An Equal Opportunity Educator/Employer

Students may take Band or Orchestra or Choir as their elective for all four quarters.

BAND

Students will:
- Play with rhythmic and pitch accuracy.
- Perform with good embouchure in developing tone and accurate intonation.
- Accurately tune their instrument.
- Improvise or compose a short musical example.
- Read basic rhythms.
- Learn to respond to a conductor.
- Learn standard music notation and vocabulary.
- Describe and evaluate performances.
- Recognize and identify music from different time periods and cultures.

ORCHESTRA

Students will:
- Play with rhythmic and pitch accuracy.
- Perform with developing tone and accurate intonation in first position.
- Accurately tune their instrument.
- Improvise or compose a short musical example.
- Read basic rhythms.
- Learn to respond to a conductor.
- Learn standard music notation and vocabulary.
- Describe and evaluate performances.
- Recognize and identify music from different time periods and cultures.

CHOIR

Students will:
- Sing unison, two-part, or three-part choral music.
- Sing choral music using appropriate diction in a variety of languages.
- Learn to read choral music scores.
- Learn ensemble skills and respond to a conductor.
- Sight read music.
- Establish a musical vocabulary.
- Study the background of music being studied as it relates to history or culture.

Students not in Band, Orchestra, or Choir must take all four electives below.

TECHNICAL EDUCATION—1 Quarter

Students will:
- Explore technology and careers in construction, transportation, manufacturing, and digital communications.
- Design and build projects in high-tech areas including: Lego robotics, drafting and design, audio communication, and video production.

WORLD LANGUAGE—1 Quarter
Spanish *and* French

Students will:
- Say numbers 1–50, alphabet, and colors in languages.
- Begin to understand spoken languages on familiar topics with picture help.
- Understand the cultures of France and Spain compared to United States culture.
- Recognize words that look similar in English.

GROWING UP READY—1 Quarter

Students will:
- Explore family and consumer skills needed to be successful in the home, at school, and in the community. Areas include: food and nutrition, child development, and sewing projects.
- Review the food pyramid.
- Learn real-life applications of math and science in the home.

GENERAL MUSIC—1 Quarter

Students will:
- Sing on pitch and in rhythm.
- Play contrasting rhythmic patterns while other students sing or play.
- Recognize standard notational symbols and terms.
- Recognize a concerto, suite, and symphony.

KENOSHA UNIFIED - NO. 1 - SCHOOL DISTRICT

Figure 9.2: Sixth Grade Success Steps—most essential benchmarks.

continued →

ENGLISH / LANGUAGE ARTS
4-Quarter Requirement

Students will:

- Write a personal narrative focusing on one event.
- Write a variety of letters.
- Write to inform and compare/contrast.
- Write for a specific audience.
- Use precise words to make writing clearer and interesting.
- Write paragraphs and multiparagraph pieces that develop and support a topic.
- Write complete sentences with different lengths and beginnings.
- Revise writing to improve sentence fluency, organization, and word choice.
- Edit writing for appropriate grammar, capitalization, spelling, and punctuation.
- Practice and use a variety of reading strategies (making connections, determining importance, asking questions, summarizing, predicting, inferring, and synthesizing) to improve understanding.
- Read a variety of fiction and nonfiction texts, including everyday texts such as newspapers, how-to manuals, and cereal boxes, in class and at home.
- Read informational and everyday text (e.g., newspapers, instruction manuals, and magazines).
- Use the format and structure of fiction and nonfiction texts to help with understanding.
- Read aloud with fluency and accuracy.
- Monitor understanding while reading, and use fix-up strategies to repair understanding and meaning.

MATHEMATICS
4-Quarter Requirement

Students will:

- Add, subtract, multiply, and divide decimals.
- Add and subtract fractions and mixed numbers with like and unlike denominators.
- Divide with two-digit divisors and multi-digit dividends (e.g., 25 $\overline{)1350}$).
- Estimate the sum, difference, and product of whole numbers, common fractions, mixed numbers, and decimals to hundredths.
- Write fractions, decimals, and percents in equivalent forms.
- Compare and order fractions and decimals using less than, greater than, and equals symbols.
- Compare and order positive and negative numbers using the number line.
- Write ratios and set up proportions (e.g., scale drawings).
- Find perimeter and area of squares, rectangles, triangles, and parallelograms.
- Find circumference of a circle.
- Use both metric and customary units of measure.
- Display and analyze data in various tables and graphs (e.g., line graphs, bar graphs).
- Complete patterns using pictures and numbers.
- Change words into mathematical expressions (e.g., four less than x is written as x-4).
- Write and solve a one-step equation (e.g., $2x = 10$).
- Explain answers to problems using correct math vocabulary.

SCIENCE
4-Quarter Requirement

Students will:

- Study the structure of the planet earth and its changes.
- Describe the characteristics of living organisms and how they are classified.
- Study commonly used models that represent scientific concepts.
- Ask questions that can be answered with scientific investigations.
- Collect, organize, and report data and observations.
- Discuss how science and technology influence and are influenced by society.

SOCIAL STUDIES
4-Quarter Requirement

Students will:

- Use a globe and a variety of maps, photographs, etc. to gather and compare information about continents, regions, and countries in Africa, Asia, Europe, and Russia.
- Identify examples of conflict, cooperation, and interdependence among societies of Africa, Asia, Europe, and Russia.
- Identify how laws are established and the types of government systems that exist in various societies in Africa, Asia, Europe, and Russia.
- Identify how the concentration of selected natural resources generates trade and shapes economic patterns.
- Describe the ways in which local, regional, and ethnic cultures of Africa, Asia, Europe, and Russia may influence the everyday lives of people.

PHYSICAL EDUCATION/HEALTH
1st and 3rd Quarter or 2nd and 4th Quarter

PHYSICAL EDUCATION

Students will:

- Demonstrate efficient and effective movements using appropriate biomechanical principles.
- Execute developmentally appropriate movement patterns in modified versions of team and individual sports.
- Use results of physical fitness assessments to guide changes in physical activity.

HEALTH

Students will:

- Identify three sides of the Health Triangle.
- Identify good health habits.
- Identify causes of injuries and ways to prevent injuries.
- Define bullying and describe the feeling of the targets of bullying.
- Define social health.

VISUAL ARTS 6
1-Quarter Requirement

Students will:

- Demonstrate a basic understanding of how to describe, analyze, interpret, and evaluate art.
- Become familiar with the relationship of the elements and principles of design.
- Recognize how artwork is manipulated into a variety of 2-D and 3-D art.
- Develop a basic understanding of the various techniques through the making of various compositions.
- Learn the styles of art and how they create symbolic cultural connections to the viewer.

KEYBOARDING* & COMPUTERS
1-Quarter Requirement

Students will:

- Demonstrate touch keyboarding skills at 20-25 words per minute, with 90% accuracy.
- Use word processing software to compose, organize, and edit information.
- Use the Internet to identify security issues, obtain information, and send and receive e-mail.
- Learn the basics of Internet safety.
- Passing keyboarding assessment will allow for more electives in seventh and eighth grade.

Source: Teaching and Learning, Kenosha Unified School District No. 1. Used with permission.

No single teacher, grade level, or school can ensure the proper assessment balance. District participation and coordination are needed. This need for commonality is not just technical for purposes of data accuracy. It is also essential for communication to stakeholders and to households with children attending more than one school. The use of common assessments with all students is also a reflection of the district and school culture, focusing on the equity issue of ensuring access to the general education curriculum and the opportunity to learn all of the most essential benchmarks.

In districts with more than one high school, common end-of-course exams are essential to ensure that patterns of instruction and low/high achievement do not follow neighborhood borders. Algebra I should be Algebra I and address Algebra I benchmarks wherever the student attends school. And if the use of common formative assessments is good practice with demonstrated results improving student learning, such assessments should also be used in content areas without state tests.

Another issue that arises and needs a common response is the use of pretesting. If one school uses a commonly developed assessment as a pretest, and another school believes that "gives away" their test, conflicts will arise from school to school. Interaction among school-wide data teams, policymakers, and supervisors of curriculum and assessment at the district level must be seamless and characterized by mutual respect.

Implications of Data Use: Professional Development Planning

The point was made earlier that schools don't set master calendars or negotiate contracts. Both of those processes impact professional development planning and must be addressed at the district level. If principals and school leadership teams are to be held accountable for change and improved performance, their needs for professional development must take priority. One district assured its principals that professional development days would be held harmless from district mandates so that they could complete the training they needed for implementation of their school improvement plan. One of the district's schools had made a major investment in new technology, but it was not paying off for students, because every time the technology training had been scheduled, the district hijacked the professional development day for some other purpose. These principals accepted the district's new assurance and began to lay out their professional development plans for the following year. Shortly thereafter, they received notification that the district had been awarded a writing grant and that professional development days would be devoted to this purpose. Such experiences not only inhibit the implementation of change at the school level, they destroy trust and system coherence.

The district that models using data itself for decision making will use the school improvement plans as data. If several schools have identified the same topic or need for professional learning, the district can protect resources by coordinating training for all who need it. If a few new teachers at each school need orientation to programs or curricula, the district can pull them together.

In addition to modeling organizational learning and flexibility, the district needs to disseminate and support best practices. As Bruce Joyce and Beverly Showers (1988) inform us, without coaching conversations, teachers' knowledge may increase but the skills and transfer to the classroom will remain low. However, with ongoing coaching, more than 90 percent of the knowledge and skills will be transferred into teacher practice in classrooms. The district needs to honor the "what," the needs that schools express from their data, while also stressing that the "how," the formats and venues of professional development, include follow-up for application and transfer, not just initial training.

Implications of Data Use: Grading and Record Keeping

Mode Middle School's teacher teams found themselves faced with a data dilemma they phrased as "What should we be keeping track of?" When teachers shift their focus to evidence of student learning, they realize that they need a steady flow of information that is organized around the most essential learning targets for the grade or course, and they need to report to parents based on the current proficiency of students, not as an average of all attempts.

Grading Policy

Typical board policies reflect traditional grading practices, so innovation at the school level may last only until one disgruntled stakeholder goes to the superintendent and then on to (or directly to) the school board with a complaint that the practice violates the policy. One approach has been to create a written waiver to pilot a different approach at an individual school, voted on in a board meeting so that the school can be supported when criticisms of confusion arise. When a waiver is created, it does remove an obstacle for the school that is examining its practices with a focus on student needs. But in a large district, it may also reinforce the idea that these standards-based, data-guided practices are radical and only appropriate in some unique setting.

The district should encourage and support school-based initiatives, but central office leaders should also initiate and coordinate discussions with groups of teachers to include the questions "Why do we grade? What and when should we report to students and their families?" Workshops on grading practices will be more productive if awareness and readiness have been created through a host of small, reflective conversations. Waivers and revisions to board policy are some of the complex procedures in which the district data team and administrative team must actively engage.

Electronic Grading and Data Warehousing

Another decision that can only be made at the district level is the purchase or development of the electronic system that manages the data on student learning as well as many other kinds of information that must be kept and reported for various purposes. As indicated in earlier discussions, the technology should respond to teachers' needs, not dictate their practice. A major role of the district data team is to gather input and create the criteria for choosing a data warehouse system. It should reflect a vision of best and future practice so it helps support, not hinder, change.

The Adams County School District 50 in Westminster, Colorado (www.adams50.org), has taken some of the boldest steps in the nation toward systemic, standards-based, student-focused teaching and learning. The Adams 50 journey began with a wake-up call when the district was placed on the state academic watch list in 2006. Internal examination revealed a trend in changing demographics, achievement gaps between subgroups, and a low graduation rate. Enrollment had declined, and 75 percent of the district's 10,000 students qualified for free or reduced-price lunch. Forty-three percent of the students resided in homes where English was not the primary language.

A member of the school board prompted exploration into practices that had dramatically improved student learning in Chugach, Alaska, and a partnering/mentoring relationship began with that district and the Reinventing Schools Coalition. School board support continued and was reaffirmed in April 2010 in a statement supporting the effort for the next five years.

Superintendent Roberta Selleck worked closely with the teacher association and assured them that implementation would not take place without the approval of 80 percent of the teachers. When the first vote was 75 percent agreement, she honored the promise and waited, gathering and responding to questions and concerns. Teacher leaders also talked with their colleagues. A second vote of 85 percent provided the go-ahead. All of the bits and pieces of time for professional development (late starts, early releases, and so on) were combined and expanded to create nine days a year for all staff.

In order to create a reliable and viable curriculum with aligned assessments, one hundred teachers worked during the summer with Robert Marzano to identify measurement topics and learning targets (similar to power standards and most essential benchmarks). These teachers counted it as a professional development opportunity and a chance to shape their own future but were not compensated on an hourly basis. Over time, the measurement topics were divided into seventeen levels, so that the traditional mindset of twelve grades could be overcome, and students could progress from level to level based on proficiency, not age. Level 14 is now the equivalent of minimum graduation requirements, and levels 15 and 16 involve postsecondary opportunities (wiki.adams50.org). Figure 9.3 (page 178) shows one level's measurement topics in math, with spaces for the student to keep track of three forms of evidence (E1, E2, E3) that he or she is ready to be assessed on that learning target.

To create a balanced assessment system that includes the state tests, a combination of commercial instruments was chosen and work proceeds on locally developed performance tasks and scoring guides linked to the learning targets. The computer adaptive Scantron Performance Series is utilized two to three times per year to provide an outside validation of student learning per national normed assessments. The Scantron Achievement Series provides item banks so that more frequent assessments can be created, administered, and scored locally for immediate feedback. At the secondary level, the EXPLORE, PLAN, and ACT assessments are used to check the rigor of other assessments using a norm-referenced instrument and to guide students in the high school's career academies.

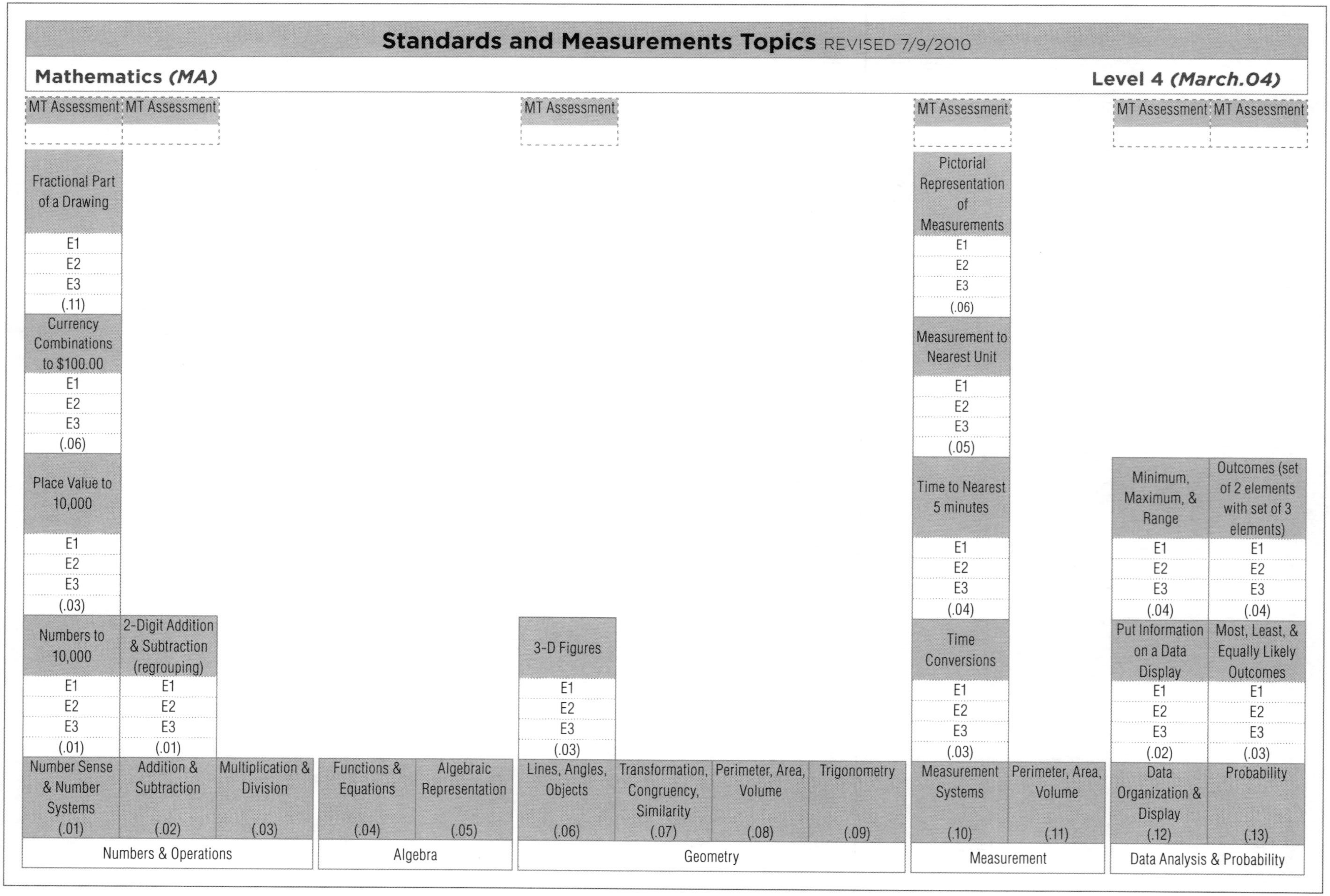

Figure 9.3: Evidence of individual student proficiency.

Source: Adams County School District 50, Westminster, Colorado. Used with permission.

The biggest question, of course, was how to manage all of this material and information in a data warehouse. Many potential users contributed to the criteria and review of possibilities. Essential criteria and questions included:

- Usability/user-friendliness
    - Who are the users, what do they know, and what can they learn?
    - What do users want or need to do?
    - What is the general background of the users?
    - What is the context in which the users will be working?
    - What has to be left to the machine to do automatically?
    - Can users easily accomplish their intended tasks at an acceptable speed?
    - What documentation and supporting materials are available?
    - What errors do users make, and how can they recover from these errors?
    - What provisions are made for users with disabilities?
- Compatibility with existing systems
- Training (initial and ongoing)—adequate support for skillful, confident use
- Single data-entry capability
- Single sign-on for multiple systems
- Cost
- Report functions
- Technical support
- Accessibility—system available to all users, including those with special needs, at home or work via a web-based interface
- Scalability—ability of system to continue responding with increasing number of users
- Ability to customize—vendor can conform to district specifications; must match reporting and gradebook to measurement topics
- Flexibility for building/developing schedules
- Rollover of existing data—students' academic history intact and able to be archived from year to year
- Ability to aggregate and report data on demand by student group, content standards, and school
- Real-time data, dynamic data transfer—interactive system with continuous change and updates as data are entered
- Access portal for parents and students to view real-time performance data
- Language translation
- Implementation time line

User groups evaluated several data warehouse systems and found a system that met the specified criteria, particularly in being able to flexibly track student progress over multiple school years. It was a web-based, standards-based education management suite that provided all users with access 24/7. It included grading tools, scheduling abilities, and reporting for individual students and groups. Data could be analyzed by student, school, grade, class, performance level, learning target, and staff member.

Implications of Data Use: Supervision and Support of Principals

A harried principal, already stressed by failure to meet the imposed target, said it well: "They call it 'giving us autonomy,' but I call it 'hanging us out to dry.'" This principal realized that achieving success for his students would require him to stimulate school-level discussion and action beyond existing policy, challenge long-held practices, and maximize creativity within legal requirements for use of funds to provide student support.

In order to survive, he knew he would need more than autonomy. He would need support and guidance, and he would need coordinated opportunities to learn from and with his colleagues. Fullan (2005) reminds us of

> two core reasons why districts or comparable regional structures are essential. First, decentralized schools will have variable capacities to engage in continuous improvement, and therefore some agency has to be responsible for helping develop capacity and for intervening (with a goal to developing capacity) when performance is low. The second reason is even more fundamental for sustainability: We can't change the system without lateral (cross-school and cross-district) sharing and capacity development. It is very much the district's role to help make the latter happen. (p. 66)

One Set of Clear Expectations

Except in very small districts, the principal likely reports to an administrator in one department, while issues of standards, professional development, and assessment are handled in another division. The line supervisors of principals approve the school improvement plans and write the formal evaluations, but other central office administrators also identify expectations regarding use of the curricula, instructional model, and assessments developed at the district level. One way of supporting principals is to ensure that they have one set of expectations that is clear and coherent and aligns with the school improvement plan for which they are accountable. Principals should be expected to set instructional leadership goals that identify the specific leadership steps they will take to ensure implementation. Based on my observations, districts would be well served to consider these recommendations:

- Review all district and school improvement plans to ensure that they include strategies for improving instruction and teacher-student relationships at the classroom level.

- Review professional development plans to ensure that they are not just a series of workshops and that they include the follow-up and feedback needed to create change in teacher performance.

- Advocate for and approve instructional coaching, but maintain ownership of the staff designated as coaches. Coaching is a powerful, but expensive, strategy for professional learning that may create tension between districts and schools. Master teachers are hired and trained to help their colleagues improve teaching. Then busy principals begin to use them as quasi-administrators and to provide direct service to student remediation groups. Districts must maintain the ability to supervise how this staff resource is being utilized in the schools.

- Review structures and schedules at the district level, asking principals which functions of central office complicate their work and how to provide greater coherence.

- As a superintendent's cabinet, review the expectations for principals that come from all departments—directives from their direct-line supervisors and the formal evaluation process, the instructional leadership roles necessary for instructional initiatives and curriculum implementation, scheduled installation and use of new technologies, and so on. Support principals by clarifying the big picture of their work that integrates all expectations. Then work as an authentic team to support all aspects of the principals' leadership in their schools and each other as district leaders.

Support

The role of the principal has become increasingly complex and stressful. External mandates, negative publicity, and unclear expectations from the central office add to the tension. Within the school, a change agenda generates additional pressures. Teachers feel new pressure to reevaluate their work and are expected to work more collaboratively, which is unfamiliar behavior for many. Lauren Campsen (as cited in Allison et al., 2010) points out that

> when blaming a student for his or her failure is no longer an option, when the data spotlight is aimed directly at the instructional program, and when teachers and administrators are asked to look in the mirror for the cause of low test scores, major staff push back is too often a predictable result. District leadership must be prepared for this and be willing to take some initial heat to provide the support that the principal must have if he or she is to move the school. (p. 124)

Fullan (2005) states that collaborative cultures are "not particularly congenial; they are demanding cultures as people continually press for better results" (p. 9). The value of such cultures is that "they push for greater accomplishments, and they avoid the debilitating effects of negative cultures" (p. 26). But collaborative cultures don't come naturally or easily, especially if a first or early experience working with colleagues did not go smoothly. Fullan (2005) further explains that regressive interactions are more likely to happen and to have staying power. They are easier to do. It is easier to opt out of a bad process than to try to correct it. It is easier to give someone superficial or no feedback or even negative feedback than to engage in the progressive interactions of effective feedback. It is less trouble to sweep conflict under the carpet than to confront it. It is safer not to count on people than to be disappointed. It is simpler to make decisions alone than with others. It is even easier to hate than to love, because you can hate all by yourself. You can hate by stereotype, but you must love by involvement. In short, regressive behavior is easier because you can do it all by yourself; progressive behavior is harder because you have to do it with others at a time that you don't feel like cooperating. . . . Progressive interactions are more complicated to establish and maintain because they require people to stay engaged over long periods of time . . . under stressful conditions, individuals and groups are more likely to revert to regressive behavior. . . . Too much stress can cause us to seize up, get angry, and get even more frustrated with the complexities of group deliberations and thus to withdraw from the fray. (pp. 100–101)

District leaders must work with principals on an ongoing basis and model the shared leadership and collaboration they expect principals to be creating at the school level. Regular monthly visits to the school should focus on implementation of the school improvement plan, with the central office administrator asking questions that empower the principal, conveying an expectation that data will be used in the responses and creating a coaching atmosphere. These simple questions can be very effective:

- What's working? How do you know?
- What's stuck? Why do you think that is?
- How can I help?

Support and professional development for secondary principals should be a specific topic within the overall discussion of principal support. Louis and colleagues (2010) point out:

Principals working in middle schools and high schools . . . face a distinct challenge, shaped by the large complex settings in which they work, and the level of support extended to them should be commensurate with their distinct needs. Simply increasing the pressure on principals is unlikely to bring about real improvements in principal-teacher collaboration and achievement levels in secondary schools. Many school districts, however, lack the capacity to do more than that. We suggest accordingly that entities at the state or the regional/national level will need to be involved. Because we know from international studies (PISA and TIMSS, e.g.) that secondary schools are the weakest link in our educational system, and that they show limited capacity for improvement under current accountability policies, we suggest that designing and providing new programs to support secondary school principals must become a policy priority. (p. 52)

They add:

Instructional leadership in secondary schools must differ from instructional leadership in elementary schools, simply because high school principals cannot be experts in all subject areas. Many of the strategies that seem to work well in elementary schools do not necessarily work as well in high schools. We cannot expect to see significant improvement until this issue is addressed more clearly. Secondary school leadership-development initiatives should focus at least as much effort on improving the leadership capacities of department heads as principals and vice principals. (p. 102)

Shared Accountability

Principals are expected to share leadership and engage all staff in building a collaborative culture, learning to work as collaborative teams and taking common action as an entire school to improve student learning and the learning conditions. Yet the accountability is placed totally on the principal's shoulders.

An approach that worked well in the Seattle, Washington, system was team involvement in review of the schools' academic achievement plans. Several teacher leaders and sometimes parent representatives attended an annual or semiannual discussion with a group of district administrators who had responsibilities and expertise connected with various aspects of the site plan, such as the director of special education, ESL director, Title I director, and professional development coordinator. Various members of the site team presented progress reports (evidence of implementation and results), and new strategies and next steps were outlined. Each member of the district team provided feedback and suggestions and helped develop awareness of how schools with common needs and plans might be grouped for support and peer interaction. Members of school teams commented that it helped them to see connections to district resources that they previously perceived just as regulators and that the entire school improvement process became much more real and important, increasing their commitment level.

Conclusion

The focus of this book has been on the importance of data use at the district, school, and classroom levels in order to impact the schoolwide conditions for learning and instruction and assessment in classrooms with a bottom line of increased student learning. In their *Learning From Leadership* study, Louis et al. (2010) noted:

> Teachers in several schools talked about the *collective* influence of teachers, not merely the influence of colleagues identified as teacher leaders. Collective influence, these teachers reported, was instrumental in school decisions and in broader decisions about school improvement. They framed it as a function of whether the principal and district authorities invited, valued, and acted upon input from teachers. (p. 59)

The collaborative work of central office leaders should include the reflective questions, How do we invite input directly from teachers? How do we show we value it? How do we act upon it? District data teams and administrative teams should also discuss the research findings directly related to use of data. For instance, summarizing districtwide use of data, the *Learning From Leadership* study (Louis et al., 2010) revealed that principal efficacy is enhanced when:

- Districts insist on data-based decision making in schools.

- Districts use data to set goals for principal and teacher professional development.

- Districts provide schools with much of the data they need to practice data-based decision making.

- Districts assist schools in the interpretation and use of data for decision making.

- Districts create structures that foster the sharing of information across schools and between schools and the district. (pp. 160–161)

Diagnosing Your Data Dynamics

This book presents the use of data as a dynamic force for change and growth at the teacher, school, and district levels. You may be reading it voluntarily and with enthusiasm because you are a data dynamo, looking for affirmation and some new ideas and more tools. You may be reading it because you already value data and want to make the data work of your team more dynamic and engaging. You may be reading skeptically because you've experienced some poor group dynamics around the use of data or you've been assigned the topic for a committee or a class paper. As you have explored each of these chapters, you have probably processed the recommendations with mental reactions varying from "Right on! I agree!" to "Good; we do that all the time" to "We need to work on that" to "Sure . . . when pigs fly." As you followed the data journey of Mode Middle School, I hope that you compared their context and efforts with yours, recognizing some similar challenges, admiring some actions, questioning others, and selecting elements that could be applied in your own situation.

This chapter introduces a tool, an Innovation Configuration (IC) Map, for more intentional review and diagnosis of the data dynamics surrounding you. The tool itself is provided as a reproducible in the appendix (pages 189–196), so you can use it and generate ratings as you read. You may also download a clean copy for other uses from **go.solution-tree.com /schoolimprovement**. You will want to consider the whole picture of your data dynamics, but any component of the IC Map or even a specific row (strand) can be used as a separate item to generate interest and discussion.

An IC Map presents the ideal *first*, at the left, so that the eye and mind first and most frequently focus on best practices. Moving to the right, each cell represents an earlier stage of development, concluding with a nonexemplar as the last descriptor. The heavier vertical lines separate the nonexemplar with a clear visual message: "Don't go there." It's not an acceptable variation, even in early stages. The IC Map will provide data for you—and, as always, it's what you do with the data that counts.

The first component of the IC Map (see page 190) for data use is *results-oriented school culture*. Chapter 2 described conditions for data use that are mirrored here. Read across each row, and place an X in the cell that most accurately (not most favorably) describes your reality. If you work with more than one level, you may find it helpful to use a code such as D (district), S (school), and TT (teacher teams) to generate three ratings on each line of the IC Map. For example, a principal would have one set of ratings for the schoolwide efforts in his or her setting but might identify variations in the progress of teacher teams within the school and might also be able to put a finger on discomfort with the district context or degree of support. A district administrator might use a different code such as H, M, and E—for high schools, middle schools, and elementary schools, respectively—to see if there are patterns by level that need to be addressed. The supervisor of principals might code each school with an abbreviation or number to reveal common successes and needs. Rich conversations could emerge from comparing how school leaders rated the district and how principals' perceptions match those of their supervisors.

Component 2 of the IC Map (page 191) describes the *school data portfolio*, or collection of available data used in decision making in the school. The first four rows describe variations in use of student achievement data, nonacademic student data, staff data, and parent/community data. They reflect the content of chapters 3–6 about the types of data that should be gathered and how they might be displayed and discussed. Rate your practices as district, school, or teacher team(s) based on the data you directly see and use. Your ratings may indicate a strong use of some data, such as state test scores, and a very limited use of other kinds of valuable information. A review of the related chapter will help you be strategic with next steps and your advocacy for district help. The fifth row of this component refers to the accessibility and utilization of the school's data, whether it is complete or not.

The third and most lengthy component of the IC Map (pages 192–193) summarizes the elements of the *use of data in school improvement*. The text and figures of chapter 7 provide the frame of reference for your ratings in each row. Figure 7.1 (page 100) and Mode Middle School's example in figure 7.5 (page 115) illustrate the relationship of the rows on mission and priorities (and how they might be stated as goals). The third row focuses on the study stage and how it has led you and your school to select strategies that will be most powerful because they truly match the data, the underlying causes, and the gaps in current practice. The fourth row of this component stimulates reflection on the design and delivery of professional development to support change strategies. This row alone could be isolated from the rest of the IC Map and used in a district meeting of principals and central office administrators to surface issues that need to be addressed in terms of how time is dedicated, how many initiatives are started, and to what degree differentiation and follow-up are taking place.

The last two rows of this component relate to how the school, district, or teams ensure that careful planning will lead to conscientious implementation and result in increased student learning. The need for formative assessments to generate real-time data about student status and progress in terms of critical skills is clear in the last row. This could also be a stand-alone item for a quick rating and discussion about assessment practices at the school or district level.

Component 4 of the IC Map (page 194) focuses attention on the *use of data in teacher teams* within the school. The levels in these rows closely parallel the activities recommended for professional learning communities and the development of provisions in models such as the pyramid response to intervention. Chapter 8 provides reminders and examples to help move your team, school, or district to more effective interaction and powerful instruction and intervention.

Component 5 of the IC Map (page 195) connects to the portions of chapter 8 about *student engagement with their own data*. The first row underscores the importance of each student knowing what the critical skills and concepts are and where he or she stands in terms of the learning targets and progress toward them. The second row shows various levels of student empowerment in describing their own data and taking responsibility for their learning. The mutual support of teachers and students in celebrations that support individuals and the community of learners is illustrated in row three.

The last component of the IC Map (see page 196) reflects the shift in chapter 9 to a focus on *supporting use of data at the district level*. The first row analyzes how the district uses data, including school-based goals and plans, for central planning. The expectations that are set for principals and schools are described in the second row. This is another strand that could be used on its own to explore the dynamics and possible ambiguities and conflicts around what principals understand as the most important aspects of their leadership. The role of the district regarding grading policies (row three) has a major impact on whether teacher teams find it valuable and feasible to keep track of individual student progress and mastery of specific skills. The support of the district to manage data in practical, accessible ways (row four) will enhance or inhibit teacher leaders in their quest to use data for instructional planning and student engagement.

The ratings you've created on the IC Map are data. Since the IC Map is reproducible, you can make copies of the whole tool, or just a component, or even a single row, and engage others in generating more data. Then it's what you do with these data that counts for the staff and students in your sphere of influence. First, summarize your ratings into the categories of celebrations and concerns as you have seen throughout this book. As you work to generate dynamics around use of data in your setting, you will want to start with the *positive* as common ground and affirmation! If any concerns came from cells to the farthest right (outside the heavy vertical lines), star those for urgent attention. Then recall the guidance of chapters 3–6 about displaying and discussing data and apply it to this new data. Who else needs to see the results of your reflection or needs to complete the IC Map on their own and then compare?

You may say that your sphere of influence is just your own classroom and your own students. Go back to figure 2.1 (page 24), and put an X on that figure to represent you. You will notice that there is no circle for "independent teacher." We can no longer afford to have teacher talent and insight hidden behind classroom doors. So you must identify yourself as part of a teacher team, even if not formally designated as such, and see the connections you have to the schoolwide data team, the school improvement/leadership team, the principal and the administrative team, and through them to the district level. You may also have informal and social contacts directly with central office staff. The point is, you have channels through which to exert energy and you *can* influence data work at any level directly or indirectly.

Based on the celebrations, concerns, and priorities you identified here, set some goals and select some strategies. In which aspect(s) of data use do you most want to see movement? State your goal(s). For example, "By a year from now, I want to see everyone in my school use assessments in formative ways and go from level 4 or 5 to at least level 2 on the first row of Component 4."

Now consider the role you will play and lay out your action steps as a member of the district, school, and/or teacher team(s) you influence. Who will you talk with? What do you do now that you will make more transparent and share with your colleagues? What will you try in your own practice? How will you describe your efforts openly and ask for help and feedback? When you try new things and struggle because of policies or practices that inhibit your efforts, how will you turn your frustration into forceful advocacy? What team will you volunteer to form or join and contribute to solutions?

Gregory and Kuzmich (2007) refer to three levels of group effectiveness. In the first case, working groups provide support for departments, sites, and individuals. Expert groups provide support *and* interact with each other, sharing their work and learning to synergize their efforts. The *highest*-performing teams prioritize, strategically allocate resources, and become adept at making midcourse changes and finding creative solutions to the problems that inevitably arise during implementation. This level of performance is the ideal for district, school, and teacher data teams and should be the express goal of all professionals—to continuously improve their individual performance and to reach beyond their own classroom or office walls to strengthen the collective efforts of their colleagues. Effective, appropriate use of data will focus growth efforts and provide the evidence of progress that sustains motivation for the hard work of preparing the leaders of the future.

So take on the challenge and become a data dynamo in your own setting. You don't need statistical expertise or technical skill to bring energy and passion to the search for greater understanding of student needs, more rigorous examination of current practice, and a drive for continuous improvement and evidence of results. Schmoker (2006) is right when he reminds us that "the life chances of many thousands of children hang on the actions we take. Their options, their ability to participate fully in the life of their communities depend on how soon and how vigorously we implement the best practices" (p. 3).

In the creation of data dynamics, there is no "lead, follow, or get out of the way." There is only *lead*. You have learned more about data use from this book, and you have generated actionable data of your own using the IC Map. Now, what will you do with it?

Appendix
Reproducible IC Map of Data Use

Component 1: Results-oriented school culture

Level 1	Level 2	Level 3	Level 4	Level 5
Staff members direct discussion to the data wall and can state celebrations and current efforts.	Staff members know where a data summary is available and who is using the data.	Staff members may state a data finding that the school is working on.	Staff can state whether the school made AYP or not.	Only staff in tested areas are aware of status.
Progress and positive status are both celebrated.	Celebrations focus on students at proficient status.	The focus is on concerns with little or no celebrations.	There is no organized, schoolwide attention to data.	
All staff embrace the use of data as a matter of course.	All staff engage in periodic, scheduled data discussions.	Use of data is limited to a designated group or team.	Use of data is considered the principal's job.	
Appropriate, accurate data terms are used by all staff.	Staff use data terms incorrectly.	Staff do not discuss data at all.	Staff only discuss students' lack of effort.	
Principal models use of data with frequent references and questions.	Principal is actively involved with data analysis in the team.	Principal forms a committee to deal with the data and develop a plan.	Principal holds faculty meeting once a year to announce state test results.	Test results are passed on to tested grades or departments only.
Principal creatively rearranges master schedule to ensure teacher collaboration time.	Principal redirects use of staff meeting and professional development time.	Principal honors district directives about use of time for collaboration and use of data.	Principal urges teachers to work together.	Principal sets no explicit expectations for collaboration.
Majority of staff questions relate to evidence of students' needs and progress.	Majority of staff questions relate to how they will manage new practices.	Majority of staff questions relate to how changes will affect personal preferences.	Majority of staff questions relate to what they "have to do new this year."	

Component 2: School data portfolio

Level 1	Level 2	Level 3	Level 4	Level 5
Student achievement data include multiple sources, both formative and summative; trends for multiple years; progress of student cohorts.	Only state test results are used to monitor student achievement; data are reviewed annually using most recent and two prior years.	Only state test results are used to monitor student achievement; data are reviewed annually using most recent year scores.	There is no routine review of student achievement data.	
Nonacademic student data include multiple measures of objective and subjective data. High schools include postsecondary data: entry, necessary remediation, and completion.	Nonacademic data include required data, objective information designated as important to answer site-based questions, and perceptual data gathered from students.	Nonacademic data include information designated as important to answer site-based questions.	Only state required data (for example, attendance) are gathered, reported, and reviewed at the site.	Only state required data (for example, attendance) are gathered and reported by the school or district.
Staff data include objective and subjective information linked to staff preparation, student learning, and staff needs.	Staff data include objective information and perceptual information.	Staff data include objective information to help plan professional development.	Only state required data (for example, licensure) are verified at the district level; no staff data are used at the school level.	
Parent/community data include objective and subjective data; community representatives help interpret the data and identify needs and possible responses.	Objective data are gathered and perceptual data are sought through surveys.	Data on parent involvement and community characteristics are compiled.	Data on parent involvement with the school are collected.	Parent/community data are not included in school decision making.
School portfolio data are summarized, displayed, and accessible.	School portfolio data are gathered and kept in the office, available upon request.	School portfolio data are gathered and kept in the office.	There is no single, organized collection of school data from multiple sources.	

Component 3: Use of data in school improvement

Level 1	Level 2	Level 3	Level 4	Level 5
Mission/vision statement is developed through stakeholder involvement and displayed and disseminated and referenced weekly; data sources are identified to provide evidence of accomplishment and revised annually.	Mission/vision statement is developed through direct stakeholder involvement, displayed and disseminated, and referenced frequently.	Mission/vision statement is developed through direct stakeholder involvement, displayed and disseminated, and revised every three to five years.	Mission/vision statement is developed in a small group with minimal stakeholder input, filed, and revised every five years.	Mission/vision statement is written by an individual or a small group, filed and revised every five years.
External and internal goals are stated as SMART goals: specific, measurable, attainable, results based, and time bound.	Some goals include specific measures and levels of accomplishment.	Goals include state targets and desired areas for improvement set by the school.	Goals are limited to meeting benchmarks set by state.	Single goal is to get out of an unfavorable state or district designation.
Strategies researched by study groups of staff; none considered without data to provide evidence of effectiveness and comparison to current context, practices, and root causes; combined strategies will affect all students, all staff.	Strategies researched by study groups of staff; none considered without data to provide evidence of effectiveness and comparison to current context, practices, and root causes; combined strategies will involve staff in selected departments/grades.	Strategies researched by study groups of staff; none considered without data to provide evidence of effectiveness.	Strategies recommended by administrators or a small group and voted on by staff.	Strategies are chosen by brainstorming in a small group or from a packaged pull-down menu; strategies are selected only for math and literacy.

Component 3: Use of data in school improvement (continued)

Level 1	Level 2	Level 3	Level 4	Level 5
Multilevel professional development plans are made for all selected strategies; staff participation is differentiated based on data; data are gathered for continuous improvement of professional development; internal capacity is built for training, and coaching cycles are repeated to support new staff.	All strategies are supported with levels of initial training and follow-up; data are gathered for feedback/improvement of professional development.	All selected strategies are supported with initial training required for all staff.	Some strategies are supported with initial training required for all staff.	Strategies selected are not supported with professional development plans.
Evidence of implementation is gathered frequently, shared with all staff, and used to adjust professional development plans.	Leaders and staff agree on indicators of implementation and methods for gathering evidence.	Leaders use external processes (for example, packaged walk-throughs) to monitor implementation.	Leaders assume that initial training ensures implementation.	
Formative assessments are used frequently to assess students' progress towards proficiency on essential standards; results are compared with large-scale assessments to check predictive value.	Assessments are in multiple formats, including some like state tests, and are at multiple levels of complexity.	Assessment items are in multiple formats (for example, selected response, constructed response, extended response) including some like state tests.	End-of-course/grade and quarterly benchmark assessments are developed by teachers across schools.	State tests are the only data used and are not linked to evaluation of whether strategies are effective.

Component 4: Use of data in teacher teams

Level 1	Level 2	Level 3	Level 4	Level 5
Results of formative assessment are used at least weekly for instructional planning. Results of summative assessments are used in formative ways to adjust programs and plans.	Teacher teams discuss results of assessments at least once a month.	Teacher teams develop assessments based on prioritized grade/course standards.	Teachers give textbook-related tests as pretests and modify for post-tests. Pretest data are used to differentiate instruction.	Teachers give textbook-related tests, record grades, and move on.
Teacher teams use data to plan instruction; common "best" lesson plans; observe each other; include Tier I interventions; varied strategies; high student engagement.	Teachers discuss instruction and attempts to differentiate and increase student engagement strategies.	Teachers plan instruction in isolation, attempting differentiation and increasing student engagement strategies.	Teachers plan instruction in isolation and attempt differentiation.	Teachers plan instruction in isolation, relying heavily on textbook teacher guides and lecture for whole-group instruction.
Teacher teams collaboratively create and deliver interventions and enrichments to support growth of all learners.	Interventions are provided for all students who are not yet proficient and do not interfere with access to ongoing instruction.	Interventions supplement regular instruction and extend opportunity to learn (for example, expand learning time).	Timing of interventions prevents students from ongoing access to the regular curriculum.	Interventions are focused on the "bubble kids" to get them to proficiency.

Component 5: Student engagement with their own data

Level 1	Level 2	Level 3	Level 4	Level 5
Students understand scoring guides and engage in peer and self-assessment.	Feedback is provided to students in terms of status and progress on benchmarks.	Students rely on letter grades to know how they are doing.	Most essential benchmarks are written in student language and provided to students and parents.	Most essential benchmarks are not identified, or are available only to teachers.
Students lead conferences with teachers and parents and describe progress, goals, and plans.	Students describe their current status, goals, and what they need to do to accomplish proficiency.	Students state what they are learning and can show how they are keeping track of their progress.	Students state what they are learning.	Students state what they are doing in class, not what they are learning.
Teachers and students design celebrations of incremental progress of individuals and groups.	Teachers design celebrations when class goals are met.	Teachers do not design celebrations.	Teachers do not openly model a focus on progress/growth.	

Data Dynamics © 2011 Solution Tree Press • www.solution-tree.com
Visit **go.solution-tree.com/schoolimprovement** to download this page.

Component 6: Supporting use of data at the district level

Level 1	Level 2	Level 3	Level 4	Level 5
District departments use school improvement plans and input from teachers as data for planning.	District departments make plans based on districtwide data.	District departments compete for access to professional development time.	There is no master plan for professional development based on data.	
All district departments coordinate expectations and supports for principals' instructional leadership; principals' goals reflect their schools' data and school improvement plan.	Expectations for principals include formal evaluation standards and school improvement targets.	Principals receive multiple/mixed sets of expectations from their evaluators and central office departments.	Expectations for principals are based solely on state/contract evaluation standards.	
Grading policies reflect academic standards achieved; nonacademic grades are reported separately; electronic systems created or purchased to reflect proficiency accomplishment.	Grading policies combine evidence of student learning with other student characteristics; grades are not aligned with essential learning targets.	Grading policies are outdated and not reviewed; practices are driven by past practice or a purchased program.		
District develops a data warehouse system to provide data on individual student proficiency on most essential benchmarks.	Teacher teams work collaboratively to create tools to track student proficiency.	Individual teachers create spreadsheets and tools in attempt to track student proficiency.	Teachers rely on traditional record keeping, not linked to specific skills/benchmarks.	

References and Resources

Agronick, G., Clark, A., O'Donnell, L., & Steuve, A. (2009). *Parent involvement strategies in urban middle and high schools in the Northeast and Islands Region* (Issues and Answers Report, REL 2009–No. 069). Washington, DC: U.S. Department of Education, Institute of Education Sciences, National Center for Education Evaluation and Regional Assistance, Regional Educational Laboratory Northeast and Islands. Accessed at http://ies.ed.gov/ncee/edlabs/regions/northeast/pdf/REL_2009069.pdf on March 29, 2011.

Agullard, K., & Goughnour, D. S. (2006). *Central office inquiry: Assessing organization, roles, and actions to support school improvement.* San Francisco: WestEd.

Ainsworth, L., & Viegut, D. (2006). *Common formative assessments: How to connect standards-based instruction and assessment.* Thousand Oaks, CA: Corwin Press.

Allison, E., White, M., Nielsen, K., Pitchford, B., Campsen, L., Peery, L., et al. (2010). *Data teams: The big picture—Looking at data teams through a collaborative lens.* Englewood, CO: Leadership and Learning Center.

Armstrong, T. (2007). The curriculum superhighway. *Educational Leadership, 64*(8), 16–20.

Assessment Reform Group. (2006). *The role of teachers in the assessment of learning.* Accessed at www.assessment-reform-group.org/ASF%20booklet%20English.pdf on March 28, 2011.

Azzam, A. M. (2008). Engaged and on track. *Educational Leadership, 65*(6), 93–94.

Bamburg, J., & Isaacson, N. (1992). Can schools become learning organizations? *Educational Leadership, 50*(3), 42–44.

Barr, R. D., & Parrett, W. H. (2007). *The kids left behind: Catching up the underachieving children of poverty.* Bloomington, IN: Solution Tree Press.

Berliner, D. C. (2010). The incompatibility of high-stakes testing and the development of skills for the twenty-first century. In R. J. Marzano (Ed.), *On excellence in teaching* (pp. 113–143). Bloomington, IN: Solution Tree Press.

Bernhardt, V. L. (2004). *Data analysis for continuous school improvement.* Larchmont, NY: Eye on Education.

Black, P., Harrison, C., Lee, C., Marshall, B., & Wiliam, D. (2003). *Assessment for learning: Putting it into practice.* Maidenhead, Berkshire, England: Open University Press.

Black, P., & Wiliam, D. (1998). Assessment and classroom learning. *Assessment in Education: Principles, Policy & Practice, 5*(1), 7–74.

Bridges, W. (1980). *Transitions: Making sense of life's changes.* Reading, MA: Addison-Wesley.

Brookhart, S. M. (2004). *Grading.* Upper Saddle River, NJ: Pearson.

Brookover, W., Beady, D., Flood, P., Schweitzer, J., & Wisenbaker, J. (1979). *School social systems and student achievement: Schools can make a difference.* New York: Praeger.

Brookover, W. B., Schweitzer, J. H., Schneider, J. M., Beady, C. H., Flood, P. K., & Wisenbaker, J. M. (1978). Elementary school social climate and school achievement. *American Educational Research Journal, 15*(2), 301–318.

Bryk, A. S., & Schneider, B. (2002). *Trust in schools.* New York: Russell Sage Foundation.

Bush, R. N. (1984). Effective staff development. In Far West Laboratory for Educational Research and Development, *Making our schools more effective: Proceedings of three state conferences* (NIE Grant No. 80–0103; pp. 223–240). San Francisco: Far West Laboratory for Educational Research and Development.

Chang, H. (2010). Five myths about school attendance. *Education Week.* Accessed at www.edweek.org/ew/articles/2010/09/15/03chang.h30.html on September 13, 2010.

Chappuis, J. (2005). Helping students understand assessment. *Educational Leadership, 63*(3), 39–43.

Chappuis, S., Chappuis, J., & Stiggins, R. (2009). The quest for quality. *Educational Leadership, 67*(3), 14–19.

Clotfelter, C. T., Ladd, H. F., & Vigdor, J. L. (2007, November). *Teacher credentials and student achievement in high school: A cross-subject analysis with student fixed effects* (Working Paper No. 13617). Cambridge, MA: National Bureau of Economic Research.

Cushman, K. (2006). Help us care enough to learn. *Educational Leadership, 63*(5), 34–37.

Darling-Hammond, L. (1990). Teacher professionalism: Why and how? In Ann Lieberman (Ed.), *Schools as collaborative cultures* (pp. 25–50). New York: Falmer Press.

Darling-Hammond, L. (2009). Teaching and the change wars: The professionalism hypothesis. In A. Hargreaves & M. Fullan (Eds.), *Change wars* (pp. 45–68). Bloomington, IN: Solution Tree Press.

Davies, A. (2007). Involving students in the classroom assessment process. In D. Reeves (Ed.), *Ahead of the curve: The power of assessment to transform teaching and learning* (pp. 31–57). Bloomington, IN: Solution Tree Press.

Deming, W. E. (1986). *Out of the crisis.* Cambridge, MA: Massachusetts Institute of Technology, Center for Advanced Engineering Study.

Deuel, A., Nelson, T. H., Slavit, D., & Kennedy, A. (2009). Looking at student work. *Educational Leadership, 67*(3), 69–72.

DuFour, R., DuFour, R., Eaker, R., & Karhanek, G. (2010). *Raising the bar and closing the gap: Whatever it takes.* Bloomington, IN: Solution Tree Press.

Edmonds, R. R. (1979). Effective schools for the urban poor. *Educational Leadership, 37*(1), 15–18, 20–24.

Edmonds, R. R. (1981). Making public schools effective. *School Policy, 12*(2), 56–60.

Edmonds, R. R. (1982). Programs of school improvement: An overview. *Educational Leadership, 40*(3), 4–11.

El Nasser, H., & Overberg, P. (2010, August 27). Ethnicity shifts in youngest classes. *USA Today,* p. 1A.

Elmore, R. (2004). *School reform from the inside out: Policy, practice, and performance.* Cambridge, MA: Harvard Education Press.

Epstein, J. (1995). School/family/community partnerships: Caring for the children we share. *Phi Delta Kappan, 76*(9), 701–712.

Epstein, J. L., Sanders, M. G., Simon, B. S., Salinas, K. C., Jansorn, N. R., & Van Voorhis, F. L. (2002). *School, family, and community partnerships: Your handbook for action* (2nd ed.). Thousand Oaks, CA: Corwin Press.

Ferguson, C., & Rodriguez, V. (2005). *Engaging families at the secondary level: What schools can do to support family involvement.* Austin, TX: Southwest Educational Development Laboratory.

Fullan, M. (1997). Emotion and hope: Constructive concepts for complex times. In A. Hargreaves (Ed.), *Rethinking educational change with heart and mind* (pp. 216–233). Alexandria, VA: Association for Supervision and Curriculum Development.

Fullan, M. (2003a, January). *Leading in a culture of change.* Keynote presented at the Office of Superintendent of Public Instruction (OSPI) Winter Meeting, Spokane, WA.

Fullan, M. (2003b). *The moral imperative of school leadership.* Thousand Oaks, CA: Corwin Press.

Fullan, M. (2005). *Leadership and sustainability: System thinkers in action.* Thousand Oaks, CA: Corwin Press.

Fullan, M. (2009). Have theory, will travel: A theory of action for system change. In A. Hargreaves & M. Fullan (Eds.), *Change wars* (pp. 275–293). Bloomington, IN: Solution Tree Press.

Fullan, M., & Hargreaves, A. (1996). *What's worth fighting for in your school?* New York: Teachers College Press.

Garmston, R. J. (2006). The five principles of successful meetings. *Learning System, 1*(4), 1, 6, 8.

Garmston, R. J., & Wellman, B. M. (1999). *The adaptive school: A sourcebook for developing collaborative groups.* Norwood, MA: Christopher-Gordon.

Good, T. L. (2010). Forty years of research on teaching 1968–2008: What do we know now that we didn't know then? In R. J. Marzano (Ed.), *On excellence in teaching* (pp. 31–62). Bloomington, IN: Solution Tree Press.

Gregory, G. H., & Kuzmich, L. (2007). *Teacher teams that get results: 61 strategies for sustaining and renewing professional learning communities.* Thousand Oaks, CA: Corwin Press.

Guskey, T. R. (2007). Using assessments to improve teaching *and* learning. In D. Reeves (Ed.), *Ahead of the curve: The power of assessment to transform teaching and learning* (pp. 15–29). Bloomington, IN: Solution Tree Press.

Hall, G. E., & Hord, S. M. (2001). *Implementing change: Patterns, principles, and potholes.* Boston: Allyn & Bacon.

Hargreaves, A. (2009). The fourth way of change: Towards an age of inspiration and sustainability. In A. Hargreaves & M. Fullan (Eds.), *Change wars* (pp. 11–43). Bloomington, IN: Solution Tree Press.

Hargreaves, D. H. (2003). *Education epidemic: Transforming secondary schools through innovation networks.* London: Demos.

Harrison, C., & Bryan, C. (2008). Data dialogue: Focused conversations put evidence to work in the classroom. *Journal of Staff Development, 29*(4), 15–19.

Hattie, J. (2009). *Visible learning: A synthesis of over 800 meta-analyses relating to achievement.* New York: Routledge.

Heifetz, R. A. (2003). Adaptive work. In T. Bentley & J. Wilsdon (Eds.), *The adaptive state: Strategies for personalizing the public realm* (pp. 68–78). London: Demos.

Hirsh, S. (2009a). A new definition. *Journal of Staff Development, 30*(4), 10–16.

Hirsh, S. (2009b). Foreword. In J. Killion & P. Roy, *Becoming a learning school* (pp. 5–6). Oxford, OH: National Staff Development Council.

Holcomb, E. L. (Ed.). (1991a). *A handbook for implementing school improvement.* Madison: National Center for Effective Schools Research and Development, University of Wisconsin–Madison.

Holcomb, E. L. (1991b). *School-based instructional leadership: Staff development for teacher and school effectiveness.* Madison: National Center for Effective Schools Research and Development, University of Wisconsin–Madison.

Holcomb, E. L. (1999). *Getting excited about data: How to combine people, passion and proof.* Thousand Oaks, CA: Corwin Press.

Holcomb, E. L. (2004). *Getting excited about data: Combining people, passion, and proof to maximize student achievement* (2nd ed.). Thousand Oaks, CA: Corwin Press.

Holcomb, E. L. (2007). *Students are stakeholders, too! Including every voice in authentic high school reform.* Thousand Oaks, CA: Corwin Press.

Holcomb, E. L. (2009). *Asking the right questions: Tools for collaboration and school change* (3rd ed.). Thousand Oaks, CA: Corwin Press.

Holcomb, E. L. (2010). Customer input through focus groups. *PAGE ONE, 32*(1), 22–25.

Hord, S. M. (1997). *Professional learning communities: Communities of continuous inquiry and improvement.* Austin, TX: Southwest Educational Development Laboratory.

Hord, S. M. (Ed.). (2004). *Learning together, leading together: Changing schools through professional learning communities.* New York: Teachers College Press.

Hord, S. M. (2007, December 2). *Professional learning community: What really is it?* Presented at the National Staff Development Council's 39th Annual Conference, Dallas, TX.

Hord, S. M. (2010). *Guiding professional learning communities: Inspiration, challenge, surprise, and meaning.* Thousand Oaks, CA: Corwin Press.

Hord, S. M., Rutherford, W. L., Huling-Austin, L., & Hall, G. E. (1987). *Taking charge of change.* Alexandria, VA: Association for Supervision and Curriculum Development.

Hord, S. M., & Sommers, W. A. (2008). *Leading professional learning communities: Voices from research and practice.* Thousand Oaks, CA: Corwin Press.

Houston, P. D. (1998). Preserving public education, not public schools. *School Administrator, 55*(8), 53.

Huebner, T. (2009). Balanced assessment. *Educational Leadership, 67*(3), 85–86.

Ingersoll, R. (2008). *Core problems: Out-of-field teaching persists in key academic courses and high-poverty schools.* Washington, DC: Education Trust.

Joyce, B. (Ed.). (1990). *Changing school culture through staff development: The 1990 yearbook of the Association for Supervision and Curriculum Development.* Alexandria, VA: Association for Supervision and Curriculum Development.

Joyce, B., & Showers, B. (1988). *Student achievement through staff development.* New York: Longman.

Killion, J., & Roy, P. (2009). *Becoming a learning school.* Oxford, OH: National Staff Development Council.

Knight, J. (2009). Coaching: The key to translating research into practice lies in continuous, job-embedded learning with ongoing support. *Journal of Staff Development, 30*(1), 18–20, 22.

Lachat, M. A., & Smith, S. (2005). Practices that support data use in urban high schools. *Journal of Education for Students Placed At Risk, 10*(3), 333–349.

Lambert, L. (2003). *Leadership capacity for lasting school improvement.* Alexandria, VA: Association for Supervision and Curriculum Development.

Landsman, J., & Gorski, P. (2007). Countering standardization. *Educational Leadership, 64*(8), 40–44.

Leithwood, K., Louis, K. S., Wahlstrom, K., Anderson, S., Mascall, B., Michlin, M., et al. (2009). *Learning from district efforts to improve student achievement.* New York: Wallace Foundation.

Levin, H. M, Belfield. C., Muennig, P., & Rouse, C. (2007). *The costs and benefits of an excellent education for all of America's children.* New York: Teachers College Press.

Lezotte, L. W., & Bancroft, B. A. (1985). Growing use of the effective schools model for school improvement. *Educational Leadership, 42*(6), 23–27.

Lezotte, L. W., & Jacoby, B. C. (1990). *A guide to the school improvement process based on effective schools research.* Okemos, MI: Effective Schools/Michigan Institute for Educational Management.

Lezotte, L. W., & Snyder, K. M. (2011). *What effective schools do: Re-envisioning the correlates.* Bloomington, IN: Solution Tree Press.

Little, J. W. (1982). Norms of collegiality and experimentation: Workplace conditions of school success. *American Educational Research Journal, 19*(3), 325–340.

Louis, K. S., & Kruse, S. D. (1995). *Professionalism and community: Perspectives on reforming urban schools.* Thousand Oaks, CA: Corwin Press.

Louis, K. S., Leithwood, K., Wahlstrom, K. L., & Anderson, S. E. (2010). *Learning from leadership project: Investigating the links to improved student learning.* St. Paul: University of Minnesota.

Love, N., Stiles, K. E., Mundry, S., & DiRanna, K. (2008). *The data coach's guide to improving learning for all students.* Thousand Oaks, CA: Corwin Press.

Marzano, R. J. (1992). *A different kind of classroom: Teaching with dimensions of learning.* Alexandria, VA: Association for Supervision and Curriculum Development.

Marzano, R. J. (2007). *The art and science of teaching: A comprehensive framework for effective instruction.* Alexandria, VA: Association for Supervision and Curriculum Development.

Marzano, R. J. (2010a). A focus on teaching. In R. J. Marzano (Ed.), *On excellence in teaching* (pp. 1–4). Bloomington, IN: Solution Tree Press.

Marzano, R. J. (2010b). *Formative assessment & standards-based grading.* Bloomington, IN: Marzano Research Laboratory.

Marzano, R. J., Pickering, D. J., & Pollock, J. E. (2001). *Classroom instruction that works: Research-based strategies for increasing student achievement.* Alexandria, VA: Association for Supervision and Curriculum Development.

Marzano, R. J., & Waters, T. (2009). *District leadership that works: Striking the right balance.* Bloomington, IN: Solution Tree Press.

Marzano, R. J., Waters, T., & McNulty, B. A. (2005). *School leadership that works: From research to results.* Alexandria, VA: Association for Supervision and Curriculum Development.

McLaughlin, M. W., & Marsh, D. D. (1978). Staff development and school change. *Teachers College Record, 80*(1), 69–94.

McTighe, J. (2010). Understanding by design and instruction. In R. J. Marzano (Ed.), *On excellence in teaching* (pp. 271–299). Bloomington, IN: Solution Tree Press.

McTighe, J., & O'Connor, K. (2005). Seven practices for effective learning. *Educational Leadership, 63*(3), 10–17.

Merriam-Webster Online. (2011). *Dynamic.* Accessed at www.merriam-webster.com/dictionary/dynamic?show on March 3, 2011.

National Association of Secondary School Principals. (2004). *Breaking ranks II: Strategies for leading high school reform.* Reston, VA: Author.

Netter, G. (Producer), & Hancock, J. L. (Director). (2009). *The blind side* [Motion picture]. United States: Alcon Entertainment.

Nichols, S. L., & Berliner, D. C. (2008). Testing the joy out of learning. *Educational Leadership, 65*(6), 14–18.

O'Connor, K. (2007). The last frontier: Tackling the grading dilemma. In D. Reeves (Ed.), *Ahead of the curve: The power of assessment to transform teaching and learning* (pp. 127–145). Bloomington, IN: Solution Tree Press.

O'Neill, J., & Conzemius, A. (2006). *The power of SMART goals: Using goals to improve student learning.* Bloomington, IN: Solution Tree Press.

Palmer, P. J. (2007). *The courage to teach: Exploring the inner landscape of a teacher's life* (10th ed.). San Francisco: Wiley.

Patterson, K., Grenny, J., McMillan, R., & Switzler, A. (2002). *Crucial conversations: Tools for talking when the stakes are high.* New York: McGraw-Hill.

Pennsylvania Department of Education. (2011). *Classroom diagnostic tools.* Harrisburg, PA: Author.

Popham, W. J. (2011). Formative assessment—A process, not a test. *Education Week.* Accessed at www.edweek.org/ew/articles/2011/02/23/21popham.h30.html on March 5, 2011.

Preuss, P. G. (2003). *School leader's guide to root cause analysis: Using data to dissolve problems.* Larchmont, NY: Eye on Education.

Reeves, D. B. (2004). *Accountability in learning: How teachers and school leaders can take charge.* Alexandria, VA: Association for Supervision and Curriculum Development.

Reeves, D. B. (2006). *The learning leader: How to focus school improvement for better results.* Alexandria, VA: Association for Supervision and Curriculum Development.

Reeves, D. B. (2007). Challenges and choices: The role of educational leaders in effective assessment. In D. Reeves (Ed.), *Ahead of the curve: The power of assessment to transform teaching and learning* (pp. 227–251). Bloomington, IN: Solution Tree Press.

Reeves, D. B. (2010). *Transforming professional development into student results.* Alexandria, VA: Association for Supervision and Curriculum Development.

Richardson, J. (2005). Focus groups zoom in on school district's concerns. *Tools for Schools, 9*(1), 1–3, 8.

Rosenholtz, S. J. (1989). *Teachers' workplace: The social organization of schools.* New York: Longman.

Rothstein, R., Wilder, T., & Jacobsen, R. (2007). Balance in the balance. *Educational Leadership, 64*(8), 8–14.

Schmoker, M. (2001). *The results fieldbook: Practical strategies from dramatically improved schools.* Alexandria, VA: Association for Supervision and Curriculum Development.

Schmoker, M. (2006). *Results now: How we can achieve unprecedented improvements in teaching and learning.* Alexandria, VA: Association for Supervision and Curriculum Development.

Schmoker, M. (2010). When pedagogic fads trump priorities. *Education Week.* Accessed at www.edweek.org/ew/articles/2010/09/29/05.schmoker.h30.html on October 13, 2010.

Sergiovanni, T. J. (1992). *Moral leadership: Getting to the heart of school improvement.* San Francisco: Jossey-Bass.

Sharratt, L., & Fullan, M. (2009). *Realization: The change imperative for deepening district-wide reform.* Thousand Oaks, CA: Corwin Press.

Shirley, D. (2009). The music of democracy: Emerging strategies for a new era of post-standardization. In A. Hargreaves & M. Fullan (Eds.), *Change wars* (pp. 135–160). Bloomington, IN: Solution Tree Press.

Silver, H. F., & Perini, M. J. (2010). The eight Cs of engagement: How learning styles and instructional design increase student commitment to learning. In R. J. Marzano (Ed.), *On excellence in teaching* (pp. 319–342). Bloomington, IN: Solution Tree Press.

Stiggins, R. J. (2007). Assessment through the student's eyes. *Educational Leadership, 64*(8), 22–26.

Stiggins, R. J., Arter, J. A., Chappuis, J., & Chappuis, S. (2004). *Classroom assessment* for *student learning: Doing it right—Using it well*. Portland, OR: Assessment Training Institute.

Supovitz, J. (2007). Why we need district-based reform: Supporting systemwide instructional improvement. *Education Week, 27*(13), 27–28.

Taylor, B. O. (Ed.). (1990). *Case studies in effective schools research*. Dubuque, IA: Kendall/Hunt.

Thompson, G. (2008). Beneath the apathy. *Educational Leadership, 65*(6), 50–54.

Wahlstrom, D. (1999). *Using data to improve student achievement: A handbook for collecting, organizing, analyzing, and using data*. Suffolk, VA: Successline.

White, S. (2007). Data on purpose: Due diligence to increase student achievement. In D. Reeves (Ed.), *Ahead of the curve: The power of assessment to transform teaching and learning* (pp. 207–225). Bloomington, IN: Solution Tree Press.

White, S. H. (2005). *Beyond the numbers: Making data work for teachers & school leaders*. Englewood, CO: Advanced Learning Press.

Wiggins, G. (2010). What's my job? Defining the role of the classroom teacher. In R. J. Marzano (Ed.), *On excellence in teaching* (pp. 7–29). Bloomington, IN: Solution Tree Press.

Wiliam, D. (2007). Content *then* process: Teacher learning communities in the service of formative assessment. In D. Reeves (Ed.), *Ahead of the curve: The power of assessment to transform teaching and learning* (pp. 183–204). Bloomington, IN: Solution Tree Press.

Yazzie-Mintz, E. (2007). *Voices of students on engagement: A report on the 2006 High School Survey of Student Engagement*. Bloomington, IN: Center for Evaluation and Education Policy.

Index

Learning by Doing
A Handbook for Professional Learning Communities at Work™
Richard DuFour, Rebecca DuFour, Robert Eaker, and Thomas Many

The second edition of *Learning by Doing* is an action guide for closing the knowing-doing gap and transforming schools into PLCs. It also includes seven major additions that equip educators with essential tools for confronting challenges.
BKF416

More Than a SMART Goal
Staying Focused on Student Learning
Anne E. Conzemius and Terry Morganti-Fisher

Successful school-improvement efforts not only set SMART goals, but also align them to the school-improvement process, curriculum, instruction, assessment practices, mandates, and professional development. Understand how to properly use the SMART goal process to effect change.
BKF482

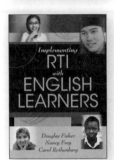

Implementing RTI With English Learners
Douglas Fisher, Nancy Frey, and Carol Rothenberg

Learn why RTI is the ideal framework for supporting English learners. Follow the application and effectiveness of RTI through classroom examples and the stories of four representative students of varying ages, nationalities, and language proficiency levels.
BKF397

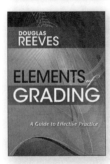

Elements of Grading
A Guide to Effective Practice
Douglas Reeves

Learn several strategies for improving grading practices, while examining the common arguments against reform. With this practical guide, you can improve grading to meet four essential criteria—accuracy, fairness, specificity, timeliness—and also make the process quicker and more efficient.
BKF410

Data-Based Decision Making
Essentials for Principals Series
Edie L. Holcomb

You're ready to start collecting and utilizing school data, but what data are you looking for? How exactly will you find that data? And how will you use it once you have it? This informative resource takes an in-depth look at best data collection practices, and guides the elementary school principal on how to reach struggling learners, strengthen instruction, and achieve full, schoolwide improvement.
BKF469

a division of

Solution Tree | Press

Solution Tree

Visit solution-tree.com or call 800.733.6786 to order.